JUSTICE AT WAR

RICHARD DELGADO

JUSTICE AT WAR

*Civil Liberties and Civil Rights
during Times of Crisis*

Foreword by Jennifer L. Hochschild

New York University Press • *New York and London*

NEW YORK UNIVERSITY PRESS
New York and London

© 2003 by New York University

Library of Congress Cataloging-in-Publication Data
Delgado, Richard.
Justice at war / Richard Delgado.
p. cm.
Includes bibliographical references.
ISBN 0-8147-1955-4 (cloth : alk. paper)
1. United States—Race relations. 2. Racism—United States.
3. Race discrimination—United States. 4. United States—
Politics and government—2001– . 5. United States—
Social conditions—1980– . 6. Minorities—Legal status,
laws, etc.—United States. 7. Minorities—Civil rights—
United States. 8. Emigration and immigration law—United States.
9. Immigrants—Civil rights—United States. 10. Intellectuals—Fiction.
I. Title.
E184.A1 D328 2003
305.8'00973'090511—dc21   2002012272

New York University Press books are printed on acid-free paper,
and their binding materials are chosen for strength and durability.

Manufactured in the United States of America

10 9 8 7 6 5 4 3 2 1

The struggle of man against power is the struggle of memory against forgetting.
—Milan Kundera

Contents

Acknowledgments

I GRATEFULLY ACKNOWLEDGE the assistance of the Bogliasco Foundation and the Ligure, Italy, Study Center, where much of this book was written, and the support of the University of Colorado School of Law Dean's Fund. Jean Stefancic provided incisive comments and an editor's sharp eye; Noah Markewich, much of the case and statutory analysis for chapter 1; Joey Lubinski, exceptionally able research assistance. Cynthia Carter, Linda Spiegler, Diana Stahl, Kay Wilkie, and Cindy Winn prepared the manuscript with care, intelligence, and dispatch. Portions of chapters 1 and 8 appeared in Georgetown Law Journal and Michigan Law Review.

Thanks, above all, to Derrick Bell for his permission to borrow Geneva's persona and to develop her family tree a little further, as I have done.

Foreword

Jennifer L. Hochschild, Harvard University

FEW SCHOLARS write with not only incisive analysis but also grace and wit, and even fewer can thread a tender love story through that analysis. But Richard Delgado has done all of those things in Justice at War, producing a book that is simultaneously charming, thought-provoking, maddening, and deeply important. I disagree with some of what he says but find his basic argument compelling and powerful. That is in keeping, in my view, with the very great virtues and occasional problems of the whole movement of critical race studies, of which Delgado is a leading light.

As Delgado points out, too many scholars, even on the "left," have retreated from attention to disparities of economic class, racial hierarchy, and political power in favor of a focus on the meanings and implications of words and symbols. Several years ago, when I asked one of my all-time favorite students (an African American) what he and his companions sought as a result of a sit-in in the university president's office, he responded, "to change the terms of the discourse." Delgado would have been as dismayed as I was, and for the same reasons—the deep injustices of the world call for something less self-referential than deconstructing meaning and language. Injustices call for anger, hard-headed coalitions, redistribution of resources across groups and national boundaries and, above all, commitment to reconfigure political and economic structures that reinforce subordinations of race or class.

Critical race theorists such as Derrick Bell, Kimberlé Crenshaw, and Richard Delgado have done a great deal to trim the excesses of scholars' move from things to symbols, from materialism to idealism, from a focus on power to a focus on discourse. More than that, they have contributed powerful insights of wide import. Bell's insistence that African Americans only gain status or resources when it is in the interests of Anglo Americans to allow them to do so is in some sense self- evident—what group in power at any point in world history has ever voluntarily relinquished its standing in favor of the scorned underdogs? But Bell's argument is no less significant for that, since it gives us analytic tools for understanding when change does and does not occur, and impels us to look beyond surface rhetoric and celebratory narratives to understand people's motivations and fears. Crenshaw's and Patricia Williams' insistence that the leverage granted by liberal rights matters to a group of people who have never had the luxury of being in a position to scorn them has been similarly salutary in its chastening of white liberals.

Critical race theorists also play a valuable role in insisting that, despite unremitting exercises of domination by the winners, the losers can and should continue to believe in and fight for their due. Derrick Bell's recent books end on uplifting, even inspirational notes; his successors are sometimes harder-edged but they too struggle to maintain optimism and even faith. We see that mix in Justice at War. Delgado's own critical outlook occasionally leads him, in my view, into being excessively Hobbesian in his analysis of the United States—as he puts it, "all of law is a war zone, just as all social life is"—and insufficiently Hobbesian in his analysis of international conflict. How can a Hobbesian, or a critical race theorist, for that matter, believe that "the easiest way to see to our collective security is simply [for nations] to make friends with each other"? This sounds excessively optimistic coming from a proponent of Derrick Bell's interest convergence theory. But, it does suggest the importance that Delgado places on not simply being a nay-sayer, not simply falling back into the luxury of complete cynicism.

We have other disagreements. Critical race theorists are rightly suspicious of formal legal principles which mostly, somehow, end up resolving political and legal disputes in favor of society's winners. But their solution to this problem—to rely on "our basic values and commitments" in Delgado's terms—seems rather like a distinction without a difference. Wouldn't it be the case that, for people with Delgado's and my sympathies, relying on our basic values and commitments would lead us to resolve political and legal disputes mostly in favor of society's losers? That, in fact, is the point of his claim. Such a move would produce better substantive outcomes, but not more defensible ones than legal formalism does from a philosophical perspective. So why not just argue over the content of the rules and values to be used for resolving disputes, rather than trying to argue that formal principles are biased but that applying basic values to particular circumstances would not be?

These disputes, however, mainly add spice and variety to my chief reaction to Justice at War, which is admiration for Delgado's combination of deep commitment and high analytic sophistication. His argument that universities should discount run-of-the-mill achievements of privileged applicants while searching for unusual promise among disadvantaged applicants seems exactly right; if implemented, it would help move the egalitarian aspirations of our educational system closer to reality. His caution against overbroad principles for redress of unfair treatment, on the grounds that they are as likely to be used against welfare mothers as against gun manufacturers, is also right; that discussion nicely demonstrates how to probe one's own preferred argument for hidden flaws and predictable unintended consequences.

Perhaps most impressive is Delgado's analysis of the moral, political and analytic dangers of black exceptionalism and the black-white binary. While always recognizing that African Americans have a different and perhaps even more severe history of racial subordination than do most other groups, he insists correctly that that difference does not necessarily imply a stronger claim on justice. What to do next is the painfully difficult issue. In my view, although perhaps not in his, we can best get past the moral morass of competing claims of injustice by focusing on empirical trajectories. On balance, can the children and grandchildren of immigrants improve the conditions of their lives and their standing in society? If so, a nation that treated the immigrants themselves unjustly owes less in recompense to their descendents than if those descendents remain stuck on the bottom of economic, social, and political hierarchies. I draw stronger inferences, in short, than Delgado does from the phenomenal upward mobility of most Asian Americans and the lesser but still considerable incorporation of many second- and later-generation Hispanic Americans. That makes me still a partly-unreconstructed black exceptionalist—but it may also make me more of a thorough-going class analyst.

Nevertheless, Delgado's willingness to address this barbed subject, his incisive observations about the difficulties of building essential coalitions across groups (would he include WASP miners from eastern

Kentucky in his biracial coalitions?), his urgent moral claims on behalf of the array of peoples harmed so that others may benefit—all of this is compelling and powerful. Justice at War moves and teaches its readers while it entertains and provokes them; if more books were like this one, it would be easier to believe that "ye shall know the truth and the truth shall set ye free."

JUSTICE AT WAR

Introduction

WHO IS RODRIGO? What about his mentor and straight man, "the Professor"? And, what are law professors doing writing stories, anyway?

The reader curious about these matters will find answers to most of them in the dialogs themselves. Written simply and with as little jargon as possible, they are intended to be accessible and engaging to the general reader interested in critical race theory, politics, and American public life. But for the reader who wishes a little reassurance in this respect, or just a bit of background before diving into this book, here is a brief overview of where we will be going over the course of the next two hundred pages and about eighteen months of my characters' lives.

Rodrigo Crenshaw, my brash, gifted alter ego, is a young Italian-educated man of color in the early stages of a law teaching career. When I first introduce him to an American audience, Rodrigo has just returned to his homeland at the recommendation of his half-sister, famed civil rights lawyer Geneva Crenshaw, to seek out "the Professor." The son of an African American serviceman and an Italian mother, Rodrigo is born in the United States but raised in Italy when his father, Lorenzo, is assigned to an outpost there. Rodrigo graduates from the base high school, then attends an Italian university and law school ("the oldest one in the world, Professor") on government scholarships, graduating second in his class.

Rodrigo seeks advice from the narrator, a grizzled veteran of many civil rights struggles and in the final years of his teaching career. The young man is thinking of returning to the United States and enrolling in an LL.M. (graduate law) program in preparation for a law teaching career of his own. Despite their age difference, the two become good friends, discussing standardized testing, the U.S. racial scene, love, empathy, the economics of race and discrimination, human cloning, and many other topics over the course of the next few years. The reader learns about Giannina, Rodrigo's great love, and follows his career as he progresses through his coursework and first teaching position. The reader also meets Laz Kowalsky ("Laz"), Rodrigo's best friend on the faculty, a young conservative who is as far to the right politically as Rodrigo is to the left, but just as audacious and brilliant.

In this book, the reader learns what two intellectuals of color think about, what worries them, and what gives them joy. He or she learns what race and racism seem like from the perspective of two characters who, despite high occupational status, are nevertheless frequently caught in discrimination's grasp. He or she follows one of them as he falls, to his great surprise, madly in love. The two discuss issues in the news—globalism, international terrorism, and the current wave of conservatism that is sweeping the land. But they also discuss ones the average reader might not have thought about, at least not in quite the same way—formalism and lawyers' discontents, hate speech, and the black-white binary paradigm of race. They discuss interracial attraction and whether a minority person who marries a Caucasian is guilty of bad politics. They ponder the recent spate of books that deal with the racial IQ gap. Are minorities less smart than whites? What is the role of law in the construction of human intelligence? Why are most American whites prosperous and minorities poor? Is the explanation genetic? Cultural? Why do the wider vistas opened by the civil rights revolution not lead to greater upward mobility for blacks and Latinos? Does a form of cultural DNA cause social relations to replicate themselves, generation after generation, and if so, what is the mechanism of that replication? Does the left bear any responsibility for the current dreary racial scene?

Like its predecessors, the current volume is an example of legal storytelling, a genre of scholarship pioneered by critical race theorists Derrick Bell, Patricia Williams, and myself. With this volume, I expand that approach to subjects other than race. As the reader will see, the interplay of different voices and viewpoints allows for the probing exploration of complex issues while avoiding the dry-as-dust quality that afflicts much legal writing.

I hope the reader finds Rodrigo as engaging as I did as author. He came into my life at a time when I was in transition, just as American law—indeed Western civilization generally—is today. In reflecting on these currents, it occurred to me that Geneva Crenshaw must have a brother, that he must be part black, part Latino, and that he would have much to say about the many matters that trouble me and my country-men.

Writing in a fever, I produced Rodrigo's First Chronicle in just a few weeks, added footnotes with the help of a computer- savvy research assistant, and sent him off to *Yale Law Journal* where a talented editor, James Forman, Jr. (whose famous father plays a small role in this book) pushed me to flesh him out even more. Then when he was satisfied I had done all I could, he edited him, brushed him up, and made him shine.

The eleven chapters in this book tell a story, with characters, adventures, and an unfolding plot. Accordingly, the best way to read it may be sequentially. But for the reader interested primarily in certain subjects—or pressed for time—Part I, and especially chapters 3 through 5, deal with a single theme: the role of conflict in American life and law. Part II deals with the current U.S. political scene, especially the role of progressive legal movements. Taking as my premise that these movements are today in disarray, chapters 7 through 11 discuss why that is so and what should be done about it. Chapter 6 is a love story.

Chapters 1, 4, and 6 through 9 are the most legal; 1, 2, 6, and 11 deal with race and racial politics. Chapters 1 and 3 supply the best insights into my principal character, Rodrigo; 2 and 6, into the narrator, "the Professor." My women characters, Giannina and Teresa, play central roles in chapters 1, 3 through 7, 9, and 11.

A final word: All the characters in this book are fictional, including the narrator. As I have drawn him, the Professor is a man of color teaching at a major law school in a city not far from Rodrigo's, and in the late stages of his career. Like his young protégé, the Professor is a civil rights scholar and activist, but, unlike Rodrigo, has suffered scars and disappointments during years in the trenches. He is as much in need of Rodrigo's impetuous energy as Rodrigo is of his caution and counsel.

As the volume opens, the Professor has taken time out from his books and students to tend to one of the necessary minutiae of life—grocery shopping. If you were there, you would see a dignified but ordinary-looking black man of advanced years wheeling his cart down the aisles of the supermarket while peering intently at some item on the shelf. Listen in, now, as he experiences one of those chance encounters—has this ever happened to you?—that set in motion a series of events that will change his life, in some ways for the better, in others not.

PART I

TEN MONTHS

I

Introducing Rodrigo

IN WHICH RODRIGO AND I MEET
IN AN UNLIKELY SETTING AND RESOLVE
TO DISCUSS POSTDIVERSITY RACIAL REMEDIES

"Professor, is that you?"

The familiar voice from behind gave me quite a start. Wheeling around so suddenly that my cart almost collided with that of an on-coming shopper, a young woman who smiled at me indulgently, I sput-tered, "Rodrigo! What are you doing here?"

The tall, smiling youth strode out from behind his own cart, shook my hand warmly, and said, "Giannina and I are in town for a few days, staying with her mother, who has a time-share condo here. She uses it every summer to get away from the Florida heat. The two of them are making plans for when the baby comes, then in about a week we're heading for Mexico for a few days' vacation. We tried calling you, but the law school says your voice mail has been down."

"I never much cared for the new technology," I said, then motioned toward his supermarket basket, which was piled high. "Looks like you're stocking up."

"Giannina's mom has to start over every time she comes to town, because the previous tenants are required to clean everything out. She gave me quite a shopping list."

"I've got a long one myself," I said, easing my basket along the aisle and motioning him to follow. "What a nice surprise. We must get to-gether before the two of you take off."

"Giannina made me promise to set something up. I was going to drop by your office on the way home and leave a note if I didn't find you. Mrs. Pellegrini said we should invite you over for tea. She's interested in meeting you. Oh, here are the anchovies." Rodrigo took a small tin and added it to his already overflowing basket.

"I'd be honored," I said. "How is Giannina doing these days?"

"Fine, except that she has these strange cravings. Just the other day, she wanted a peanut butter sandwich with anchovies on the side."

I smiled, remembering the time, many years ago, when my late wife had been pregnant with my own two daughters. "And what is her mom like?"

"You'll like her," Rodrigo said. "She's an ardent environmentalist. In fact, she's at a meeting of the local wildlife federation right now."

"Then I know just the present for her," I said, reaching for a long, narrow box of transparent sandwich wrap that I used to pack my lunches for work. Then, after a pause to allow a pair of fast-moving teenagers with baskets speeding down the aisle to clear us, I said, "And what are you working on these days?"

"Oh," replied Rodrigo, frowning and peering closely at two pricing labels for almost identical-looking packages of crackers. "Let's see, this one looks like it's . . . twenty-four cents an ounce, while this other one . . . okay, I'll take this one. . . . Oh, what am I working on? Well, I've got my vacation reading right out in the car, as a matter of fact—four books on the current racial scene. An advance copy of the National Urban League's *State of Black America*,[1] Terry Eastland's diatribe against affirmative action,[2] Bowen and Bok's *The Shape of the River*,[3] and *The Good Black*."[4]

"That's quite an assortment," I said, slowing down to round the corner of the aisle and head down the next. "What made you select those four?"

"Just keeping up on my reading." Rodrigo paused a moment at the meat counter to scrutinize some pink-looking filets of salmon. "Mmmm. Those look good. Giannina and her mother love salmon. But, as I was saying, after reading three of them and nearly finishing the fourth, a hypothesis occurred to me. I was just starting to talk it over with Giannina when an old friend stopped by to drop off a baby present, so we had to put it on hold. Maybe we can discuss it when you come for tea."

"Sounds good to me," I said. "I've read Eastland, which struck me as a particularly remorseless dissection of affirmative action, as cold and uncaring as I've seen. And of course I've read Bowen and Bok, which everybody has been talking about—even the tables and charts. I asked the librarian to get me *The Good Black* the other day. But I haven't seen the latest from the Urban League."

"I can lend it to you when we get outside," Rodrigo said, fishing his credit card out of his wallet and holding it in his teeth as he slid a heavy bottle of water onto the lower shelf of his shopping cart. "Giannina's mom drinks only the bottled kind. She said we would too, if we saw *A Civil Action*.[5] Oh good, there's not much of a line."

As we waited for the checker to finish ringing up the purchases of the shopper ahead of us, I asked Rodrigo, "Where in Mexico are the two of you going?"

"A little fishing village in Baja California," Rodrigo replied. "One of my colleagues told me about it. It's not too touristy, and the prices are lower than in the big resorts. We decided to go before Giannina gets too uncomfortable to travel."

"Send me a postcard," I said. "I'll be down there myself on my semester off. But that won't be 'til a few months later. I'm afraid we won't cross paths."

Rodrigo paused as our cashier rang up the final items and handed him the bill. He examined it quickly, then handed the cashier his credit card. "My mother-in-law said to give you these coupons," he said.

Minutes later, we were wheeling our baskets through the supermarket's huge parking lot. "Hey, you parked practically next to me," Rodrigo said. He opened the hatchback of his little car, and I helped him stow his groceries inside.

"Thanks," Rodrigo said, opening up the back passenger-side door and reaching inside. "Here's the National Urban League book. Now, let me help you with your stuff."

He did, and after exchanging phone numbers and promising to get together soon, we drove off to our respective destinations. Rodrigo was true to his word. When I returned to my apartment, I heard Giannina's familiar voice on my answering machine inviting me to her mom's place the following Thursday for tea and thanking me for making sure that Rodrigo got all the food items she wanted—especially the anchovies.

IN WHICH RODRIGO, GIANNINA, MRS. PELLEGRINI, AND I DISCUSS RECENT BOOKS DEALING WITH AMERICA'S RACIAL PREDICAMENT

"Good afternoon," I said. "Are you Mrs. Pellegrini?"

The handsome, white-haired woman standing at the doorway took my hand, smiled warmly, and invited me inside. "You must be the Professor. Welcome. Giannina has told me so much about you. It looks like you brought something."

"It's for you," I said, handing over a package I had wrapped myself. "Open it now, if you like."

After ushering me into the attractive, sunlit condominium, Mrs. Pellegrini tilted her head and looked at my rectangular, flat package with interest. "It must be a stuffed animal," she laughed.

As she began removing the wrapping paper, I said, "I hope you don't already have one. Rodrigo told me you're an environmentalist."

"Oh, an animal clock!" she exclaimed, clapping her hands together. "A friend of mine has the bird kind that plays songs every hour on the hour. I've always wanted one like this." Looking at it closely, she said, "I've got the perfect place for it." As she picked it up and motioned me to follow her in the direction of the kitchen, I heard the sound of familiar voices and noted to myself the resemblance between mother and daughter.

An attractive woman—maybe after the young ones head off to Mexico, I'll ask her to lunch. I hope Giannina won't be scandalized, I thought, and cautioned myself not to be too forward. Perhaps a sedate invitation to a lecture at my university, followed by a bite to eat at a campus restaurant. Surely the young people could not object; she is, after all, about the age my late wife would have been had she lived. And I had been wanting to learn more about environmentalism, especially the new environmental justice movement. But I warned myself to proceed discreetly, remembering how the young often did not like to think of their elders as having any sort of social life and not wanting to jeopardize the fine relationship I enjoyed with Rodrigo and Giannina.

"Oh, there you are," Giannina said, looking up from some two-person cooking project with which she and Rodrigo were busily engaged. "We hope you like Italian soup. We're making it for later, in case we get hungry after tea and cookies. What do you have there, Mom?"

Mrs. Pellegrini showed the two young people her present, which brought much laughter and exclamations as she plugged it in and turned the hands to the various animal positions.

"There's a way to turn it off at night, if you want," I said. "The instructions are in that plastic bag over there. The warranty, too."

Rodrigo covered the large pot, adjusted the heat to low simmer, and took off his white chef's apron. "Come on out," he said. "Everything's ready."

We followed Giannina as she carried the tea and cookies on a tray to the dining area adjacent to the kitchen and placed them down on the table, which I noticed was nicely set. A far cry from my bachelor simplicity, I thought, stealing another glance at Mrs. Pellegrini, who was adjusting a spray of yellow flowers in a glass bowl on the table.

"Have a seat, Professor. Why don't you sit over here next to me? That way, we can keep an eye on the young people and make sure they don't get into trouble."

I laughed and pulled the chair out for her. She smiled, thanked me, then said, "I know Rodrigo and Giannina have been waiting all week to talk to you about some books they've been poring over. Go ahead and don't worry about me. I taught at the community college before I retired, including classes in government and U.S. history. I know next to nothing about law, but I'm willing to make the effort."

Rodrigo thanked her and immediately got up and brought some familiar-looking books from the hutch nearby and set them next to him on the table. They were the same ones he and I had discussed in the supermarket the other afternoon.

"May I offer you a refill, Professor, before my son-in-law gets started?" Mrs. Pellegrini asked. "By the way, you can call me Teresa."

As Rodrigo looked up expectantly, I took the bait: "And so, Rodrigo, you have a hypothesis of some sort. Something that occurred to you on reading those four books?"

"I do," Rodrigo said, smiling. (He's never at a loss for an intriguing theory. Their baby is going to be really something, I thought, catching a glimpse of Giannina's mother out of the corner of my eye as she reached to pass around a plate of some sort of homemade cookies.)

But instead of pursuing Rodrigo's theory right away, I said, "Before you jump into that, maybe we should take turns summarizing the four books. Your mother-in-law may not have read them all."

As Mrs. Pellegrini smiled appreciatively, Rodrigo looked up at Giannina and said, "Why don't you start?"

NATIONAL URBAN LEAGUE, *THE STATE OF BLACK AMERICA*

"I read the first book, *The State of Black America*,[6] the other afternoon, while waiting for a baby shower to start. It almost ruined the event for me. The editors of this annual volume, published yearly since 1976, commissioned nine authors to write essays on the African American condition. The general tenor is measured, even upbeat at times. Yet I was struck by how far this country has to go to make good on its civil rights promises. In one way or another, most of the chapters deal with barriers to upward mobility. Essays on building community[7] and the racial asset gap[8] focus on economics and the dire need to provide development and jobs to a community whose lower end, at least, seems to be slipping further and further behind. Community revitalization programs are fighting a losing battle[9] as the nature of the workplace changes and jobs leave the inner city for the suburbs."[10]

"Or even abroad," Rodrigo pointed out.

"Indeed," Giannina continued. "Periodic economic expansions have not helped African Americans, because they create jobs mainly in information technology and computers, sectors containing few blacks. And when a contraction sets in, they're the first fired. Recent reforms force welfare recipients into part-time jobs that go nowhere, instead of providing full-time jobs with a future."[11]

"One essay points out that neighborhood joblessness is in some respects worse than poverty,"[12] Rodrigo chimed in. "Employment provides an anchor of disciplined habits, along with a cluster of hopes and attitudes. These are passed on to children, who see their parents getting ready for work in the morning, depositing a paycheck, giving them their allowance, and discussing their hopes for a promotion. With technology and the suburbanization of jobs, more advantaged or stable families leave the inner city, accelerating the decline in essential services. Over time, conditions deteriorate to the point where employers will not hire anyone from inner-city neighborhoods, a sort of statistical discrimination."[13]

"Another problem the authors point out has to do with schools,"[14] Giannina went on. "Two chapters warn that creation of new state and national standards for school achievement will do little good without better teaching, curriculum, textbooks, and buildings. The reduction in number of low-skilled jobs means that education is even more necessary than ever. But spending disparities ensure that schools in poor neighborhoods, the ones most in need of the best teachers and computers, possess few of either. Tracking assigns African Americans and Hispanics to low- level, dead-end classes, while suburban kids learn computer programming and how to navigate the internet."[15]

When Giannina paused as though to remember a final chapter, Rodrigo jumped in: "Which brings us to politics. Even modest electoral gains by African Americans, due to federal intervention and the increase in numbers reaching voting age, have done little to improve the quality of life in the black community. Coalition- building has been a problem—black politicians need to court whites, thereby diluting programs and political strength."

"Right," Giannina said. "Colin Powell raised the hopes of African Americans but, unfortunately, his presidential campaign went nowhere. He now seems content to play second fiddle—although he does that very well. The book closes with appendices on African American demographics and vital statistics on education and earnings, including the disconcerting news that the racial gap in college enrollment rates has been growing, not shrinking, in recent years."[16]

TERRY EASTLAND, *ENDING AFFIRMATIVE ACTION*

Giannina looked up at Rodrigo and said, "Your turn."

Rodrigo picked up a silver and black book with familiar lettering on the cover. "This second one, by former Justice Department official Terry Eastland,[17] could not be more different from our first. Taking as his target our national commitment to affirmative action, he turns nearly every legal advance made by African Americans and other minorities against them. Under the guise of showing how we arrived at our national scheme—now being speedily dismantled—of what he calls racial preferencing, he argues that judicial and executive rulings corrupted the noble civil rights ideal into a system of patronage. Equating actions designed to level the playing field for Latinos, African Americans, and other minorities with discrimination against whites, he rehearses the tired stigma argument under which even high-achieving minorities are thought to owe their positions to affirmative action.[18] He also conveniently ignores that the civil rights laws of the last few decades and the court decisions of the 1950s and '60s that prohibited race discrimination were meant to help minorities, not advance some abstract ideal of color blindness."[19]

"It seems to me that Eastland ignores the context in which minorities won civil rights victories and misreads history,"[20] Teresa said. "The Constitution was no godsend for blacks; indeed, it contains several passages that specifically protect the institution of slavery.[21] The Declaration of Independence may say 'all men are created equal,' but African American men didn't even get the vote until Congress enacted the Fifteenth Amendment in 1870. Eastland conveniently forgets all this when he says that we need to get rid of affirmative action and return to the color-blind principles that made our nation great."

Rodrigo shot his mother-in-law a quick look. "For a nonlawyer, Mom, you sure know your legal history. But speaking of history, Eastland certainly offers up a warped and selective view of it. He devotes little space to the legacy of slavery, conquest, and Jim Crow laws that made affirmative action necessary in the first place, instead relying on the feeble excuse that 'My grandfather may have hated blacks, but I don't. And it's unfair to make me pay for the crimes of my ancestors.'[22] His book is essentially a rehash of the standard arguments that we've all heard a thousand times: affirmative action discriminates against whites, stigmatizes blacks, is potentially limitless because it could be extended to Ukrainians and Romanian gypsies, and rewards people who lack conventional merit. On that latter point, Eastland should read our next book, *The Shape of the River*."[23]

WILLIAM G. BOWEN AND DEREK BOK, *THE SHAPE OF THE RIVER*

"Eastland sounds like he has a deaf ear for equality," said Mrs. Pellegrini, with a look of distaste. "Although my family is not black, it is Italian. And my relatives told me stories of how society treated our people in the early days that you wouldn't believe. So, naturally we're sympathetic to the plight of blacks and Latinos. How a patrician writer like

Eastland, writing from a position of privilege, can say some of those things is beyond belief."

I gave her a look of admiration and thought, I very much hope she will agree to have lunch with me. Then, sensing an opening, I said, "Maybe you and I can compare notes sometime. Our families seem to have followed similar paths. Speaking of paths, I think we all know about our next book, which followed the career paths of over forty-five thousand African American undergraduates. Beneficiaries of affirmative action, they all matriculated at twenty-eight elite colleges and universities in the falls of 1976 and 1989. William Bowen and Derek Bok, past presidents of Princeton and Harvard respectively, wrote the book to answer the question, 'Has affirmative action worked?' After carefully comparing the careers of African Americans admitted to elite schools under affirmative action programs to those of whites at elite schools, and of African Americans admitted to less competitive schools without the help of affirmative action, Bowen and Bok conclude that by most criteria, affirmative action has indeed improved the lives of black graduates.[24] As the first major statistical study of the effects of affirmative action, their work provides a compelling rebuttal to conservative attacks on it."

"Their main findings, if I recall," Giannina continued, "were that African Americans at elite schools received higher grades than African Americans at less competitive schools, graduated at higher rates, went on to law, medical, and other graduate schools in greater numbers than their counterparts from less competitive schools, and reported higher earnings. On these same measures, they also found smaller gaps between black and white college graduates from elite schools than between black and white college graduates in general. In response to the stigma argument, they investigated whether African Americans from elite schools were dissatisfied with their university careers. They found instead that African Americans who got into elite schools under affirmative action were happier than ones who went to less competitive schools where affirmative action wasn't necessary for them to be admitted. They also assumed positions of civic and community leadership in large numbers and contributed to a racially diverse learning environment while in college."[25]

"In short, Bowen and Bok provide strong evidence that African Americans are much better off with affirmative action than without it,"

Rodrigo concluded. "Ending affirmative action would almost eliminate the African American presence at elite schools,[26] while increasing white enrollment by, at most, 2 percent.[27] But for conservatives like Eastland, nothing African Americans have suffered at the hands of white society can justify an infinitesimally smaller Euro-American enrollment at the top colleges. Think of all the interesting careers that would have been denied if Eastland had had his way."

PAUL BARRETT, *THE GOOD BLACK*

"Some of those graduates did pursue interesting careers," Mrs. Pellegrini said. "I wish all young people were as public spirited as the ones in that sample. But I think it must be harder these days. At the wildlife federation, we have two young interns from the local college. They would love to go to work for us after they graduate, but say they can't because they have to get high- paying jobs to pay off their student loans. One is going into investment banking, the other to law school."

"Speaking of law school and lawyers," Giannina said, "the last of our four books[28] deals with a young lawyer, Larry Mungin, who followed a different path from the ones we've been discussing. The son of an absentee father and an ambitious secretary mother, he decided early in life to play things straight. Starting in the mid-1960s, his mother had him bused to white schools, where he earned good grades and became senior class president, despite a somewhat reclusive nature. Mungin's brother and sister remember social discrimination, such as being followed by store clerks, but Mungin remembers none, saying he 'wasn't fixated on [race].'[29]

"A graduate of Harvard College and Harvard Law School, he worked at several law firms before bringing his six years of experience to the Washington, D.C., office of the big Chicago firm Katten Muchin & Zavis. There, he was promised challenging work and a partnership track. When he received routine assignments that should have been given to a first-year associate or paralegal, he would politely ask his supervisors to give him ones appropriate to his level of expertise. But they ignored him, then later told him they couldn't make him a partner because he wasn't doing challenging enough work.[30]

"Even then, he did his best to smile and keep his feelings to himself, perhaps remembering his mother's admonition to be a human being first, an American second, and a black third. When his mistreatment became intolerable, he decided to bring a race discrimination suit. The firm argued in defense that it mistreated everyone, not just minorities. The jury didn't buy it; they awarded Mungin $2.5 million. The firm asked the trial judge to overturn the verdict, but he refused, finding the jury's verdict reasonable based on the evidence. But an appellate court reversed the jury verdict, and Mungin got nothing."[31]

"And what do you make of this rather horrific tale?" I asked.

"His case is an object lesson in the dangers of assimilation," Giannina replied. "Mungin did his best to deny that race was important. He played by the rules and made every effort to fit in. But in the end, he realized race still counts. His discrimination suit cost him his career—few, if any, large firms will hire someone who has sued a former employer. Maybe it would have been worth it if Mungin had been able to keep the jury award. But for all his efforts to fit in, Mungin gained nothing and lost a lot. Assimilation is a dangerous strategy: it can cost you your soul, career, and self-respect."

We were all silent for a minute, absorbing the bleak quandary our analysis had left us in. Then I looked over at Rodrigo. "I believe you were going to tell us about a hypothesis of some sort. I hope it has to do with a way African Americans and other people of color can break out of doomed or shopworn strategies like the ones the four books cover."

When Mrs. Pellegrini also nodded encouragingly, Rodrigo picked up his cup and saucer. "Giannina and I think we need to clear away some of the clutter and start over with some new approaches, including one or two we think will knock your socks off. Speaking of clutter, why don't we clear the table and start over. Would everyone like soup and bread?"

We all nodded and carried the dirty dishes into the kitchen in exchange for bowls from Mrs. Pellegrini into which Giannina ladled out servings of steaming soup with colorful vegetables floating on top. As we filed back into the living room, I noticed that Mrs. Pellegrini allowed the young people to go ahead of us. I took advantage of the moment to pose the possibility of lunch next week and was delighted when she quickly agreed. "I'll call you tomorrow," I said, then wondered if Giannina, just ahead of us, had overheard. Did I just imagine that she smiled at me slightly as we sat down again? I quickly looked away. Come now, I thought to myself. I am, after all, nearly seventy years old and a widower. We old-timers are entitled to a little companionship from time to time, are we not?

IN WHICH RODRIGO AND GIANNINA PUT FORWARD THEORIES FOR PROTECTING THE INTERESTS OF PERSONS OF COLOR

I pulled myself together as Rodrigo began.

"Well, as you can imagine, I think we need some wholly new approaches. These books show that litigation has been producing fewer and fewer gains, affirmative action is on the way out, and self-help aids only those who have something to invest. Playing it straight—assimilation—exacts a terrible cost and even then guarantees no sure reward."

As Rodrigo paused for effect, Mrs. Pellegrini asked if I would like some coffee. As she leaned close I noticed the faint scent of apricots. I nodded gratefully, "Decaf, if you have it," after which she took orders from the others.

"Talk about something else," she said, disappearing into the kitchen. While Teresa was away, I asked Giannina a little about her family history and learned that she had been raised in Sardinia, off the coast of Italy, where her father, a captain in the Italian navy, had been assigned to an outpost. After he died, Giannina and her mother emigrated to Canada, spending several years in Calgary, then relocated to New York where Teresa worked as a translator for the United Nations. I learned that in addition to loving animals and wildlife, Teresa was a devotee of the theater. Aha! I thought, remembering that my campus's theater department was about to start a run of Beckett's *Waiting for Godot* and relishing the possibility of attending it with the beauteous Teresa.

I snapped to attention as our hostess emerged from the kitchen with a tray full of coffee cups and decanters of coffee. Placing them on the table and looking over at her son-in-law, she said, "Now, where were we?"

"Rodrigo was about to entertain us with his thoughts on the future of civil rights theory," I replied. "Since traditional approaches are not working, new ones need to be explored."

"I have a few in mind," Rodrigo said. "Giannina and I were think-ing about this recently in connection with a grant application we were filling out." He looked over at his wife expectantly.

The First Approach: International Human Rights Law

"One new approach that occurred to us is international human rights law," Giannina began. "Indigenous groups, including Native Hawaiian people, have been invoking this body of law recently to good effect.[32] And not long ago, Amnesty International criticized the United States for tolerating widespread police brutality toward minorities, mistreatment of female inmates, including selling women to male prison guards or prisoners as sex slaves, shackling, and the use of devices like Tasers, stun guns, and stun belts. The organization also flagged America's fre-quent resort to the death penalty, mistreatment of political asylum seek-ers, who are often thrown into jail like ordinary criminals, and the prac-tice of executing juvenile offenders.[33] All these violate several interna-tional treaties, including some to which the United States is a signatory."

"The news created quite a stir, if I recall," I interjected.

"It did," Giannina agreed. "The United States is not used to being fingered as a violator of human rights law. That body of law is sup-posed to apply to other countries, usually our enemies. The idea that we ourselves might be brought to the attention of the United Nations or charged in an international tribunal goes against our self-image. Human rights violations are what those other people do, not us."

"Hmmm," Teresa mused. "It occurs to me that even if formal charges are not brought, merely framing things this way could do some good. Recent studies rank the United States low among Western indus-trialized countries in access to health care,[34] infant mortality,[35] and life expectancy in minority communities.[36] Furthermore, the gap between the wealthy and the poor in income and assets,[37] educational achieve-ment—particularly in math and the sciences[38]—and salaries paid to public school teachers[39] is disturbingly wide. The United States is used to thinking of itself as the best, freest country in the world, with the highest standard of living. Pointing out how the plight of minorities and the poor belies this image—through charges that the United States is in violation of international law—might supply a powerful stimulus for change."

"I'm not so sure," I grumbled. "In the old days, when we were competing with the Soviet Union for the hearts and minds of the uncommitted third world—most of which was black, brown, or Asian—that might have been true.[40] Then, we had to be concerned with our domestic minorities, otherwise the communist bloc could argue that unaligned countries should side with them, rather than with us, their racist rival. With the dismantling of the Soviet Union, this no longer holds true. Without the spur of Cold War competition, I don't see why this country could not just let black and brown misery—like that documented by the Urban League[41]—deepen. Without a crisis of some sort, the occasional report by an international organization isn't likely to spur more than cosmetic changes. We could ignore world opinion just as we ignore domestic organizations like the Urban League or NAACP. I hope the two of you have more arrows in your quiver than that."

The Second Approach: Judicial and Jury Nullification

"We know it's not the final answer. A second strategy, for lawyers, would be to promote nullification of unfair laws and practices," Rodrigo continued. "I'm sure you remember Paul Butler's proposal in the *Yale Law Journal*.[42]

"Even I've heard about that," Teresa chimed in, "and I'm not a lawyer." I looked at her with respect and admiration. She blushed slightly and went on. "I heard him on NPR the other day. He urges African American jurors to acquit African American defendants, particularly young black men charged with nonviolent crimes, if the jurors believe that the police are racist or that the young man is more valuable to the community free than behind bars."

"We were discussing this in my criminal law class the other day," Giannina interjected. "The problem is that it's illegal for the lawyer to mention to the jury that they have this power, one that is as old as the institution of the jury and that has been used to block enforcement of laws that offend the community. A lawyer who even hints to the jury that they consider nullification can be cited for contempt or even disbarred.[43] It seems to me like a right without a remedy."

"But that's the beauty of what Professor Butler has done," Teresa added excitedly. "He has gone on radio, especially black radio, and TV telling everyone about his approach."

"Isn't he risking bar sanctions?" I asked.

"Possibly," Giannina said. "Although in my professional responsibility class, we learned that lawyers may advocate law reform outside the courtroom.[44] This is a right protected by the First Amendment. They may even discuss civil disobedience, so long as they don't expressly advocate it."[45]

"What about parts of the country where African Americans and Latinos fall below, say, 30 percent of the population?" I asked. "There, juries may contain no minority members, or too few to make a difference."

"That reminds me of a case I heard about on NPR," Teresa said, touching me lightly on the arm. "Just the other day, a reporter described the case of federal judge Nancy Gertner, who refused to apply a three-strikes type law against an African American whose prior offenses had to do with automobiles and driving.[46] She reasoned, based on studies that show that the police pull African American motorists over on suspicion more often than whites, that the defendant's previous record was likely tinged by race. So she gave him a lesser sentence than he would have received if he had not been black with the same number of prior offenses."

"A type of judicial nullification," I said admiringly. "I think I'm going to increase my contribution to National Public Radio. I hadn't heard about that case."

"I actually volunteer for the station," Teresa said, modestly. "If you send in your check before the fifteenth of this month, we'll invite you to our fall party. I don't suppose professors dance?"

The idea of dancing with the beauteous Teresa made my head swim. "In my youth, I wasn't too bad," I mumbled, trying to sound nonchalant. "I might need a few refresher lessons."

"I doubt it," Teresa said, her eyes twinkling. I made a mental note to write the check as soon as I got home.

While I was pondering what it would be like to dance a sedate foxtrot with my apricot-scented dinner companion, Rodrigo spoke up. "Judicial nullification could, of course, cut both ways. Do you remember how in *The Good Black*, Larry Mungin considered that the appellate court nullified his victory before the jury?[47] A perfectly reasonable jury found that Mungin had suffered discrimination. The trial court refused to overturn the verdict. But the appellate court did.[48] Judicial nullification, perhaps even more than the jury variety, can turn against us as easily as it can help. For this reason, we need other approaches. Would you like to hear more?"

The Third Approach: Class-Based Affirmative Action with a Twist

"Of course," Teresa and I said at the same time. After we had exchanged laughs, Giannina began as follows.

"We're sure you know that a host of commentators have been urging that race-based affirmative action, now under siege, be replaced with a version based on socioeconomic status or class."[49] When Teresa and I both nodded, she continued, "Whether we like it or not, many oppose affirmative action and want to end the program. In that sense, Eastland's book merely articulates what many are thinking."

"Such as the voters in California[50] and Washington,[51] conservative legislators in a host of states,[52] and litigators at right-wing think tanks and foundations around the country,"[53] I added.

"And do you recall Paul Barrett's concern about reckless affirmative action?" Giannina asked. "Companies hire minorities to feel good about themselves, then let the new hires wither on the vine. With conservatives attacking affirmative action, the public growing disenchanted with it, and employers performing it recklessly, we had better be ready with something better."

Once again, I took the bait. "What do you have in mind?"

"I'm not sure it's better, but many are calling for a shift to class-based affirmative action,"[54] Giannina said. "In this version, disadvantaged applicants, such as those who experienced early childhood poverty, frequent moves, a broken home, and similar challenges, would receive preference in jobs and college admissions. This will supposedly help minorities, because many are poor and suffer social disadvantage, including discrimination."

"But we all know that won't happen," I said. "The number of poor whites will swamp that of African Americans and minorities. So if a university decides to reserve, say, 15 percent of its entering class for SES-based affirmative action candidates, only a small portion of that group will be candidates of color. The number of minorities on the nation's campuses will plummet."

"Just as it did at Berkeley and Texas in the wake of the referendum and *Hopwood v. Texas*,"[55] Teresa added.

"Right," Giannina continued. "But there's also what Deborah Malamud calls the 'top of the bottom' problem.[56] Are you familiar with the term, Mom?"

When Teresa looked dubious, I admitted, "I'm not sure I am, either."

Giannina explained, "Conservatives are fond of pointing out that current race-based affirmative action benefits mainly those who need it least. The sons and daughters of middle- or upper-class African American and Latino families get into Harvard or Berkeley, not ones from the inner city or barrio. That's because admissions officers at elite schools, not surprisingly, look for minority kids most likely to succeed in their highly competitive environments—ones who resemble their white classmates as much as possible."

"Assimilated, in other words," I said, "privileged, graduates of prep schools, sons and daughters of families with book-lined living rooms."

"And do you think this would occur all over again if the nation shifted to a deracinated approach based on socioeconomic status or class?" Teresa asked.

"Consider," Giannina said: "With class-based affirmative action, admissions officers will examine a potential pool of, basically, poor kids. And who will they select out of that pool?"

"The top candidates, of course," I said.

"And those will in most cases be white,"[57] Teresa seconded.

"Exactly," said Rodrigo. "Which brings us to what Giannina and I were talking about the other day. Do you know, Professor, how conservatives have been challenging race-based affirmative action as a violation of *Regents of the University of California v. Bakke*?"[58]

"You mean because colleges really don't compare all the candidates with each other?"

"That too," Rodrigo conceded. "But we were thinking more of the way *Bakke* requires schools to make race just one factor among many.[59] According to affirmative action's detractors, that's exactly what they are not doing. Rather, they are allowing race to serve as the only diversity-making factor. In other words, they are not giving comparable weight to being a Republican, a war hero, or a successful operator of a small business."

"What's wrong with that?" Teresa asked. "Why shouldn't schools prefer blacks, say, to war heroes with crew-cuts, if that's the kind of diversity they want?"

"It's because of the law's definition of a compelling state interest," Giannina replied. "We talked about this in my constitutional law class the other day. A school can't call diversity a compelling interest if it applies it selectively. So, diversity must be uniform; it cannot serve as a cover for race. If it does, it loses its reason for being and becomes unconstitutional."

"I see," Teresa said. "So that if schools change to a class- based diversity plan, the same requirement would operate. They would have to admit all people who suffered demonstrably severe handicaps, not scoop off just those who were both disadvantaged and black, say."

"We do have a twist, however, that might give these programs some bite," Rodrigo said.

I don't see how, I thought glumly. But I said, "If you have any ideas that will brighten up the current dismal landscape, I'd love to hear them."

Giannina's Variation

"We were talking about this just the other day," Rodrigo began. "As you remember, Giannina's a second-year at that other law school in our city. We were comparing notes on the kinds of jobs her classmates were seeking and my own research assistants' plans. We both knew students who began by professing great interest in public interest careers but changed their goals as they went through law school and wound up in corporate practice. We also thought of students from strong academic backgrounds who did only average work in law school, and ones from small, unknown colleges who wound up at the top of their class. This led to a revelation about affirmative action. But I'll let her explain it. Giannina?"

Giannina and her mother both smiled as the impetuous Rodrigo yielded the stage to his brilliant wife, who had been patiently waiting.

"Do the three of you remember how we were saying that conservatives have been jumping up and down, insisting that an interest stops being compelling if it is not applied consistently?" she began.

I said, "Right. Another way of looking at it is that the interest is not precisely tailored if applied in an overbroad or excessively narrow fashion. Conservatives argue that liberal college admissions committees are guilty of just that when they admit just African Americans and Hispanics and not the full range of diversity."

"Exactly," Giannina said. "High school chess champions, and sons and daughters of military attaches who had to attend thirty schools when they were growing up. Members of the Young Republicans and junior chamber of commerce. Concert violinists. Kids who made harpsichords in their garages out of a kit."

"And you think this has some bearing on programs for diversity based on class?" I asked. I did not see the connection my two young friends were trying to draw and wanted them to spell things out a little more.

"We do," Rodrigo obliged. "Consider how a focus on privilege could work if applied across the board. Imagine a school that is comparing two applicants. Applicant A has a grade point average of 3.2 from a famous prep school and SAT scores of 1210. As the son of a famous family, he spent summer vacations in Europe and his junior year in an exchange program. He has no particular plans in life, but wants a liberal education to broaden his horizons. His essay describes how hard he worked to make his school's cross-country team and how it fortified his character. Applicant B has a 3.4 average from an inner-city high school in an all-Chicano neighborhood and 1050 on his SATs. As a high school student, he stepped in when his father went to jail, worked part-time, and helped his mother raise his five younger siblings. His essay describes how he wants to make his life work adapting Cesar Chavez's collectivist, religion-based activism to the plight of the urban working poor."

"I'm sure all of us would favor the Chicano candidate," Teresa said.

"Without question," Rodrigo agreed. "But what about the other one? All of us know students like that, advantaged, conventional—and fairly dull. Most of them want to just get by, graduate, then go to work in Dad's company. Sometimes you hear of them years later when they finally pass the bar exam on the third try or operate Dad's company so badly that it drops fifty million dollars in value."

"And your plan would single out students like that?" I asked.

"Yes," Giannina said. "We call them paradise-lost kids. Given their advantages in life, they should be performing at a much higher level. We'd apply a discount, to eliminate them from the pool and to clear away the competition for hungry minority kids like Applicant B."

"Now I see the parallel to the conservatives' lament!" I exclaimed. "If advantage and disadvantage are going to be the touchstone of the new regime, we have to apply them across the board, penalizing candidates at the upper end of the scale who have had great advantages of birth or fortune, but are not doing much with them. Ingenious—with advantage the new criterion for diversity, you need to look at who has been dealt an overly kind hand in life, just as you look to see who has received a harsh one."[60]

"A sort of bottom-of-the-top corrective to the top-of-the- bottom problem you mentioned before," said Teresa.

"Something like that," said Giannina, smiling. "Maybe I'll call it a complacency discount. Conservatives could, of course, reply that it's wrong to penalize someone for how much money their parents have. Yet they might well go along with your argument, because they detest laziness and sloth."

"As well they should," said Teresa. "How about moving into the living room? These straight-backed chairs are a little hard."

Giannina gratefully agreed, and so we cleared the remaining dishes and followed her into the comfortable living room. I noted a photo of a handsome man wearing a military uniform, resting on the piano. With a pang, I realized it must be Teresa's late husband.

After we had settled down on sofas and upholstered chairs and Teresa had brought out a tray of fruit and cheese, I noticed Giannina and Rodrigo looking up expectantly. "I gather you two have more up your sleeve?"

The Fourth Approach: Environmental Law

Physical Habitats

"We were just starting to discuss this the other day," Giannina said, accepting my invitation. "We didn't get very far, because something came up and we had to put our discussion on hold. Then, as our trip approached, we thought we'd wait and get your input."

"I gather you're referring to the environmental justice movement?"[61] Teresa asked. Giannina nodded. "That's been a big issue in my organization. In fact, it's on the agenda for the next directors' meeting. The board is thinking of polling the membership to see if they want to move decisively into this area."[62]

"What are the prospects?" Rodrigo asked.

"Fairly good, I think. The membership is liberal, and the idea of joining a movement that examines the siting of biohazards in minority communities should appeal to many members. No one could quarrel with distributing toxic waste sites, sewage treatment plants, and similar noxious installations equitably instead of concentrating them in poor or minority communities. The board is also considering adding arsenic, lead, and rats—big- city hazards that afflict slums and minority neighborhoods—to our list of environmental concerns."

"You said no one could quarrel with these objectives, Mom. But courts do. I've been learning about the history of the environmental justice movement in my reading group. Most of the cases find that the plaintiffs have no cause of action.[63] If they sue under the Fourteenth Amendment or a civil rights statute, they lose because they can't prove discriminatory intent.[64] In most cases, the company or utility located the nuisance where it did, not because it hates black or brown people, but because the land is cheap or the residents unlikely to object as vociferously as they might if the biohazard were placed in Beverly Hills."

"And one or two cases that were not brought under civil rights laws, but under environmental statutes, fared only slightly better, if I recall,"[65] I added. "These laws don't require intent, but the usual solution is to remand the case for a fuller hearing. They don't require a substantive result, just due consideration; if the court or agency below skipped steps or moved too fast, the remedy is to slow things down and do it again."[66]

"And in the meantime, Native American children are playing on radioactive waste piled up on the reservation," Teresa added sadly. "So what's the solution?"

Species Protection
"We're almost afraid to say it," Rodrigo said. "We think it's a different environmental statute: the federal Endangered Species Act.[67] For people, we mean."

"Do you mean we should ask Congress or the courts to declare blacks, Chicanos, Indians, and so on endangered species?" I asked, thunderstruck. When Giannina and Rodrigo nodded, a little warily, I continued, "What an audacious idea. It reminds me of something I read by Chris Stone,[68] but in reverse. I also read somewhere that only nine hundred Ute Indians are left in Colorado, all the rest having been slaughtered early in history or wiped out by white man's diseases,[69] and that almost 25 percent of American Indian women of childbearing age have been sterilized, many at U.S. Public Health Service hospitals.[70]

And, of course, the black community sometimes describes African American males as an endangered species, constantly harassed by the police and plagued by high rates of homicide, high blood pressure, incarceration, and early death. As we mentioned, infant mortality and sudden infant death rates are much higher in the African American community than among suburban whites. So, I suppose that in a sense African Americans, Indians, and Chicanos are endangered. The Urban League study certainly shows that for blacks. But are you suggesting that the Endangered Species Act should, literally, be applied to them—that blacks should have standing, as it were?"

"Like Professor Stone's trees and rocks in that famous article," said Teresa.

"Yes," Rodrigo said with conviction. "Even though the idea sounds novel when you first hear it, no insurmountable barrier prevents its being done, either by judicial construction or express legislative amendment. People are animals, too. We're all part of the great web of life. Protecting human beings is surely as worthy a goal as safeguarding snail darters."

"This idea of yours definitely takes a little getting used to," I said. "I hope it wasn't in your grant proposal." Rodrigo smiled and shook his head. "But I don't want to reject it out of hand." I foresaw some interesting sessions down the road with Teresa, learning more about killer whales and spotted owls while getting to know each other better, but my curiosity got the better of me. "How about a quick tutorial on the ESA and what it provides?"

"Sure," Giannina said. "Our study group was reading up on it. And I bet Mom can help us fill in the gaps."

Endangered Species

"Lone among environmental statutes," Giannina began, "the Endangered Species Act provides substantive, not just procedural protection."

"That's right," Teresa interjected. "I've been working on an ESA project at the Federation. We were going over *Tennessee Valley Authority v. Hill*,[71] the snail darter case, just last week. For some reason, Justice Burger's words stuck with me. He wrote that the ESA 'is substantive in effect, designed to prevent the loss of any endangered species, regardless of the cost.'[72] Scholars call the Act the strongest environmental law in the world.[73] But Giannina, I interrupted you. You know how I get carried away on this subject. Why don't you go on telling the Professor how the ESA works?"

"No, you go ahead, Mom," Giannina answered. "You know this stuff better than I do. Besides, I have a feeling the Professor would prefer to hear your voice than mine."

Was Giannina catching on to my interest in Teresa? I thought fast, but only managed an awkward answer. "You both have wonderful voices and intelligent things to say. But if Teresa can shine on environmental topics, let's hear her."

"Thank you, Professor," Teresa replied. "Back to the ESA. The Act contains two basic provisions that operate to protect endangered species. One section commands '[A]ll federal agencies to insure that actions authorized, funded, or carried out by them do not jeopardize the continued existence of an endangered species or result in the destruction or modification of habitat of such species.'[74] Another applies to private action.[75] It prohibits any person from 'taking' any endangered species.[76] Taking includes any 'significant habitat modification or degradation [that] actually kills or injures' an endangered species.'"[77]

"It sounds like you were quoting verbatim," I said, dazzled by her intelligence and lamenting my own fading ability to bring up texts in class in that fashion, something I had done so well in my youth.

"The Act is so powerful that its words and those of the cases and regulations really stick with you," Teresa said. "Together, these two sections make the ESA applicable to all persons and entities, whether state or federal, public or private. They protect endangered species by focusing on critical habitat, the areas in which species live and depend upon for their survival.[78] They assign protection of 'endangered species . . . the highest of priorities,'[79] even exceeding the economic gains expected from, say, dams."[80]

"You used the terms endangered and threatened species," I said. "Do they have specific technical meanings?"

"Yes, they do," answered Rodrigo, not one to stay quiet for long. "I've become familiar with the statute through my discussions with Mom and Giannina. 'Endangered species' means 'any . . . which is in danger of extinction throughout all or a significant portion of its range.'[81] 'Threatened species' means 'any . . . which is likely to become an endangered species within the foreseeable future throughout all or a significant portion of its range.'[82] See Mom, I'm quoting too. What do you think?"

"Not bad, Rodrigo. You've learned your lessons well," said Teresa, with a humorous tone that only increased my already strong liking of this spirited woman. "I bet you even know about the 'God squad.'" When Rodrigo furrowed his brow, she explained, "In the wake of *Hill*, Congress established a committee empowered to grant exemptions from section 7 that requires interagency consultation and cooperation, a mandate that has been interpreted to impose a duty on the part of every branch and agency to pursue a policy of species preservation."[83]

Extending the Act to Human Beings

"That's quite a statute," I said, feeling that I now knew enough to understand my young colleagues' astonishing proposal. "Thanks for sketching it out for me. But do the three of you really think it might be extended to human beings, in particular minority communities?" Rodrigo and Giannina nodded. "I still have huge doubts. But I can see why you might find it attractive. It draws, potentially at least, on all the approaches you've mentioned today. It would take the best aspects of international human rights law, in that it demands that we treat minorities humanely—like animals." My three companions smiled at the irony. "Teresa, you mentioned that the international human rights approach frames things in such a way as to embarrass violators. Calling attention to the way the United States treats animals better than some minorities can certainly do that."

"For one thing, most dogs have doghouses; people even worry about displaced prairie dogs. Yet the United States, unlike many Western industrialized countries, has a homelessness problem," Teresa interjected. "Most dogs and cats get vaccinations and a nutritionally balanced diet. The FDA monitors animal products to make sure this is so. Yet, many ghetto kids get neither."

"Not just that," Rodrigo added. "In some cities, dogs and cats have their own private cemeteries, with gravestones and carved monuments.[84] Many indigent people have to resign themselves to a much less fancy disposal of their remains. In fact, I was just reading that in certain counties in Colorado where the sugar beet industry attracts large numbers of migrant workers, local governments have persuaded the state legislature to pass a bill prohibiting the use of public funds for the burial of indigents, whose remains would instead go to a medical school for dissection. The bill struck terror in the hearts of Mexican field workers, many of whom bought burial insurance they could scarcely afford."[85]

"Many cities offer boutique dog kennels for pets whose owners are going on vacation.[86] And in Los Angeles and other cities, a dog or cat that is neurotic or acts out can be taken to a psychoanalyst for therapy,"[87] I added. "Not to mention obedience training."

"The other day," Rodrigo added, "Giannina and I saw a TV program showing a team of veterinarians who were trying to diagnose and cure a sick eagle.[88] The bird, which had no broken bones or other obvious injuries, was listless and apathetic. They finally concluded it was suffering from lead poisoning."

"Just like many black children in inner cities," I said. "Many show dangerous levels of lead in their bloodstreams from old, peeling walls that were painted with lead-based paint. It would be ironic if the eagle received first-class medical attention and the children did not."

"Lead poisoning leads to permanent brain injury and impaired mental functioning," Teresa added. "So, pointing out the way we treat people less solicitously than some animals should at least get people's attention." She paused for a moment, then added: "Just the other day, I watched an award-winning documentary, *Defending Our Lives*, which made a similar comparison."

"I saw it, too," Giannina said. "It pointed out that society funds more shelters for stray animals than battered women."

I jumped in: "Not long ago, I read about a New Zealand group that is seeking human rights for higher apes.[89] They point out that these noble creatures share many human characteristics, such as self-awareness, the ability to reason, and empathy—the capacity to imagine what others are feeling. I'm starting to come around to your position. In some respects, our society treats animals—pets, anyway—better than it treats the urban poor. And your suggestion is that we point this out and ask for equal treatment?"

"Well, yes," Rodrigo replied. "I don't think that's too much to ask."

"At least it's an arresting analogy," I conceded. "And it does recall affirmative action arguments in urging that people receive at least as much consideration as animals."

We were all silent for a moment. Then Rodrigo said, "Positive law in the United States protects flags,[90] state flowers,[91] agricultural products from defamation,[92] and the institution of heterosexual marriage.[93]

It would be ironic if it could not protect poor African Americans, Asians, and immigrant farm laborers just as assiduously."

After another pause, Giannina said, "And do the two of you see how all this ties in with another approach we discussed—judicial and jury nullification?"

When I must have looked blank, she continued, "Imagine the effect of minority scholars advocating inclusion of minorities under endangered species protection! Whole new areas of debate might open up; people would need to face that, at least in the environmental arena, the law treats minorities worse than it treats animals. One of the chief benefits of nullification is its ability to force attention on law reform and the role of racist cops and unpopular drug laws. The ESA approach has some of the same potential."

"Even if not directly enacted," I said. "And I suppose you think the ESA approach borrows from class-based affirmative action, as well?"

"That's right," she continued. "As we know all too well, conservatives like Eastland and increasingly the courts insist that any affirmative action program based on race is unconstitutional. It's a type of favoritism or special treatment. But the notion of 'endangered species,' if extended as we urge, would include any human community that presently bears or is likely to bear a disproportionate burden of environmental hazards. Worded this way, it should easily survive a charge of reverse discrimination. Listen to me go on—does somebody else wish to speak?"

"I have a concern," said Teresa.

"What is it? I'm sorry I hogged the floor for so long."

"Industry and resource developers already hate the ESA the way it is. They'll dislike it even more if it expands. I can hear them already: Where are we going to site any environmental hazards if we have to contend with an ESA that covers human beings?"

"You may have a point," Rodrigo conceded. "And these criticisms are beginning to get the ear of government. But the revised Act would only prevent the siting of environmental hazards in communities that already endure, or are likely to endure, a disproportionate impact from such hazards. Industry could still build so long as it spreads its sites evenly instead of targeting minority communities as it does now. When the original ESA was passed, they asked, 'How can we afford this?' But industry found a way to survive protection of snail darters and spotted owls. If we can force industry to protect them, we should certainly be able to force it to protect human beings, too."

"You've got me half sold," I replied. "Although at first I thought it was off the wall, I now see how your proposal is at least rhetorically and strategically appealing. But could it really be put into effect, do you think?"

"A five-part argument suggests so," Rodrigo replied. "The first two parts have to do with emotions and plausibility, the last three with logic and analogical reasoning."

"Stranger things have happened," I said. "Go ahead."

PLAUSIBILITY AND WHITE RESISTANCE

Otherness and Familiarity; Terror and Reassurance

"Have you ever noticed how a certain type of Euro-American thinks nothing of lavishing affection on an African American or Latino baby?" Rodrigo began.

"You mean on sidewalks and in supermarkets, that sort of thing?"

"Yes. They coo over the infant, say how cute he or she is. They'll stop the mother, who may be walking the baby in a pram, and ask the baby's name and how old it is. If the toddler is standing, the white person may pat him or her on the head. They demonstrate genuine affection."

"And you don't think it's a facade, to show how liberal the white is?"

"No," Rodrigo replied. "In contrast to African American male teenagers and adults, who strike terror in Euro-American hearts, especially when walking in groups on a darkened street, African American babies seem safe and cute, like little animals. Their hearts go out to them."

"I see where you are going," I said. "The idea is to frame the problem in a way the dominant group will accept. Affirmative action won't work because whites hate to think of themselves as guilty participants in an iniquitous scheme or undeserving beneficiaries of privilege.[94] It also requires that they think of black and brown people as victims, when to their way of thinking these people are getting away with all the jobs and advantages, while their young are committing crimes. International human rights law, while intriguing, won't work because Anglo Americans don't like to think of their country as an international terrorist or violator of human rights, even if it is. But your endangered species approach only asks them to think of minority people as small animals. Quite unthreatening, even appealing. It's a little demeaning, but heaven knows, we need all the help we can get. What's your other argument?"

Interest-Convergence

"It's simply interest-convergence.[95] As you know, Derrick Bell proposed that the twists and turns of blacks' racial fortunes respond not so much to altruism or evolving notions of decency and human rights as to the self-interest of elite whites.[96] He refined this notion lately in the form of 'racial realism,' which holds that African Americans and, presumably, other people of color, must realize that their fortunes are unlikely to improve significantly, and that the only thing left is struggle."[97]

I looked up at Teresa and was intrigued when she seemed familiar with this idea. As though reading my mind, she said, "I'm familiar with Bell, even used some of his work in one of my classes. And I can see how your ESA approach would converge with the interests of the Wildlife Federation, at least. We have a lot of trouble getting minorities to sign up. The environmental movement is often accused of being the province of white elites. If minorities see that the movement is on their side, they are more likely to lend their support. The environmental movement will gather strength at the same time that environmental racism will weaken. There you have it: interest-convergence. What do you think?"

"I think Mom is onto something," Giannina said. "I also agree with you two. White people hate being made to feel guilty or like the bearers of undeserved privilege. One thing they do like is animals. If we could get them to see African American adults, just as they do small black children, as animals, they might be kinder."

"Their treatment is, indeed, at times inhuman," I mused. "Police stop us, even if we are business executives taking a commuter train to work.[98] Early in our history, whites stole the lands of Mexicans[99] and Indians,[100] rioted against the Chinese,[101] and passed racist immigration laws against groups of color and southern Europeans merely looking for a better life.[102] Treating us as full equals may be an unreasonable goal. Sadly, the best we can hope for may be to be treated like spotted owls or wild mustangs."

"Someone once wrote that American society feels about the African American community roughly as it does about saving the whales," Teresa added. "Perhaps even less strongly; the whales, at least, are not threatening anyone. But I think you said you had a few final arguments, based on logic and analogical reasoning, for changing this equation?"

Enabling Society to Accomplish Directly What It Now Is Doing Indirectly
"We do," Rodrigo began. "The arguments are threefold, and to some extent overlap. The first has to do with the basic policy objective of all environmental law—to protect human beings by protecting our environment.[103] The current ESA aims to achieve this objective, but in an indirect, attenuated fashion. The theory is that every living thing is part of the web of life on which human beings rely and that removing a single animal from this web may have a future unknown impact on human health.[104] But we know as fact that environmental racism kills human beings by forcing unsafe concentrations of toxins upon minority communities.[105] Our proposal would protect against grave and certain harm to human beings, while current law protects against unknown, potential harm to human beings. Certainly it is better to protect human health directly, as our proposal does, rather than merely indirectly."

"Sounds reasonable," I conceded. "It also occurs to me that environmental law assumes a frequent tendency to distance ourselves from the natural world and sets out to counter this propensity, just as civil rights law seeks to curb the tendency to treat persons of other races as things. An interesting argument. What's your second one?"

Enabling Society to Protect Settled, As Well As Wild, Environments
"It overlaps with the first," Giannina said. "Some environmentalists assume the ESA intends mainly to protect wild environments uninhabited by human beings. But is it not just as important to protect the settled environments in which we live? Maybe the answer to this is subjective and can't be answered with logic. But consider, for a moment, the elitism of many environmentalists, most of whom are well-to-do whites.[106] Unlike impoverished inner-city minorities, most environmentalists live in nice neighborhoods, close to the country. On weekends, they can get in their cars and drive to the mountains to hike, camp, fish, and play. No wonder they want to preserve the wilderness.

In contrast, most inner-city minorities never get to see a forest tree or wilderness creature, let alone a redwood or spotted owl. Impoverished African Americans or Latinos in Compton or the South Bronx, living among abandoned, burned-out buildings and shuttered storefronts, have more pressing needs than saving distant old- growth forests—namely, saving their own neighborhoods. This is true even in rural areas in the deep South, where many of the worst industrial hazards and many of our poorest African Americans are concentrated.[107] These threatened communities—our endangered species—need help. But environmentalists, living many worlds away, have yet to offer that help. We should be concerned about the entire environment and not create toxic ghettos to segregate pollution and degradation."

When Rodrigo paused, Teresa added quietly, "If the wildlife federations or the Sierra Club want minorities to become participants, these groups need to do something for them. It may be out of self-interest, and not altruism, but as you mentioned, Rodrigo, interest-convergence may be the best hope at this point. We have to convince the environmental movement that protecting minority communities is as much in its interest as protecting the wilderness and that polluted neighborhoods are as worth saving as polluted forests. What's your third argument?"

Protecting the Intrinsic Value of Human Life

"Oh!" Rodrigo started, having been lost in reflection for a moment. "Our third argument parallels the second. It's simple. Animal lovers love the ESA. To them the statute finds its justification in its generous protection of the animals they hold dear. But surely human life is just as worthy of protection as that of animals such as Preble's Meadow jumping mice. I don't mean to be speciesist about it, but, after all, we're surely as deserving of protection as a snail darter."

"I certainly hope our fellow citizens agree," I said. "Which raises a question, at least in my mind: Why do you think the ESA has not been extended to people?"

"I think elitism plays a role," Giannina replied. "Environmentalists love their playgrounds, while poor, environmentally threatened minorities have too much to worry about to be concerned with Bambi's safety. Their kids are inhaling carcinogens and dodging rats all day long! Wildlife concerns are an unaffordable luxury when you're surrounded by smokestacks and toxic waste dumps."

"Another reason might be that minorities, except for Indians, are not in danger of extinction. Instead, minority population numbers are increasing.[108] What do you say about that?" I asked, determined to press my two young friends as long as possible.

"That's true," Giannina replied, "but the Act does not require that a species be at imminent risk of extinction, only that it be endangered. Am I right, Mom?"

"You are," Teresa replied. "But an analogy from hunting comes to mind. I'm sure you've heard that deer hunters insist that their favorite sport is necessary to thin the herd."

"I've heard that," I said. "They say that if X number of deer were not killed every year, the population would rapidly increase so that a deer would eventually be standing on every square inch of land."

"But we all know that's not true," Teresa replied. "Most wild animals automatically adjust their procreative rate to the amount of food available.[109] If hunters stopped their barbaric sport, the number of wildlife would increase, but just for a short time, until equilibrium were reached."

"And the three of you think that something similar operates in communities of color?" I asked.

"It seems likely," said Giannina. "Anthropologists tell us that in other societies, poor farmers have more children because many of the children die young, and so the parents produce more to have enough to help them with the farm and to take care of them in their old age."[110]

"Better prospects and a higher standard of living may be the best contraceptive," Teresa added. "There's nothing like hope to start women thinking about the future in positive terms. What's true in other societies may hold here, as well."

"So that the seemingly high reproductive rate in U.S. minority communities may be a function of desperation—of the high homicide rates, poor nutrition, and the blighted life choices that society offers them?" I asked.

"It's at least a plausible hypothesis," Rodrigo said. "Everyone knows the middle and upper classes have much smaller families than everyone else.[111] If the high reproductive rate of the minority poor is a function of terrible living conditions, with constant threats like those the deer receive from the hunters, then the term endangered might well be applied to them despite their numbers' remaining constant or even growing."

Just then, Teresa's new clock, which until then had remained silent, let out a thunderous bellow; I imagined the sound of a buffalo or similar animal. "Oh, my," I said, looking up. "It's five o'clock already. Time certainly flies. . . ."

"When you're having fun," said Giannina with an impish smile. "Well, you two had better set up your date if you're going on one. For our part, Rodrigo and I need to get going. Our Lamaze class starts in half an hour, and we don't want to be late. We could drop you off, Professor. It's on our way."

Minutes later, I was taking my leave of Teresa ("By the way, call me Gus") and walking down the steps wishing we had had more time. As I stooped over to get into the back seat of Rodrigo and Giannina's little sports car, I said something vaguely complimentary to Giannina about her mother—I think, how rare it is to find a Euro-American of her generation with such a passionate commitment to both racial equality and the environment.

As Rodrigo smoothly accelerated the little car into the traffic in the direction of the women's center and my apartment, Giannina gave me a quick but warm smile, and said, "She's a rare species. We'll all have to take good care to keep her well. Even without a statute."

I resolved that I, at least, would do my part, and looked forward to our meeting Wednesday and a new chapter that I hoped would include talk of children, race, the environment—and each other. I reminded myself, as well, to ask her (perhaps after we had built up some rapport) whether she thought Giannina and Rodrigo meant their Swiftian proposal about minority communities and the Endangered Species Act to be taken seriously or were proposing it only for effect.

Just then I heard a sudden intake of breath, Giannina said "Watch it!" and Rodrigo braked sharply to avoid a squirrel skittering across the roadway.

Well, well, I thought. I think I have my answer.

2

A Terrible Tale

AFTER THAT HAPPY AFTERNOON at Teresa's apartment, Rodrigo and I saw each other only once over the next three months, an unusually long interval for us. Our next meeting took place in his city, where I had gone for the funeral of a onetime colleague of mine. I had dropped in on Rodrigo's law school unannounced, having a little time on my hands, and found him pinned down in his office by counseling duties. In between students dropping off course registration forms or asking Rodrigo his advice on what classes to take, we talked about the career of my friend, Yancey, an old- line civil rights litigator who was immensely popular in the black community, hundreds of whose members had turned up for his funeral. We discussed Yancey's growing disenchantment, toward the end of his life, with the course of the civil rights movement to which he had devoted his entire life and which he considered had been almost entirely stalled for some time, if not moving backward.

We talked about the potential for a racial cataclysm in this country, another stage of extreme violence triggered by right- wing attacks on affirmative action, the welfare net, HeadStart, and other programs of vital concern to minorities. We discussed how even some liberals had turned to the right, starting conservative think tanks that bankrolled snappy position papers, sent speakers around the country spreading the neo-conservative gospel, and training a new generation of right-wing youth for positions in journalism, academia, and government.[1]

Rodrigo reported a conversation with his friend, Laz Kowalsky, in which the devoted freemarketer had told him that the West sees social life as one round of unceasing warfare and social competition after another, with peace the exception, and that whenever two people of radically different kinds meet, one is destined to conquer and subjugate the other.[2] Kowalsky, who admired the principle of competition in the marketplace of commerce and inventions, deplored its extension to international and domestic relations. He thought that some of our greatest judges were social Darwinians who embraced an adversarial approach to justice because they believed that courts could not, in most cases, find the truth but could only determine which party had the stronger argument. A bleak, unattractive view of judging and human affairs, with the strong bound to dominate the weak and little role for love, sharing, kindness, or the arts.[3]

I mention all this because it contrasted so sharply with the ebullient mood that marked our meeting that glorious day at Teresa's apartment, and because it explained, in my mind, some of the events that followed. Toward the end of our short session in his office, Rodrigo and I had discussed whether current liberal and radical thought, including Critical Race Theory, offered any hope for redemption. Again, Rodrigo was uncharacteristically downbeat. Although the movement had demonstrated tremendous energy and creativity in its early years, developing ingenious theories and approaches, in recent days it had softened its stance and adopted an ingratiating manner toward the white establishment, emphasizing coalition, making friends, and talking more about racial discourse—the terms and language with which we discuss issues of race—than about race itself.[4] He considered all this an evasion and commented somewhat offhandedly that what was needed was a program of reform and resistance. I recalled that he said the movement might have to go back to W. E. B. Du Bois, Martin Luther King, Cesar Chavez, and Mahatma Gandhi. He mentioned as well Antonio Gramsci's prison writings and the work of Oscar "Zeta" Acosta, the radical lawyer-novelist whose life apparently ended in an accident off the coast of Baja California in 1972.

Afterward, we drove to his and Giannina's apartment for a quick bite. Laz was there with his new partner Enrique, a documentary filmmaker and playwright, and we spent most of the evening learning about the film industry. During the course of it, I learned when Giannina's baby was due and also observed her husband taking out a pad of paper from time to time and writing on it. I thought the latter unusual, for the quick-witted Rodrigo had never struck me as weak of memory or at a loss for words or ideas. Yet he was obviously compiling a list of some kind.

The evening ended with warm embraces and vows all around to get together soon. But as luck would have it our paths did not cross. Rodrigo was not at the annual AALS law professors conference, although his name was in the program. And once or twice, when I was traveling near his city, I gave him a call, but he was out. My curiosity about the content of his notebook was not to be satisfied until, some weeks later, I received a six- page, single-spaced letter, on plain non-letterhead paper, postmarked from an unfamiliar city. It began with an apology for the long gap in communication, then continued as follows:

> And so, Professor, I hope you'll forgive me for not being a better correspondent. At our last dinner, I was hoping to share with you some news of Giannina's and my plans. As you know, I've been up for a research leave for some time. Well, it finally came through, along with a modest grant that Giannina and I had put in for to a small liberal foundation. As you can tell from the postmark, we've set up a small nonprofit organization, with seed money from the grant, in a storefront in a factory town not too far from where I went to school and not that far from you. Part think tank and part activist center, the institute combines scholarly activity and grassroots mobilizing. Giannina, whose pregnancy is going very well—she's feeling fine, now that a short bout of morning sickness is behind her—is the center's director. I'm in charge of development (which means fundraising—a new role for me!) and research. Laz plays a small role as well. The enclosed booklet describes our three-part program which, as you'll see, includes policy analysis, community organizing, and youth training in a unified effort aimed at counteracting the right-wing juggernaut and, we hope, serving as a model for similar centers around the country. I see no reason why the left should meekly give in, when we have just as much brainpower, ideas, and will as the right, and, in addition, are better positioned to appeal to students, workers, and the community of color. Our general approach is resistance—the very theme you and I were discussing that day in my office. In fact, you'll see from the booklet that we've stolen an idea or two from you. Currently, we have five scholars on full-time fellowships, including some whose names I'm sure you will recognize, at least the ones in law. In addition, we have up to eight others who bring their own funding or are on sabbatical, their salaries paid by their schools. We're about

halfway through raising money for a megachair for you. I realize I should have asked you about this, but I assumed you'd be
interested and that your institution wouldn't mind lending you
to us for a couple of years. If the timing's bad, I'm sure we can
get a lesser figure to keep the chair warm for you until you're
ready.

   You may have seen coverage of some of our efforts, although reporters are not always good about attribution which,
as a fundraiser, bothers me. I've included press clippings, stuck
inside the booklet, showing what we've been up to. We have
had a few threats, which we hope will settle down by the time
you get here. One anonymous letter took issue with something
one of our fellows proposed in an op-ed column, and not too
subtly pointed out what happened to those black churches and
abortion clinics. I don't take these threats too seriously, but I
have arranged for a security guard, especially when I've been
away. Laz's brother actually turns out to run a private security
agency. Giannina thought it a waste of money, but I considered
it a wise investment, especially since sometimes the scholars
prefer to work at home or go off to the library, and she's there
alone. We hope to get away to Mexico again next month for a
few days of rest and recreation. You know how much she loves
desert plants and scenery.

   Well, that's all the news for now. Please let me know what
you think of our agenda, and whether you'd consider a one or
two-year fellowship sometime soon. We'd be honored to have
you—you could work on any of a number of things within our
broad areas of interest—and despite the plain, storefront appearance of the place, we have pretty good support inside.
You'll find an office manager, a secretary (maybe we'll have a
second one by the time you get here), copy machines, and some
new computers, although I know you're not much into technology yet. We can also help you find nice but inexpensive
housing nearby, if you don't want to commute. If you come the
year after next, I will be back at my school, but Laz, who is up
for a sabbatical, has agreed to run things, and will be sure
you're comfortable and have what you need. After that, we'll
reevaluate where we are. If one or two big grants come
through, we'll hire a full-time director (are you possibly inter-

ested?)—and maybe install a sprinkler system, just in case that character who wrote to us is actually serious.

Best regards,

The letter was signed by Rodrigo and ended with a postscript by Giannina, who described how her pregnancy was going, told about a book she was finishing, and how much they hoped I would say yes to Rodrigo's offer. The envelope included, as well, a folded-up brochure describing the new center, which featured a plain, storefront exterior inside which stood clean, spacious offices, computers, a conference room, and a small library. Canvasing the roster of fellows and staff, I noted a number of well-known figures in civil rights, including, I was happy to see, a few of my generation.

Other features of the program jumped off the page—an almost dizzying list of speaking engagements undertaken by the current fellows and by a group of affiliated fellows working from their home institutions but sympathetic to the aims of the institute. My attention was riveted by courses the institute offered for ordinary people on resistance to military spending, new weapons production, and standardized testing that disadvantaged black and Latino test-takers, as well as anyone else who attended poorly funded schools or could not afford an expensive test-prep course.

An order form offered, at remarkably low prices, twenty- to thirty-page pamphlets, apparently prepared in-house, on such issues as the war on drugs, community control of the police, how to organize to combat racial profiling, and how to counteract the conservatives' co-optation of Martin Luther King's quotations. Another offered guidance on how to set up a campus or high school newspaper to counter the host of new ones now being sponsored by conservative organizations; yet another dealt with ways sympathetic whites could tap the "Race Traitor" ideas of Noel Ignatiev and John Garvey and put them in practice in their daily lives.

But the section that most caught my eye was one devoted to current faculty scholarship being carried out by the resident fellows. In case Rodrigo was really successful at raising the money for that megachair, I thought I'd better peruse it carefully. I was glad I did. What I saw there was an astonishing array of creative projects, some theoretical, many practical, aimed at tapping the resources of midlevel and senior academics for the benefit of the country's poor and marginalized. One professor, on loan from a major private institution, was researching strategies that would harness the current federalist tide, jiu-jitsu fashion, so as to coax favorable consumer- protection and workers'-rights remedies out of local and state courts in situations where the federal courts were likely to turn a deaf ear. Another two, a married couple, were researching state and regional racial histories, looking for instances of official discrimination likely to have lingering effects today. Their premise seemed to be that with the Supreme Court likely to jettison or greatly curtail affirmative action under the old *Bakke* rationale—namely, diversity—the only basis on which schools and other institutions could continue race-conscious decision making would be remediation—making amends for past discrimination. Consequently, the two were examining state and institutional records, looking for official barriers set before minority families seeking educational opportunities for their children.

Other scholars were researching hate speech, sexism in science curricula and instruction, and the movement for racial reparations for blacks and Latinos. The compilation was so enticing that I immediately sat down and began drafting my own proposal for a year at the institute and a sabbatical request I would turn in to my dean, in the event I was successful.

Not thirty days later, the half-drafted research proposal still in my computer, I received a second letter, this one from Giannina. Handwritten on small, neat notepaper, it spoke in urgent but anguished tones:

Dear Professor,

I have hesitated to write to you until I was more certain of what has happened. It seems Rodrigo has disappeared. We do not know whether foul play was at work, or not. As you may know, our center had come under withering attack by the right. At least two conservative congressmen called for an investigation of our tax-exempt status, and one dean summoned one of our fellows home in midyear, charging that the professor had received his sabbatical under false pretenses and that the work of the center had nothing to do with serious scholarship. One of our grantors got cold feet and backed out. And, as Rodrigo may have mentioned, we received all those threatening phone calls

and letters. One morning, we came to work to find that someone had forced open the back door and started going through
our files. Apparently, they didn't count on leftists having a
work ethic similar to theirs, for when we arrived a little before
7:30, they took off, not having gotten very far in their dirty
work. It cost us several days photocopying everything to guard
against loss.

Then, the most terrible thing of all. One afternoon, during
our vacation in Baja, while I was resting in our hotel, Rodrigo
simply disappeared. When he didn't return for supper or his
evening run, I became worried and went searching for him
with the hotel security chief. It seems Rodrigo may have rented
a small boat. The operator of a charter business reported someone who looked like him setting off in a launch, piloted by a
competitor, in the direction of some nearby offshore islands.
Usually tours like this last only an hour or so, but even so, Rodrigo would have let me know before setting off by himself.
Then again, he knew I was feeling slightly ill and planned to
sleep a little. At any rate, a storm sprang up, and no one knows
what happened. The skipper of the boat that might have taken
Rodrigo out did not return that afternoon, although another
operator reportedly saw him that evening packing his belong-
ings into a trailer hauling his boat somewhere. I called you fran-
tically several times, but you were out. I don't know whether
Rodrigo is alive or dead. I stayed in Mexico for three solid
weeks in the hope he would show up, contacted the embassy,
the local police, and even the FBI, which was not at all helpful,
insisting he must have run off with a local woman or to escape
a gambling debt, which we both know is of course ridiculous.
They even asked if he used drugs!

I'm back at my law school, planning to take my exams
early in case the baby arrives ahead of schedule or I hear something about Rodrigo. I have a full-time detective working on
the case and plan to go to Baja as soon as I finish the term and
the baby is born. My mother has agreed to look after the baby,
and I'll let you know immediately if I find out something. In
the meantime, I'm afraid we must both expect the worst. It's a
bitter irony. As you know, another well-known Latino activist

disappeared in much the same way.[5] Send your prayers that this disappearance will have a happier ending.

I immediately contacted Giannina, who had just gone into the hospital with early symptoms of labor. She had heard nothing new of Rodrigo and, when the labor pains subsided in what the doctors decided was just a false alarm, we had a longer conversation. In the course of it, I offered to serve as acting director of the institute, beginning at the end of the quarter. She immediately accepted, saying that she had been about to broach the idea herself, and offered to continue my salary at the current level, which I declined. We both speculated briefly on the possibility that the tumult over events in New York City could have had something to do with Rodrigo's disappearance, but seeing no possible connection, discarded the possibility. I had some old friends in Mexico City, one of whom had lived through a terrible two weeks when a family member was kidnapped for ransom in the wave of kidnapping that had swept the country a few years ago. Not wanting to alarm Giannina, I merely mentioned that I knew someone who might have contact with a good detective agency, which was true, and offered to see what they could do.

LIFE WITHOUT RODRIGO

My friend's detective agency, which indeed turned out to be the best one in the country—and priced accordingly—turned up nothing. Nothing, that is, that Giannina had not learned already, except for one tantalizing piece of information. One day, one of the agency's detectives, a bright young, English-speaking operative, turned up at the Institute, which I was by then running, and asked to see copies of any materials Rodrigo might have had with him on his trip to Baja. I immediately called Giannina, who told me where to look, and the young fellow, called Hector, spent the afternoon poring through them. "Thanks, Profe," he told me before leaving, then volunteered that he hoped to go to law school in the States sometime. Maybe the next Rodrigo, I thought, but my train of thought was cut short when Hector pointed out to me the same notebook I had seen Rodrigo writing in that night in his and Giannina's apartment and just before, in his office. But the section entitled "Notes for an Institute" was almost entirely missing. Only the first page and the torn edges at the top of the notebook, ringing the metal spiral, marked where Giannina said extensive handwritten notes had stood. Had someone taken them? Had Rodrigo torn them out to take with him on their trip? I asked Giannina about it later, but she had no idea.

We never returned to the meaning of the missing pages. She went into labor only a few days later, her delivery was long and arduous, and she and the baby both arrived home totally spent. Teresa, whom I had seen only a handful of times since that evening at her apartment but with whom I had had several long phone conversations, including one that went on (according to my phone bill) for almost two hours, arrived on the scene to help out with the baby. When she felt she and her daughter had things under control, she suggested an evening out together, which I delightedly accepted. I made the mistake, however, of buying theater tickets without checking with her first. Sleep-deprived, she fell asleep in the darkened theater during the second act, then again in the taxi on the way home, her head on my shoulder.

When, arriving at the darkened doorway of Giannina's apartment, Teresa looked up at me intensely and tried to apologize, I told her, a little lamely, that we had all been going through an incredibly bleak and stressful period, first with Rodrigo's disappearance, then the awful events in New York City, and now the demands of a newborn infant. She said she felt terrible that she had not been able to spend as much time with me as she knew we both wanted, promised to make it up to me later, and said she was pricing one of the condos in her unit that was coming on the market soon, because she was considering moving there permanently and selling her place in Florida.

When I told her that nothing, short of Rodrigo's safe return, could make me happier, she threw her arms around me and, on the darkened stairway, gave me a soft, lingering, but intense kiss on the lips. I kissed her back, and we remained locked in each other's arms until, what seemed like hours later but was probably no more than three minutes, the lights went on, we heard the door open and Giannina's sleepy voice saying, "Mom?"

Aside from a few—too few!—stolen moments like these, Teresa and I struggled to keep everything from falling apart. For my part, the days were one round of meetings with fundraisers, the office staff, which had decided to unionize and press for better benefits, and the resident fellows, some of whom were unhappy when I had to let one of the press liaison workers go in an economy measure. During winter break, Laz showed up early, wrote out a large check ("Enrique is donating half of it—his new show was a big success"), and agreed to take on the humble duties of press officer, in addition to grading the seminar papers he had brought with him and drafting three grant applications start to finish. He said he'd be back at the end of the semester, if we still needed him, which I assured him we would.

For her part, Teresa had me for company on the few evenings she could spare away from Giannina and the baby, and, of course, on the telephone, which we kept tied up so often we joked that we would have to get our own private line. When I thought I had things under control at the institute, I began taking lunch breaks with her and Giannina at the flat. I would pick up some delicatessen food on my way over, taking care to buy at least one little treat for the two women, in addition to the main course of sandwiches or pasta salad, which I knew both of them liked. We talked about events at the institute and the baby's development. I learned that both of them had decided he looked like Rodrigo.

Then, three things happened in short order: My dean called, asking when the law school could expect to see me back, and implying that next semester (not next year) would be ideal. Two of Laz's grant proposals were successful. With the money from one, we advertised for an interim acting director. We received over three dozen applications, but the independent search committee picked Laz, who accepted after the local arts council hired Enrique to direct a major theater initiative. Laz, who had just received tenure at his law school, arranged to take unpaid leave in order to put the institute on a sound footing. And Teresa, after a long talk with me while walking in the park one day, sold her home in Florida and bought that condo in her complex that had come on the market recently. That would put her no more than ten miles from my law school and sixty from the institute. We both joked that it would certainly cut down on the phone bill, but I knew from the look on her face that we both knew that something else was likely to happen, and soon.

That was the setting when I moved my few things out of the institute office, vacated the room at the "Y" where I had been staying temporarily, and returned to my law school late in the summer. We all felt frozen, as though time had stood still. But, of course, it hadn't. The institute was thriving, Giannina's baby was growing and developing a new repertory of cries and tricks, Giannina's energy was returning to normal, and Teresa and I looked forward to resuming our relationship away from the daily demands of domestic life and the institute. As glad as I had been to take leave from it a half-year earlier, I thought my tenured professorship has never looked so good.

3

Rodrigo Returns

I STARTED, as the telephone on my desk rang with unexpected loudness. Then I remembered why. I had gone next door to check a detail with a faculty colleague about our last faculty meeting a few days ago. For years, our dean had been in the habit of assigning the most junior member of the law faculty the onerous duty of recording and distributing the minutes of faculty meetings. This fall, in an excess of democratic spirit, she had decided to assign the task to the most senior faculty member: me. After our first faculty meeting in early October, I had procrastinated a few days until her secretary called me up to ask, not too diplomatically, when they might be seeing the minutes. So I had been spending precious morning time trying vainly to recall whether a certain motion—to increase the number of hours of extern credit a student could earn in pursuit of a degree—had passed or been tabled. I had gone next door, first switching my telephone ringer to the "high" volume position so I could hear if a call came through while I was talking with Professor Weinrib, whose memory was much better than mine.

I should take one of those memory courses, I thought, as I reset the volume to normal and picked up the receiver. The older I get, the more I seem to be forgetting.

"Hello."

"Is this the Professor?" The familiar voice in my receiver gave me a second, even greater start.

"Rodrigo, is that you?"

"It is. I just got back. My plane from Baja landed this morning. You're the second person I called, after Giannina."

"Where on earth are you?"

"In that little coffee shop around the corner from your law school. I couldn't get into the parking lot. Your school must be having a conference of some sort."

"It's the annual water law conference. I skipped it in favor of the dullest task you can imagine. I'll be right down. How much time do we have?"

Rodrigo explained his immediate plans, I hand entered the last items on my minutes, marked them "draft," and dashed to the elevator, dropping them off at the dean's office on my way. Odd: in my excitement, I remembered clearly the outcome of the vote that had escaped me just minutes before, and that I had just asked Weinrib about. Maybe I don't need that memory class after all, I thought.

Minutes later, a familiar tall figure leaped to his feet, smiled broadly, and motioned me over to his table. When I got there, he clasped my arm warmly with both hands, then pulled a chair out slightly for me. "I bet you want me to explain myself," he said, smiling, I thought, a little sheepishly.

"It has been a while. How long—almost four months? I didn't know if you were alive or dead."

"I did manage to get an ambiguous message to Giannina," Rodrigo said. "I didn't want to make her an accomplice, in case they went after her. I'm sure all of this doesn't make any sense. Order your drink," Rodrigo indicated the waiter who had approached and was waiting, note pad in hand, "and I'll start from the beginning."

IN WHICH RODRIGO EXPLAINS HIS LONG ABSENCE

After the waiter took our orders—his usual double cappuccino for my ebullient friend, a herbal tea for me ("doctor's orders," I reminded him)—Rodrigo looked up:

"I'm sure Giannina told you about that offshore island," he began. When I nodded, he went on: "Well, as you know, we had taken a short vacation in Baja. We both love Mexico and it gives us a chance to practice our Spanish. We had only been there a couple of days when I decided to take a short trip to some offshore islands. I wanted to see a certain Indian village that had stood there for centuries, virtually untouched. Giannina was feeling tired—she was pregnant, as you know—so I arranged for the owner of a fishing boat to take me out there in the morning and come back for me in the afternoon."

"What happened?" I asked. "Giannina told me you never returned, and that the fisherman was seen leaving hastily later that evening. He never came back."

"I never found out what happened to him," Rodrigo replied. "It seems he disappeared, along with his family. Some of his fellow fishermen told me that he might have been dealing drugs on the side and had to leave in a hurry."

"So he abandoned you on the island?"

"Yes, although I didn't learn this right away. What happened was that we had a mild dispute about his fee on the way over. I told him I wanted to be left off at a certain point near the Indian settlement. He said that would cost extra, even though it was the only docking point on the whole island, which is not very large. We agreed on a new price, and I thought everything was set. When he didn't come back that afternoon, the Indians tried to send a radio message to the hotel so Giannina wouldn't worry, but an electrical storm had set in and the radio wasn't working. At first, I thought the storm was the reason the fisherman never showed up."

"So you had to spend the night with the Indians?"

"Not just the night. The storm quieted down by the middle of the day, but the Indians' little radio for some reason still couldn't reach the hotel. So I used my credit card to call the American Embassy on the mainland. I started to explain my situation, intending to ask them to call Giannina so she wouldn't worry, and arrange for another boat to pick me up. That's when things started to take a strange turn. The consulate asked my name, said 'Hold on for a moment,' and after a click I found myself talking to someone from the Immigration and Naturalization Service somewhere in Iowa."

"In Iowa? Why on earth did they want to talk with you?"

"I never got the full story. It seems I was on some sort of INS watch list."

"Watch list?" I asked. "I've never heard of such a thing. I taught immigration law once when my friend Hiroshi Hato was on sabbatical and the students petitioned for someone to cover his class. So I know a little about that field. But I've never heard of a watch list."

"I hadn't either," Rodrigo replied. "But I'm sure you've heard of preventive detention.[1]

"After a fashion," I said. "It's one of the most disputed notions in the law. The idea is that society has the power to detain someone, not for what they did but for what they might do. It goes against the grain of our entire criminal law, which is based on the idea that a person is innocent until proven guilty. Short-term psychiatric commitment is an example, say for someone who is suicidal or raving mad and likely to hurt someone."[2]

"Exactly," said Rodrigo, moving aside his water glass for the waiter to set down our drinks. After motioning to the waiter that he wanted sugar and cream, he continued as follows:

"But right after the World Trade Center attacks, the U.S. Attorney General asked Congress to give him powers of that sort for individuals thought to be threats to the country. Congress quickly passed formal legislation."[3]

"He started detaining people even before the bill passed," I interjected. "I was reading just the other day that federal agencies detained over 1,200 people for questioning.[4] Most they never charged with a crime. They just wanted to talk to them about their Muslim friends, their travels in that part of the world, and so on."

"And what fewer know," Rodrigo went on, "is that some of them were held for quite a long time and never charged. One even died in captivity.[5] Most of the names were not even released until recently. And the situation for American residents traveling outside the United States was even more perilous. That's where I came in."

"But you?" I asked, incredulous. "You're an assistant professor of law at a major state law school. They wanted you for questioning?"

"I never got the full story," Rodrigo said. "When the Iowa agent said I shouldn't hang up and that they would send someone out to talk to me in the nearest big town, I got off the phone in a hurry and started making phone calls to friends, including a onetime student of mine who works for the I.N.S. She confirmed that I, indeed, was on some sort of watch list and was not to be allowed back into the United States under any circumstances. She told me the reasons were confidential and that she could lose her job if she told me. But she intimated that it had something to do with that line you wrote about me almost ten years ago."[6]

"Oh, no," I said, my heart sinking. I remembered full well that passage in an essay reporting our first conversation. "You mean that casual remark about terrorism? That didn't amount to hardly anything."

"Yes, that," Rodrigo said. "Plus a few student groups I belonged to in Bologna, before I came back to the States. But the thing that really made me decide to lie low for a time was when my grandmother, back in Italy, told me over the phone that some men with porkpie hats and American accents were snooping around our old neighborhood, asking about a certain incident I took part in when I was really young—a teenager."

"What did you do?"

Rodrigo looked down. "I really don't want to get into it. Typical teenage behavior that backfired and got me into trouble with the Italian authorities. Nothing serious."

I noticed that Rodrigo was blushing slightly—the first time ever I had seen my confident young friend display embarrassment or self-doubt. I recalled how mortified my late wife and I had been, years earlier, when one of our daughters had been charged with juvenile shoplifting. No charges were filed, but the visit by the police officer and our trip to apologize to the department store manager were engraved on our memories.

"So you decided to go underground?"

"Yes. My ex-student intimated that I would be wise not to try to reenter the country. It would precipitate a hearing, and I might find myself officially declared persona non grata. I'm still an Italian citizen, as you know, with a green card. I'm eligible to reinstate my citizenship, now that Giannina and I are married, but I haven't gotten around to doing so."

"Small wonder," I said. "A country that treats promising young scholars like that, people with impeccable records."

"Not completely impeccable, Professor," Rodrigo reminded me. "At any rate, I found my Indian hosts fascinating and friendly. As long as I gave them a little money for my room and board, they were glad to have me stay with them. I learned some of their language, and a lot about Subcomandante Marcos. Even though they're not really in his neighborhood, half the village consider themselves loyal followers of his."

"So how long were you with them?"

"Months. Then I learned from a different friend that I was no longer on the watch list. Maybe they considered me dead or lost at sea. I quickly packed up, drove a rental car back across the border, caught a plane, and here I am."

"That's quite a story," I said. "You certainly fooled me. When I didn't hear from you, I assumed you were, in fact, lost. Giannina was frantic too. Either that or a good actress."

"I had to let her think I was gone, so she could tell the authorities, truthfully, that she didn't know where I was. She even hired a detective, who came awfully close to finding me once."

"So, does the dean of your law school know you're back?"

"Giannina called her this morning. She was very relieved. They were just starting a search for my replacement. Laz had been covering my classes. He never gave up hope."

"Good old Laz," I said.

"I left a message for him. He'll be glad to see me back."
After a pause, I said, "I hope we can spend some time together before you head back. You must be anxious to see Giannina and the baby."

"Actually, they're going to be here tonight. In about . . ." Rodrigo looked at his watch, "three hours. We're meeting at her mother's. How are you getting along with Teresa, by the way?"

Now it was my turn to stammer. "Just fine." Actually, I was hoping against hope that I would be invited to the grand reunion, but worried that I would be out of place at that happy family event. "We've gone out a few times. Nothing heavy," I added, noticing his smile and the quick look he shot me. "Just a play or two at my campus theater and dinner at the faculty club. Very sedate."

"She's a lovely woman. And I thought she liked you that time we got together at her place last summer. You're about the same age, aren't you?"

"Funny. I've never asked her. But I was going to see her this Friday for the opening of a new art gallery in her neighborhood. She said she'd cook dinner for us beforehand."

"Well, it sounds like you've been busy too," Rodrigo said. "I kind of thought you two would hit it off. I'll check with her when I get to her apartment. Maybe we can all do something before Giannina and I head back."

"That would be great," I said. "Use your judgment, though. I don't want to intrude."

"I'm sure she'll be as anxious to see you as you are to see her. I'll give you a call." Rodrigo looked up for the waiter and waved his credit card to show that he wanted to pay. "We'll have a lot to talk about."

"I want to hear more about life on that island."

"And I want to hear about how the institute is doing. Plus, I want to run a lot of ideas past you. As you can imagine, I've had a lot of time to think. I almost filled up two notebooks."

4

Justice at War

I ARRIVED AT Teresa's townhouse on the other side of town a few minutes early. With a little repressed pleasure, I recalled her slightly breathless voice when she had called, just two days earlier, to invite me over. Rodrigo, her daughter, and the new baby had been staying in her extra bedroom, getting caught up with each other. But they were going to go for a stroll that afternoon to pick out some wine for our dinner. If I dropped by around four, we would have a little time for ourselves and I could help her set the table.

I held onto the railing, the flowers I had purchased just moments before in my other hand, and my heart beating hard. The willowy, mature woman who answered the door wearing a simple dress cut from some elegant gray Italian cloth took my breath away.

I gave her a quick, chaste kiss on the cheek and handed her the flowers. Did I notice a look of concern, mixed with pleasure, on her face? It seemed to me that she looked over my shoulder, almost anxiously, to see if the young people were looking.

"Thanks, Gus. They're beautiful. Let's put them on the table over here. The young people just went out."

For the next few minutes, we busied ourselves setting the table and talking about inconsequential things. I noticed that the photograph of her late husband, a handsome Italian naval officer, which had stood on the mantelpiece, was nowhere in sight. I also learned that her daughter and Rodrigo had named the baby Gustavus. "After you, I think. Although Giannina has a favorite uncle by that name too." As she returned from one of her many trips to the kitchen, I noticed, in the mirror, the fine, soft lines at the corners of her eyes, barely visible in the afternoon light. I wanted to reach out and smooth them, but resisted the temptation. Down, boy, I told myself. You have no idea how she would take that. Why endanger a pleasant evening? Besides, the two of you, like it or not, are role models for the young people who would be here any minute now.

As luck would have it, they were, a stylishly dressed Rodrigo waving the two bottles of wine they had just purchased and Giannina holding up the baby, who was sound asleep, for my inspection.

"He's starting to look a lot like his father," I said, putting on my glasses to look more closely. "But he has your cheekbones. What does he like to do these days?"

"Eat, mostly. And wiggle all his parts. He takes after his father in that respect. Can't keep still."

"And liking food," I added, referring to his father's famous appetite.

"Let me put him down in Mom's bedroom, so we can take advantage of his rare nap."

When Giannina returned, I caught a glimpse of a pink room with a small, tidily made up bed in the center. Next to it stood a nightstand with a single candle. I could imagine myself and the sweet Teresa standing there, blowing it out together some day.

"All right, you two," Teresa announced, emerging from the kitchen. "Wash your hands, if you're going to, and come to the table. Rodrigo's already sitting down, and the baby will be interrupting us soon enough."

IN WHICH RODRIGO EXPLAINS HIS THEORY
OF JUSTICE AT WAR

Minutes later, we were all seated around the festively decorated table, having made great inroads into the savory veal scallopini that Teresa had prepared, when Rodrigo looked up. "I bet you want to hear more about my detention, Professor," he said. When I nodded emphatically, he said, "And on my part, I want to hear more about your activities. Giannina tells me that the two of you ran the center in my absence."

"It was the least we could do. We never gave up hope you might show up alive. It actually didn't do too badly. One or two of your grants came through. And, as Giannina no doubt told you, Professor Cranston finished up his book ahead of schedule. All the other fellows are amazed and redoubling their efforts. He's rumored to be in line for a prize from the American Political Science Association. His book on suing international terrorists and torturers in American courts could not have come out at a better time."

"Ironic," said Teresa. "The very same government that is cracking down on terrorists abroad is limiting civilian trials at home, all in the name of Americanism and American values."

"The right to a jury trial is not all they have been abridging. The newspapers have been full of stories about how the United States will need to curtail civil liberties, perhaps permanently, to deal with the threat of terrorism.[1] They were even in the Mexican editions."

"Then you know that measures have been put in place providing for freezing the assets of persons, companies, and regimes thought to be harboring terrorists.[2] You and I talked, just the other day, about preventive detention and watch lists.[3] And I was just reading an article in which a high-ranking intelligence official bewailed the inability of his agency to do anything about a suspect who remained silent and refused to answer questions about his role in a terrorist cell or group. He said our elaborate system of civil liberties may be inappropriate in situations like this, that we may have to adopt some of the procedures foreign intelligence systems, such as that of the Israelis, use to get suspects to talk."[4]

"I saw that same article," Giannina interjected. "The official mentioned the possibility of using truth serum or physical threats.[5] My advanced criminal law professor distributed it in class yesterday and asked us to think about what constitutional amendments those tactics might violate, and what case law might be used to get around them. The class seemed to think it would be a good idea—to get around them, I mean."

"Shocking," Teresa chimed in. "I'm not a lawyer, but the idea that the police could beat or drug a possibly innocent person reminds me of the Fascist regime I lived through in Italy when I was a child. Or those Latin American oligarchies that torture peasants to break up unions of land-reform activists. Not the United States that fancies itself a paragon of liberty and defender of justice. Do you think this sort of thing can happen here?"

IN WHICH RODRIGO ARGUES THAT, YES,
IT CAN HAPPEN HERE

"It not only can, it has," Rodrigo replied. "Many times, in fact. I was thinking about this while cooling my heels and feeling sorry for myself in that village on the island, hoping the government would eventually get tired of me or think I was dead. Now that I'm back and reading about the new American unilateralism, it looks like the problem is unlikely to go away."

"I suppose you have a theory," I said, casting a quick look at Teresa, to see if she seemed as interested as I in hearing her brilliant son-in-law hold forth. I recalled that her late husband was a military officer and didn't know how she would react to Rodrigo's antiestablishment stance. In truth, she and I had never discussed politics, aside from civil rights and the environment, and I was almost afraid to find out where she stood. I found her an extraordinarily attractive woman—in her way, as much so as my own late wife. And she seemed to like my company, even knowing that I was a critical race theorist and an unabashed liberal. I was most relieved when she nodded vigorously and said,

"Yes, go ahead. Like a lot of people, I am worried where this country may be going. Living under fascism once was one time too many. I don't remember if I told you this, Professor, but my late husband, Gianni, was thrown out of the Naval Academy when he and one of his teachers had a big argument about following the leadership of the Fascist regime. He took the position that an officer need not obey an unjust order. After the war, he got back in and completed his education toward a commission. This was before we knew each other."

I hadn't known any of that. I had wondered about her early upbringing and her marriage, just as I had wondered about her politics. I assumed she was at least a liberal, with a daughter like Giannina and her devotion to environmentalism. But one is never sure. And, as they say, love is blind. I had hoped, more than once, that I had not been ignoring cues that would turn out to pose stumbling blocks in our relationship later.

Seeing that he had an interested audience, Rodrigo began. "I actually do. Have a theory, I mean. The current wave of hysteria. . . ."

"Which, as you explained, includes preventive detention, border watch lists, and official wiretapping and electronic surveillance of citizens,"[6] I interjected.

"Right. Over twelve hundred individuals were detained for questioning, only a handful of whom have been charged with having any connection to the events in New York. Several thousands more have been asked to come in, supposedly voluntarily, for questioning."[7]

"And with relatively little protest," Giannina added, looking up at Rodrigo. "In fact, when the FBI and Justice Department floated the idea that they might need to use torture to penetrate the silence of suspects in custody who refused to talk,[8] one or two famous liberals actually backed it."[9]

"We must read the same stories," Rodrigo smiled. "Even though I've been reading them in translation."

"Your Attorney General wanted the power to detain suspects, not for a few hours or days, but indefinitely,"[10] said Teresa, looking warmly but fervently toward me. "Even after an acquittal."[11] It occurred to me, in a flash, that she might have been just as relieved as I was to learn that I was not one of those crusty old neoconservatives of color that have been commanding so much attention these days. "That would remind me of fascism in no uncertain terms."

"Indefinite detention I had not heard about," Rodrigo said. "But it makes sense. A Pakistani died in custody after thirty days behind bars.[12] He hadn't been accused of anything. His questioners just thought that if they held him long enough, he might tell them something."

"Unforgivable," I said. "Our system is not supposed to deprive people of their liberty without good cause and a warrant issued by a judge. This is a protection built into our Constitution, but it's as old as the Magna Carta."

"Not only that," Giannina added. "Officials insisted on the authority to inspect logs of internet use, including the subject lines of private messages.[13] And they wanted the same power to listen in on people who communicate by cell phones and other forms of wireless technology—including lawyers.[14] I guess they assume that because you're on the move, you might be suspicious."

"So that if I called you from a conference and mentioned a certain keyword that a computer was trained to pick up—say, 'virus,' or 'Allah'—I could end up with an intercept operator listening in."

"Just don't tell me you ordered a meal a la carte," Giannina said. "I'm sure the computer can't tell the difference between a la and Allah."

"Just the other day an American columnist suggested requiring all Americans to carry national ID cards, like the ones Jews had to display in Nazi Germany,"[15] I added.

"Britain is considering the same thing,"[16] Giannina said. "Among their virtues is that airlines and border authorities could match them against national watch lists. Everything would work together nicely, one columnist said.[17] It would not be a big change, because practically everybody has an ID of some kind now, and loyal Americans, who have nothing to hide, would be glad to make this small sacrifice in return for the added security it would bring."[18]

"Britain actually required citizens to carry such cards during World War I and again during World War II. But they abolished them in 1953 when a court ruled that the police powers that accompanied them, including the power to stop citizens randomly and require them to show their cards, bred resentment and caused British citizens to fear the police rather than want to cooperate with them,"[19] Rodrigo added.

"A sensible nation," I said. "I hope we follow their more recent example, and that they don't go back to their former ways."

"Talking about former ways," Rodrigo went on, "recall that executive order that authorized the United States to try any noncitizen suspected of terrorist activities in a special military court, with military officers serving as both judge and jury, without the opportunity to see the evidence, without the right of appeal and, perhaps, without the right of habeas corpus."[20]

"We did that once or twice in our history," I said. "And, under the original order, the proceedings could be entirely secret.[21] Fortunately no such trials have been held—at least that we know of. A famous liberal, Laurence Tribe, thought they were a perfectly good idea,[22] even though they would prosecute the war crimes of only one side—theirs—and without the most basic elements of due process. At least one other nation informed us they would not cooperate with U.S. extradition requests under those circumstances."[23]

"No wonder the Pentagon issued new rules preserving at least the presumption of innocence and the defendant's right to see the evidence against him,"[24] Giannina added.

Teresa, who had just returned from the kitchen with our desert, a light-colored flan in a round mold, said: "I could hear you. And I brought a couple of stories I'd like to share. In this one here"—(she shuffled a newspaper)—"a major paper reports a Lebanese citizen who had been held two weeks, with hardly any questioning other than a few perfunctory queries having to do with his immigration status. The article says a lot of this has been happening. People are being detained based merely on coincidental factors—their appearance or national origin— rather than anything targeted to a specific investigation.[25] The Attorney General bragged that federal police were apprehending immigrants from Middle Eastern countries for 'spitting on the street'—on pretexts, in other words.[26] Even some local police departments have refused to go along with his department's request to interview thousands of Middle Eastern men."[27]

She began spooning out flan in our bowls. "You said there was a second story?"

"Oh, yes. Some supporters of the mayor of New York urged that he stay on indefinitely, even after his term was up. He was very popular, but the state's term limitation law meant that it was time for someone else to take his place."[28]

"King Giuliani," I said. "Reminds me of the old notion of the divine right of kings. Regardless of whether or not you think he did a good job while in office . . ."

"And many don't," Rodrigo interjected. "You remember his crackdown on crime, which included brutal beatings and arrests of innocent people."

"Right," I said. "But even if he did a good job of rallying the people of New York during the recent crisis, you have to admit it's extraordinary in American history to want to get around a recently enacted law, applicable to all, merely to have a familiar figure remain in power."

"Better sense prevailed," Rodrigo said. "But the very idea that politicians would go along with such a suggestion, even momentarily, tells us something about justice at war."

"Speaking of good sense," Giannina said. "Why don't we pick up and move into the living room? We're less apt to disturb the baby, who could wake up any time now." She looked at her watch meaningfully, and we all leaped up to carry our plates into the kitchen. As we did, I noticed Teresa looking at me in a familiar way that reminded me of the good times we had had on our handful of outings together. She had a way of looking directly into my eyes, holding my glance for a moment, smiling, then looking away that made my heart leap.

After we had cleared away everything and settled down in the comfortable living room, Teresa took our orders for after-dinner beverages—espresso for my two high-energy young friends, a soothing camomile tea for me—Giannina came back from a quick check in the bedroom to see how the baby was doing, and Rodrigo resumed as follows:

IN WHICH RODRIGO EXPLAINS
WHY JUSTICE AT WAR SEEMS DIFFERENT

"Have the three of you ever noticed how everyone concedes that justice during wartime is, somehow, different?"

"Liberals deplore it . . ." I said.

"But usually end up going along," Giannina added.

"While the right welcome and embrace it, sometimes using the opportunity to push through programs they had been hankering for all along,"[29] Teresa said. Then, turning to her son-in-law: "I gather you have a theory for why this is so?"

"I do," said Rodrigo. "But first notice how, in other systems, when something breaks down or goes seriously wrong, they change the government. The ruling party resigns, directors or prime ministers are fired, and they move ahead with someone else in charge. The system stays the same, but someone new takes the helm."[30]

Rodrigo looked around the room expectantly, so I took the bait. "And I suppose you think the United States is different in some way?"

"Yes," Rodrigo replied animatedly, whether from the high-octane espresso he was sipping or intellectual excitement, I wasn't sure. "We keep the same leaders in office, but just blame someone else—usually some segment of the civilian population, or some minor government bureau."

"So, not only war, but lack of preparedness for one, seem exceptional. They require an explanation. Someone to take the blame," said Teresa.

"In the Vietnam war, it was the students," I said. "And when the economy tanked recently, we blamed greedy yuppies and investors. Who do you see taking the fall today?"

"Easy," said Rodrigo. "The intelligence agencies. Believe it or not, for not knowing that a handful of Islamic extremists were planning to hijack planes and fly them into the World Trade Center."

"And don't forget the two national religious leaders who said that the attack came about because God was punishing the nation for tolerating homosexuals and women's lib,"[31] Giannina said.

"And what do you make of this displacement?" Teresa asked. "Is it just that we revere our leaders so much we're reluctant to blame or replace them? Or does it show something about the way we think?"

Rodrigo was silent for a second. Then, looking up from his flan, he said, "Good question. We do have a bit of king-worship in our national character, perhaps because we don't have one of the real kind, like the British do. But I think the displacement is a symptom of something deeper."

When he paused, Giannina jumped in. "Do you mean what we were talking about before—the unwillingness to recognize conflict?"[32]

"You read my mind," Rodrigo said. Then, looking at me: "Recall, Professor, when you and I were discussing alternative dispute resolution—ADR. We agreed that that movement, which features mediation, arbitration, neighborhood justice centers, and various deformalized judicial innovations, is guided by the unstated premise that conflict is pathological. It's not. Rather, it's the ordinary state of affairs, with women vying with men, minorities with the majority group, workers with management, consumers with sellers and manufacturers of goods, and so on. Treating it is an anomaly, as the proponents of deformalized justice do, sweeps under the rug—adjusts away—social problems that are better dealt with forthrightly. And it sets up the weaker parties for dispositions that disempower them even more than formal, in-court proceedings do."[33]

"And you think this applies to the current situation?"

"I do," Rodrigo said. "When we're at war, as we are now . . ."

"And, as our leaders keep telling us, we are apt to be for the foreseeable future," Teresa interjected.

"Right," Rodrigo acknowledged. "When we're at war, everyone believes things are radically different, so that different rules apply. But they think our basic system of civil liberties remains intact. It's just that another set of rules clicks in, temporarily, for the duration of the war."

"So it is like ADR, after all," Teresa said. "We make the same mistake advocates of deformalized justice do when they react to a dispute between neighbors with horror, as though it were a blot on an ordinarily peaceful neighborhood."

"And this mind-set is self-reinforcing," I said. "Once it clicks in—once we officially deem ourselves in the exceptional situation—the ordinary rules of discourse change. A columnist once accused the president of running away and hiding during the early hours of the attack on New York. After a flood of criticism, the newspaper ran a front-page apology.[34] In another case, a TV comedian criticized the U.S. military for cowardice for lobbing bombs at the Taliban from a nice safe distance instead of going in and getting its hands dirty. A White House spokesman rebuked him, saying that media people need to watch what they say.[35]

"The administration also asked U.S. TV stations not to cover the press releases and tapes of Osama bin Laden, although stations in Europe and elsewhere did so freely," Teresa said. "All this in a nation devoted to free speech and the First Amendment.[36] In ordinary times, if someone like me or you, Professor, proposes mild-mannered rules curtailing campus hate speech, the First Amendment's defenders get very excited.[37] *That's* what we mean by censorship, they say. But when the government cracks the whip over a newspaper columnist or TV satirist for criticizing public policy—something you would think lies at the heart of the First Amendment—the silence is deafening."

Teresa looked at me, causing my heart to leap: Did I just imagine a look in her eye that said she would like to continue this conversation with me privately later? Then she said, "The government has even been freezing assets and bank accounts of people and organizations thought to be sympathetic to the rebels, in some cases doing real harm to perfectly legitimate businesses.[38] I think you mentioned, Rodrigo, that you had trouble accessing your account in Mexico."

"I did," Rodrigo said. "Although I'm not positive it was the government. Giannina says that after I was missing for several weeks and got that ambiguous message to her, she decided, perfectly on her own, to close our joint credit card. Her idea was to make it look, to anyone who might be keeping track, as if she really thought I was gone forever. But even before that, I stupidly tried, once or twice, to bill long-distance calls to my calling card, which is backed by a separate credit card in my name only. That came back blocked too. I tried it the other day, and it's working again."

"How *did* you manage to call out?" I asked.

"Oh," Rodrigo grinned. "You know I've always been something of a technological whiz. I also hate lying and cheating, as you know. But I figured that if someone was not only trying to keep me out of the country but tying up my assets, all holds were off. With the help of a friendly village radio-telephone operator, who turned out to be a whiz at computers and switching technology, I managed to get through to my grandmother in Italy, Giannina at home, and two ex-students of mine who held government jobs and whom I needed to talk to about my predicament. Where were we?"

"You were telling us how everyone thinks wartime is different, so that you cannot expect government to work normally. They get the benefit of every doubt. We refuse to believe that our ordinary ways of doing business were defective, so we don't reexamine them or the people who, employing them, made mistake after mistake. Instead, we say, we just need to change the rules. It's always some impersonal, external force that is forcing our hand."

"An abdication of responsibility," Giannina observed.

"Not just that," her mother added. "Our leaders, in addition to refusing to accept responsibility for their mistakes, demand new latitude. The world is so changed we have to suspend our usual ways of doing business, including the system of civil liberties that ordinarily stays their hand."

"And we buy it," Rodrigo said. "Telling ourselves that it's just for a short period. If I were a psychoanalyst I would say it's a form of denial. But I think the answer is more straightforward."

"Namely . . . ?" I wheedled.

IN WHICH RODRIGO EXPLAINS LAW'S DUALITY: ONE REGIME FOR PEACETIME, ONE FOR WARTIME

"We confuse the ordinary and the extraordinary," Rodrigo began. "It's like our ADR example. I'm reminded of a speech one of the Supreme Court justices gave recently. Sandra Day O'Connor had just come back from India, where she first learned about the terrorist attack on the World Trade Center. When she returned, she spoke at NYU law school, saying Americans should expect more restrictions on their freedoms than have ever been imposed in the country's history."[39]

"I must have missed it," I said. "How did she square that with her duty to defend our system of constitutional liberties?"

"She didn't. Or rather, she said the new situation would require a balancing between the old regime, which respects the rights of criminal suspects and ordinary citizens, and the new one, in which the need to root out terrorists is the number one priority."[40]

"I saw it," Giannina interjected. "She spoke at the dedication of a new law building. Ironic. A new regime comes in both at that school, and nationally."

Rodrigo looked up with surprise and pleasure at his wife. "For someone who has spent the last several months caring for a new baby, going to school, and running an institute, I'm impressed at how you've managed to keep up."

"Sandra Day O'Connor is one of my principal puzzlements. I try to keep up with her, not because I admire or see her as my role model. Nor because she's frequently the swing vote in many 5–4 Supreme Court decisions, or even because she's one of only two women who have ever served on that court. Rather, it's because her view of law and judging is so statist it serves as a bellwether on where the establishment may be wanting to go."

"And you think that her idea of balancing provides a clue?" Teresa asked.

"It does," Giannina said. "The government made a series of policy errors in the Middle East, leading up to the current wave of terrorism. In our system, we can't blame the leaders, at least unless they behave very badly. So we blame the messengers, the CIA and FBI, for bringing us the wrong message."

"Or not bringing us the right ones," Rodrigo interjected.

"Precisely," Giannina continued. "And now for these bureaucrats and underlings to do their jobs better, we fool ourselves into thinking we must change the rules. As though locking up a thousand people and giving them truth serum will make up for the deficiencies in our role in the world and our failure to come up with a sensible Middle Eastern policy."

"Did Justice O'Connor address any of that?" Teresa asked.

"Not at all," Giannina replied. "She said, instead, that the national trauma will . . . let me see. I have the story right here." She riffled through some newspaper clippings on a shelf under the coffee table nearby. "Yes, here it is. Will cause us to 'experience more restrictions on our personal freedom than has ever been the case in our country.'[41] She went on to say that lawyers will play an important part in striking the right balance."[42]

"By which she means, of course, forfeiting our freedoms from criminal surveillance, wiretapping, and travel in and out of the country," Rodrigo added. "Odd. I don't feel very reassured by that."

"Nor should you," I said. "The history of justice during wartime gives little ground for comfort. During each major war, the United States cracked down on dissenters. Eighty years ago, the United States suffered a wave of bombings, including one at the home of Attorney General A. Mitchell Palmer. In the raids that followed, government agents in dozens of cities arrested six thousand suspects, many of them foreigners or immigrants, on suspicion of nothing more tangible than being sympathetic to unionism or radical causes. The agents beat many, detained them in crowded quarters, and forced them, on penalty of violence, to sign fraudulent confessions."[43]

"Before that, Congress in 1798 passed the Alien Enemy Act in anticipation of war with France. It authorized deporting alien males over the age of fourteen.[44] In 1918, Congress passed a similar measure for World War I,[45] and in 1940 the Alien Registration Act required all noncitizens residing in the United States to register and be fingerprinted,"[46] Rodrigo said. "Laz mentioned these to me the other day, as a way of getting my goat, I think. Most of these measures were enacted by Democratic administrations."

"Not to mention Lincoln's suspension of the writ of habeas corpus," I added. "He suspended the Constitution, supposedly to save it."

"And during World War II," Giannina continued, "we detained over one hundred twenty-thousand Japanese Americans in makeshift internment camps on trumped-up charges, never tested in a hearing of any sort, that the entire ethnic group might be contemplating sabotage.[47] We were discussing this in my constitutional law class the other day. Most of the class thought it was indefensible. But only a few compared it to the detention of those twelve hundred Muslims."

"And I bet you remember the period in the late forties and early fifties, when we imposed criminal and civil sanctions on persons thought to be members of communist groups or writers sympathetic to the left. Many went to jail rather than name their friends. Others left for Mexico, where they spent years in exile writing under assumed names. These included some of Hollywood's most noted figures,"[48] I said.

"I read about that period," Giannina said. "Anticommunist fervor ran high, just like today with Arabs and other foreigners. Although we now think Senator McCarthy and his allies overstepped, at the time few offered any protest."

"And I bet you ran across yet other occasions, Professor, when you taught that immigration law class, when the United States adopted racist or anti–civil libertarian rules in times of threat," Rodrigo prompted.

I thought for a moment. "Yes, indeed. During World War II, the United States refused to admit Jews fleeing Nazi Germany under sanctuary provisions.[49] And, in addition to the examples you mentioned, you have the more recent situation that prevailed after the 1996 Oklahoma City bombing when Congress authorized the Immigration and Naturalization Service to use secret evidence to deport immigrants.[50] It also made it a crime to provide aid to any foreign organization thought to engage in terror, as defined by the United States."[51]

"Very good, Professor," Rodrigo said. I thought to myself, the young guy has probably forgotten that us old codgers know a thing or two. He probably thinks he's the only one around this table who has all his marbles. Much as I liked and admired him, I made a mental note to show him sometime what I could really do. But I realized he was on something of a roll and undoubtedly wanted to tie his theory up in some sort of bow. So I tossed him a softball:

"And so, Rodrigo, given all this evidence that things change radically during wartime, what accounts for it?"

"I have a theory," he said. Teresa and Giannina smiled simultaneously. But the irrepressible Rodrigo continued undaunted. "Actually two, or, depending on how you count, three." Noticing his wife toss a glance in the direction of the bedroom—where the baby was sleeping, he said, "Maybe I'll just outline the first two, and save the grand theory for next time."

"Good plan," said Giannina.

"Although I, for one, very much want to hear it," said Teresa. "Maybe we'll get Gus back here again soon for a makeup session."

I'm an old guy, but the reader can imagine my reaction to that latter remark. When I shot a quick glance at her, I noticed Teresa smiling at me with the sweetest, most indulgent look you can imagine.

IN WHICH RODRIGO EXPLAINS
HIS FIRST THEORY ABOUT JUSTICE AT WAR

How the Analogy to Courts Martial and
Military Justice Unconsciously Colors Our Thinking

"My first theory is simple. Almost one-quarter of American families contain a member who has served in the Armed Forces in some capacity or other. Either they attend a military school, perform actual military service, or serve in the reserves or national guard. If you add in citizens who join paramilitary organizations like the police, FBI, CIA, DEA, or police auxiliary units, the number is even larger."

When Rodrigo paused to let the impact of these figures sink in, I said, quick as a flash, "And so, Rodrigo, you are saying that all those Americans gain some exposure to a form of justice, the court martial or an equivalent of it, that accustoms them to the idea that justice during situations of duress can be, shall we say, streamlined, with different rules and less procedural nicety? This exposure then disposes them to respond the same way years later, when they consider what the national response should be to a threat of some sort."

Rodrigo looked up with a look of respect. "You said it better than I could have myself, Professor. I keep calling you that, but I should be calling you Gus, I know. We're colleagues and on the same plane. Or rather, I hope I'm on the same plane as you, Professor. Oh, I'm making a fool of myself. Never mind. But well put. We let this other model click in."

"It doesn't just click in as some sort of background figure or trope," I went on. Now, I'm on a roll, I thought. Maybe my memory's not failing after all. "In fact, just the other day I was reading that Giannina's role model Justice Sandra Day O'Connor"—I looked up at her to see her quick smile—"in that same article Giannina told us about, said that in our treatment of suspected terrorists, even in our civilian population—men, women, and children of Arab descent who may have done nothing more suspicious than attend a mosque, criticize our Israel policy, or share a last name with a known terrorist—we may have to adopt a new approach or paradigm."[52]

"And that paradigm is . . . ?" said Teresa, looking at me intently.

"Why, a quasi-military one, like the one that got your late husband in trouble for merely suggesting that a loyal Italian officer might harbor concerns over state fascism. For at least one Supreme Court justice, unusual situations of national threat mean that we can and should suspend our cherished constitutional guarantees—I believe she actually used those precise words—and instead replace them with international rules of war."[53]

When all three of my interlocutors looked shocked, I added, "I'm quite sure. We could look her up on Lexis, if Teresa's computer has the software." She nodded, so I went on. "But I don't want to preempt a second discussion, or prolong this one past the point where we'll be joined by a probably very hungry and cross fifth participant. So, in the interest of hearing Rodrigo's second theory, I think we should quickly spell out what Justice O'Connor's remark means, then move on."

"Professor, your mind works fast. If you take her seriously. . . ."

"As we must," Teresa interjected. "I'm sure she chose her words with care."

"Indeed," said Rodrigo. "It would seem to follow that one could detain a member of the enemy in a prison-type camp indefinitely, until the war ends, and without any need to provide a lawyer and a hearing. We don't supply those for POWs, and under O'Connor's model, we probably wouldn't have to for Muslims and foreigners rounded up during the current crisis."

"O'Connor's rules-of-war model does fit a great deal of what we were talking about," said Teresa. "Take surveillance. POWs are subject to constant surveillance through watchtowers and guards. This is expected and normal, and no one gets excited when it happens or thinks a constitutional violation has occurred. We take away their valuables, just as the current regime feels no compunction about freezing the assets of anyone thought to be connected in any way with a regime it believes is supporting terrorism. Even national ID cards. Prisoners are forced to wear easily recognized uniforms with their names on them, to answer roll call several times a day, and to have their mug shots taken."[54]

"Exactly," said Rodrigo. "We may use the language of a wartime emergency, as though we were merely bending peacetime rules a little. But if you look more closely, you see that really we are talking about a wholly new way of looking at due process. Justice at war is a misnomer. What happens is that we first decide we're at war. Then the approach changes, so that we apply, sometimes without knowing it, international wartime rules, even to civilians and civilian problems like a newspaper editor who writes a column questioning national policy."

"A heavy thought," I said, after a short pause. "But I think you had a second theory for us."

IN WHICH RODRIGO EXPLAINS WHAT CALLS UP
THE MODEL OF INTERNATIONAL RULES OF WAR

"Oh, yes," Rodrigo said. "The final thing I need to do is set out what situations call up the second paradigm—the one in which prisoners only get an occasional visit from the Red Cross and protection from outright torture or isolation."

"If that," Giannina interjected. "When the United States transferred the first group of Taliban prisoners to Guantanamo for detention, the administration at first maintained that they were not even prisoners of war protected by the Geneva Convention.[55] Fortunately, international pressure caused them to back down.[56] But you were explaining what causes this paradigm to click in."

"I assume that it has to do with some sort of perceived threat," Teresa said.

"That's part of it," Rodrigo replied. "But the threat need not be external. Everything is on a sliding scale. I was thinking about this on that island."

"Sliding scale?" I said. "The threat part I understand. But I don't know what you mean by that term, in this situation, at least. I hope you explain yourself later—assuming Teresa is willing to have us back."

"All of you, separately or individually," Teresa said, smiling. I could feel my cheeks getting warm and my temperature rising, so I said nothing. Fortunately, Rodrigo jumped in without seeming to notice my confusion:

"What calls up the wartime exceptions, then, is any sort of situation that prompts society to draw simple we-they distinctions. Friends and enemies. Us and them. Western civilization versus the forces of darkness. Rationality and democracy versus fundamentalist zeal. Once you get that, jettisoning constitutional niceties and embracing the barebones minimum we afford prisoners of war who five minutes ago were trying to kill our boys begins to seem reasonable." Rodrigo looked up to see our reaction. Seeing no dissent, he concluded:

"And that explains why the U.S. president, in the weeks following the New York City events, so many times declared 'Either you're with us or against us.'[57] He demanded that the nations of the world take sides. They either sided with us against the terrorists, or the United States would consider them part of the problem, part of the terrorist network—the axis of evil."

After a short pause, I added: "The U.S. Attorney General went even further. Testifying before the Senate he said that those who challenged him only aided the terrorists and gave ammunition to America's enemies."[58]

"And, to make sure that America's youth have the right attitude, a different Supreme Court justice, with help from the ABA, launched a Dialogue on Freedom. He wanted to counter all that academic shilly-shallying that always sees two sides to a story and 'shades into excuses' for terrorism. He called it a nonpartisan effort."[59]

"And, once again, what is it that calls up this behavior on our part?" Teresa asked.

"Any situation that fills us with either uncertainty or a sense of threat. Then we don't want anyone remaining neutral, like Switzerland. Even the UN and organizations like the Red Cross come under suspicion. You're either friend or foe, as in actual wartime. Which explains much of what we were talking about before. The internment of innocent Japanese Americans. The raids against domestic protesters during times of stress. Racial profiling of Arabs. The recent closings of the border. The key thing is whether the country sees you as friend or foe."

"Or at least foreign," Giannina added. "Do you remember those two hundred fifty Dominicans who were killed in that plane crash in Queens shortly after the World Trade Center disaster?" When we all nodded, she continued: "You don't hear any more about them these days. As soon as the country determined that the crash that killed them was not part of a terrorist plot, we lost interest."

After a short pause, I said, "Rodrigo, you mentioned racial profiling just now. Just to play devil's advocate, what's wrong with that practice? After all, eleven Arabs did fly those planes into our towers."

"Not to mention their support groups," Rodrigo acknowledged, "Arabs all. What's wrong with that argument is that it ignores the one billion Muslims who did not. Also, that our own kind may well pose an even greater danger."

"Which we conveniently ignore," I said. "Perhaps because of that very same we-they thinking you've been describing. This reminds me of an earlier conversation we had."[60]

"On black and white crime, and the social construction of threat," said Rodrigo. "There, we showed that white-collar crime, undeclared wars, unsafe products, and other behavior associated with white perpetrators cause more deaths, injuries, and property loss, on an aggregate as well as per capita basis, than all street crime combined."

"Yet we focus on the crimes committed by other groups all out of proportion to their frequency and lethality," I said. "But still, isn't terrorism different—weird, foreign, alien, the sort of thing committed mainly by foreigners?"

"Yes and no," Rodrigo replied. "The Unabomber, Oklahoma City bombers, and school shooters were all Americans. The anthrax mailer probably, as well."

"Not to mention the arsonists who burned down all those black churches," Teresa added.

"Plus many more examples we could name, if we went back in civil rights history," Giannina added.

"The Enron crisis, caused by ruthless predatory behavior in corporate suites, cost three thousand workers their jobs and pensions. That's probably twelve thousand people facing destitution," Teresa said.

"Yet nobody suggests racially profiling whites or requiring every corporate executive, design engineer, or accountant at a major firm to have his or her briefcase checked every day," Rodrigo pointed out. "In the World Trade Center tragedy itself, public health authorities kept quiet about certain risks . . ."

"Including levels of dioxin, asbestos, benzene, and other chemicals several hundred times higher than those the EPA considers safe," Teresa interjected.

"Right," Rodrigo continued. "They said they didn't want to alarm the public. Yet their failure to warn exposed hundreds, perhaps thousands, of people to the risk of deadly cancer."

"Including the brave fire fighters, police, and rescue workers who rushed to the scene."

"And could have worn masks, or waited a short time until they became available," I added.

"Nobody suggests profiling government authorities to see if they may be lying to us on important matters," Rodrigo said. "It's because of that same we-they thinking. The sorts of action committed by our own kind seem ordinary and normal."

"I'm reminded of those debates over immigration you hear in environmental circles and some right-wing policy reports," Teresa interjected. "Immigrants consume social services and cause wear and tear on certain public facilities, like roads. Whether they make up for that in their economic contribution to the regions in which they settle is anybody's guess. What no one mentions is that their impact on the economy, medical services, gasoline consumption, and so on, is apt to be much less than that of the baby boom generation reaching old age. Yet no one damns the boomers or suggests that they have no business getting old."

Just then, Giannina cocked an ear toward the bedroom and gestured that we should be quiet for a minute. Then, tiptoeing toward the room, she opened the door slightly and peered inside. Then she closed it and tiptoed back. "By my reckoning we have about five minutes. Rodrigo, if you're going to summarize, you'd better start. I'll get the baby's things together."

Rodrigo took a deep breath. "It's been a long conversation, with a lot of unexpected twists and turns."

"Okay," Teresa said. "Let me start out. I think we agreed that the quality of justice America affords militants, dissidents, communists, immigrants, and especially wartime enemies is a function of how foreign and threatening we think they are. In short, we try them first in the court of public opinion, then decide what quality of justice they are to get. History shows that in every era, we tailor even our most basic constitutional guarantees to the type of defendant and the situation in which he presents himself.[61] Today is no different. And Rodrigo has given us the beginnings of a set of criteria that the nation implicitly uses to determine the degree of justice a defendant is due."

"Right," Rodrigo said. "And the main one is how threatened the nation feels by virtue of what the defendant has done, and how many others seem likely to do so as well. In short, war, metaphorical or actual."[62]

Just then the baby let out a lusty cry, Giannina jumped up, Teresa gave me a wistful look, and I told Rodrigo, "Looks like your grand synthesis is going to have to await another time."

"Oh, well," said my irrepressible young protégé, picking up empty plates and starting toward the kitchen. "Mom seems to like the idea of getting together again, so . . ."

Just then Teresa materialized at my elbow. "What are the three of you doing tomorrow?" she asked. Trying not to seem too eager, I said, "I have a seminar, but I'm free after three."

5

Taming Terrorism

WHEN WE RECONVENED next afternoon, I had to force myself to concentrate and seem normal. Rodrigo's voice welcoming me and asking how my seminar had gone seemed to be coming out of a pink-tinged fog. Teresa had met me on the steps of the townhouse and, glancing around to see if anyone was looking, given me a quick hug and kiss on the cheek. Except that the kiss had ended, somehow, with a quick brush of her lips on mine. So soft!

Taking my hand in hers, she led me up the steps, warning me in a low voice that the young people were upstairs waiting. I felt like a teenager as I emerged in the entryway of her apartment to the sound of Rodrigo and Giannina talking inside. Teresa gave my hand a quick squeeze, then let go. "They're in there."

Minutes later, Teresa was bringing tea and cookies from the kitchen and gesturing that we should begin. "I have a few things for dinner later on if you can stay, Gus." I nodded, mutely but gratefully, and Rodrigo began:

"The baby's just had his feeding. So we should have a little time. Yesterday, we stopped just as I was going to suggest a way of generalizing the lessons of justice at war. I was talking about this with Laz."

"You're lucky to have such a good colleague," I said.

"Even if he is a conservative. He keeps me honest. And we end up seeing eye-to-eye on more than you might imagine."

"Not to mention his helping with the institute while you were away. Some of the younger fellows who hadn't read his work assumed he was a lefty like you. Even when they realized he was not, they still really liked him and were sorry to see him leave at the end of the summer."

"He's one of a kind," said Rodrigo. "And a great role model for the gay students at my school."

Giannina gave Rodrigo a quick look, and my young colleague, catching her meaning, said. "We'd better start. Giannina wants to be in on this, and the baby may sleep for only an hour or so."

IN WHICH A YOUNG COUPLE AND TWO STAR-STRUCK OLDER LOVERS DISCUSS THE ORDINARY AND THE EXTRAORDINARY IN CONSTITUTIONAL ADJUDICATION AND A BETTER APPROACH ON THE PART OF THE WEST TOWARD ISLAMIC NATIONALISM

"What I want to propose is simply stated," he began. "I think I mentioned last time that my mechanism operated in other areas as well, and was not confined to war."

"I think you described it as a sliding scale," prompted Giannina. "In some settings, it looks like a duality. But I gather you think it's part of something broader."

"I do," Rodrigo replied. "Consider how many areas are riddled with what we call exceptions. A general rule, such as that patients have the right to informed consent for medical treatment, turns out to contain an exception if the doctor thinks the situation is an emergency and you'll die or do something drastic to yourself if not treated. And the same is true if telling you about the risks of treatment may cause you to reject it."[1]

"That's the so-called therapeutic exception,"[2] Giannina said. "We studied that in torts."

"By the same token, the doctor needn't disclose risks a reasonable patient wouldn't consider material, even if they might be quite important to you."[3]

"That's the materiality exception," said Giannina.

"Informed consent isn't the only area rife with exceptions," Rodrigo continued. "Consider immigration law, which Gus taught recently. Usually the government cannot deprive you of your liberty or right to a livelihood without a hearing and good cause. But if you're an immigrant, it can, based on secret evidence.[4] And the government may change the rules without any input from people like you."

"That's the plenary power doctrine,"[5] I said.

"Right. And criminal law is full of the same sort of thing. In civics class, we're taught that the police can't enter your home or search your car without a warrant signed by a judge and a showing of good cause.[6] But that rule is riddled with exceptions."

"Such as the good faith one,"[7] Giannina said.

"Or the plain-view rule,"[8] I added.

"And didn't I read the other day that the police can enter your home or car if your housemate or roommate gives permission?"[9] Teresa asked.

"That's one of the more illogical ones," Rodrigo replied. "And then consider tort law. Generally, someone who performs a negligent act that foreseeably causes harm to another person is responsible if that harm materializes. But powerful commercial forces have engrafted so many exceptions that this rule might as well not exist."

"I can think of several," I said. "Such as the rule of privity—that you can't recover from a defendant in a chain of commercial dealings, only the one who sold the product directly to you."[10]

"And consider all those exceptions having to do with warranties. A seller who does not want to be liable only has to include a disclaimer, 'I am not responsible for any damage resulting from use of this product.'"[11]

"Sounds one-sided and illogical," Teresa said.

"Not to mention the host of rules protecting particular industries, such as pharmaceuticals, or limiting liability to a certain amount, such as five hundred thousand dollars. Or ones that say you cannot recover for pain and suffering.[12] A manufacturer of a defective product, say a hammer, that flies apart and hurts someone only has to pay for that person's medical bills and rehabilitation."

"As though that squared the accounts," Teresa said. "My late husband once had a bout of an illness, namely shingles, whose only manifestation was terrible pain. He would have paid a million dollars to avoid having it. Me too."

"So, Rodrigo, many areas of law, maybe all, have exceptions. Is your point that legal principles lie on a sliding scale? Because if so, this is not exactly new. Unless, of course, you plan to connect this to your wartime theory in some fashion."

"Let's see if I can," Rodrigo said. "Laz, at least, thinks the idea has promise." Rodrigo drew a deep breath, caught a quick glance at the bedroom door behind which a sleeping infant, I imagined, lay sucking his thumb, and continued as follows:

"Do you remember how Robert Cover wrote that law writes on a field of pain and death?"[13]

Giannina and I both nodded. Teresa looked puzzled, so Rodrigo explained: "A leading liberal legal writer, Cover wrote that many of his contemporaries overlooked the coercive aspect of law—the way in which legal prescriptions, backed by force, have real consequences for the lives of ordinary citizens."[14]

"That stands to reason," Teresa commented. "But go on."

"Well, as Laz pointed out, that's true of our social system, as well. We may not like to acknowledge it, but our free enterprise system is based on conflict and competition, winners and losers. Labor clashes with management, adults with adolescents. . . ."

"Professors with deans," Rodrigo and I added at the same time, then laughed.

"Men and women over family law doctrines," added Giannina. "And over rules and expectations in the workplace, including family leave, career tracks, and the kind of corporate culture that decides who gets ahead based on what sort of style and way of communicating."

"Amen," Rodrigo said. "And now do you see how warfare enters in, as one extreme of a continuum the other end of which is mild social conflict, like that of husbands and wives in an otherwise good marriage?"

I was thunderstruck by the idea, whose magnitude hit me with the force of a blow to the solar plexus. I looked around the table to find my companions equally nonplussed. "Rodrigo, among all the ideas I have heard from you, and I have heard many, I think this may be your most audacious yet. If I understand you correctly, you are saying that, because our social system is the way it is, law, which mediates conflict, also sets the stage for who wins and who loses in those many inevitable conflicts. It does so by choosing the rules of engagement—really, the rules of war. And the actual rules of war—the Geneva Convention, the rules against mistreating prisoners, allowing the Red Cross to drop off a care package once a year or so, the rules for court-martialing traitors and soldiers who abandon their posts under fire—are not just an anomaly, exceptions to an otherwise scrupulously fair system. Rather, what you are saying is that all of law is a war zone, just as all social life is."

"We just think that the fate of justice during war is an aberration, like those exceptions to informed consent. Instead, it's the rule, the most obvious, most visible case," said Rodrigo. "We repress the idea, because we don't like to come out and say it. We want to think that law is a neutral arbiter of conflict, that it gives equal consideration to every party in a dispute, the weaker as well as the stronger. It doesn't. As in wartime, it chooses a model, a rule, a mind-set, or a presumption of some sort, based on who we want to win. Usually it's the party most like us."

"Like those who run things," Giannina said. "Those best able to get their wishes translated into law."

After a pause, I added, "I know someone who thinks criminal and constitutional law contain a Mexican exception.[15] He's Mexican American, of course. But when I heard him give his paper, I was nearly convinced. Search and seizure law, English-Only laws, laws against bilingual education, immigration policy—it's practically as though the law included an unstated exception that holds that 'these rights do not apply if you are a Mexican.'"[16]

Teresa chimed in, "I'm not a lawyer. But when I was teaching citizenship courses for immigrants in the adult school, I was struck by how often my students would ask whether a particular constitutional guarantee, such as freedom of speech or of religion, really applied across the board. When I said it did, many of them were skeptical—although they agreed readily enough to spout the approved answer on the citizenship exam. After class, many described to me what they had thought to be exceptions to various rules in the behavior of American officialdom."

"So, Rodrigo, let's say we agree with your thesis that American law is a collection of doctrines set up to facilitate successful wars of one sort or another," I began.

"Usually ones in which the strong win out over the weak," Giannina interjected.

"Because of a subtle, nearly unnoticed patchwork of burden- shifting rules and exceptions," Rodrigo added.

"And which are so numerous and influential as to constitute the ordinary state of affairs," I said. "But allowing all that to stand—your parade of examples is all but overwhelming, Rodrigo—what *is* the solution to the problem with which you began several days ago now? What about international terrorism?"

"Yes," agreed Giannina, I thought a little remorselessly. They are starting to behave with the directness of many long- married couples.

"It's not enough to point out that we are treating the Muslim world in the ways we reserve for we-they, quasi-wartime situations, with the gloves off and the ordinary rules of civil and criminal due process suspended. Nor is it enough to deplore, as I know you do, the overbroad rules of engagement we adopted during the opening days of the so-called War on Terror, bombing villages and aid stations in the hope of flushing out the leader and replacing the government that harbored him with a more friendly one. What policy would you put in place of all that?"

IN WHICH RODRIGO LAYS OUT
A THEORY OF RESPONSE TO INTERNATIONAL TERROR

"Yes," I agreed. "You need to revisit that matter. Recall that it was that famous line of yours about terror that I reported, as accurately as I could—because I was quite struck by it—when you first spoke it nearly ten years ago. A line that as you mentioned may have come back to haunt you, indeed may have caused you to miss the birth of your first son."[17]

Noticing Giannina wince a little, I hastened to add: "Not that I think it was your fault that the government seems to have quarantined you in Mexico for the first part of the Middle Eastern crisis. They had no business doing that, and if you were interested in pursuing legal remedies against them, I would gladly represent you. But most Americans do not think of their country as terrorist, and even fewer can contemplate the idea of terror waged against them with any degree of equanimity, much less consider that it might be justified. So, I for one would love to hear two things from you before this conversation ends. Number one: What did you mean by that original remark? And two: Now that terrorist forces have been unleashed against this country—your country now, Rodrigo—what do you advocate doing in response? I realize these are tough questions, but I'm sure you are up to them."

"We'll see. I've been giving them some thought. And, as I mentioned, Laz has been helping me think about them."

"My two points, Rodrigo. My two points," I persisted.

RODRIGO EXPLAINS WHAT HE MEANT BY ADVOCATING
SELECTIVE TERRORISM, YEARS AGO

"It's been a while," Rodrigo began. "But I think I can recapture my thought. We were talking, if I recall, about how the dominant paradigm of environmental and racial thought resists change.[18] Like a frog in a pot of water on the stove, the West adjusts to a declining quality of life, higher levels of white-collar crime, and increasing disparities in social well-being and wealth by blaming the victims—the minorities and outsiders whose vision and experience can supply answers to the very questions haunting us. Most people think that the problems of the Western democracies are temporary, that they have the best system of social organization in the world, and that their problems will go away if they only try harder, when the exact opposite is true."[19]

"What you called perseveration."

"The solution, as I saw it, is for the West to reach out, embrace, and learn from the outsiders. But this it steadfastly refuses to do, insisting instead that they become like us," Rodrigo continued. "So the solution, when confronted with a social system that won't abandon its hidebound modes of thought, dependence on extractive industries, and marginalization of large groups of its own citizens, is to do something dramatic that illustrates its vulnerability. You show it how interdependent it really is, how it needs the cooperation, energies, and genius of all its people to succeed and enjoy peace."[20]

"What Martin Luther King called raising creative tension,"[21] Teresa ventured.

"Precisely," Rodrigo replied. "Although he meant marches, sit-ins at lunch counters, and peaceful demonstrations, while I meant something a little more dramatic."

"You certainly did, Rodrigo," I exclaimed. "If I recall, you spoke of guerrilla-style disruption of telephone and computer lines, maybe even more than that. That's not just calling one's grievances to society's attention through peaceful means. It's affirmative, destructive action designed to shut things down."[22]

"Well, I was quite a bit younger then," Rodrigo replied a little defensively. "But I think I would affirm the same principle even today. Did not your revolutionary, Thomas Paine, and his compatriots advocate much the same thing? I seem to recall a few incidents in your collective history, tea thrown into harbors, that sort of thing."

"Rodrigo, you've made your point, although most people would think your analogy to the early American revolutionaries more than a little far-fetched. And I certainly hope you are not going to equate the lethal and suicidal terrorism of the September 11 hijackers with your own theory about softening up society so that it will begin listening to visionaries and minorities. If anything, recent events show that acting that way has the opposite effect. People shut down, become super-American."

"Ouch," said Rodrigo. "I see you are trying to catch me in a contradiction, Professor. And I may have come close to trapping myself. I concede that the civil disobedient who sets out to shake up the power structure by doing something dramatic is apt to have wartime rules—the kind we talked about before—applied against him or her.[23] And I believe that's what would have happened had the Brits managed to get their hands on Thomas Paine or Paul Revere. They would have hanged them. That's the risk you take. That's how law works."

"And you were in fact deported once.[24] And almost again, a second time,"[25] I pointed out.

"Yet, when society is complacent and incapable of seeing its own downward drift, because it has been so gradual. . . ."[26]

"Or blinded by superpatriotism," Teresa added.

"Right," Rodrigo said. "Then, if one loves one's country and believes in the idea of progress, one must be prepared to make sacrifices. And, as we said before, Professor, a society often rejects the very voices, the very ideas, it needs most."[27]

"A little like what you often see from young children," said Giannina. "I've been reading about infant psychology."

"But not every society rejects those voices," added Teresa. "In Italy, we experienced a wave of terrorism a few years back when the government persisted in excluding leftist voices. A few kidnappings and the establishment changed its tune in favor of coalition politics.[28] Not to condone what they did, of course. I had a friend who was badly burned in one of the bombings."

"I mentioned that to the Professor at the time," Rodrigo said.

"You did," I recalled.

"I'd like to talk to you sometime about some parallels I see between individual and social maturation," Rodrigo said. "In some ways, the

West has managed to grow up without certain formative experiences that would have been helpful to it.[29] Not all of the West, just certain regions. But let's save that for another time. I wonder if I have satisfied the Professor on point one."

Rodrigo looked at me expectantly. I nodded, then said: "It's not me you have to satisfy. If you're going to have a career—not to mention raise a family—in this society, Rodrigo, you will have to learn to temper your remarks. The American people have never much liked the idea of civil disobedience being used against them. Against other people and other societies, fine. Against recalcitrant Southern sheriffs and school boards, maybe. But let's let that go for now and move on to your second point. What about a campaign of deadly terror like the one we've seen this year and which our leaders warn us could go on a long time? Surely you must condemn that?"

RODRIGO'S RESPONSE TO INTERNATIONAL TERRORISM

"Of course," he said. "Anyone would. The difficulty lies in figuring out what to do about it. The problem, as I pointed out before, is that a complex society like ours is highly vulnerable to disruption at a million points.[30] Someone willing to die can always hijack a jetliner and fly it into a skyscraper full of people. We can seal off the doors between the passenger compartment and the pilots, at great expense, on every jetliner. But nothing prevents a terrorist from circumventing that by hijacking a plane while it's parked on the ground overnight, or by impersonating the crew and walking aboard at the last minute. Or blowing up the same skyscrapers in one of any number of ways that don't require a jetliner but a truck, a helicopter, or a fake delivery vehicle left in the basement garage. We can try closing every loophole, but we'd end up practically an armed camp, something our society is not—and should not be—willing to tolerate."

"So, what's your solution, Rodrigo?" Teresa asked softly. "This is no small issue. Half the world is hungry and blames the United States for it. Are we who live here always going to be at risk of alienated people carrying out acts of deadly terror? If so, it's not a very appealing prospect. Gus and I are old—I mean, compared to you. You're going to raise families. Is life for them going to be one round of disasters—school shootings, World Trade Center bombings, bioterrorist scares—after another? Will they live their lives, as you put it, in armed camps?"

"I certainly hope not," Rodrigo said.

"Me too," echoed Giannina. "If things don't get better, I've thought about picking up and leaving for a more civilized country after I get my degree. With Rodrigo and little Gustavus, of course. I have these fantasies of starting over in Latin America or a small European country, maybe practicing international or immigration law with an American firm."

"That's news to me," Rodrigo said, giving his wife a quick smile. "Although if it comes to that, I can think of worse fates. We do have the advantage of speaking four languages between us and having relatives and friends around the world. My Italian law degree could come in handy too."

"But neither Gus nor I want that," Teresa said. "I've been waiting all these years for grandchildren, and I'm not ready to have the two of you take off for Montevideo or Geneva, where I'll see you and the young one once a year. Besides, your responsibility to the world, as I see it, is to use your fine minds to solve problems, not run away from them."

"Okay, okay," Rodrigo said. "I'll do my best. Here's what dawned on me while whiling away my hours in that Indian village, hoping for things to simmer down. Imagine that you live in a stone house."

"I actually do," said Teresa with a smile. I remembered that her townhouse, the most attractive one on her block, was faced with soft brownstone.

"Well, a stone cottage, then," Rodrigo picked up. "One day, your cottage turns to glass. You're living in something like a greenhouse. Knowing that one of your neighbors could throw a rock through your roof one day, what do you do?"

He looked around at our quizzical expressions. "Well, would you all go and buy guns?"

"They wouldn't be much use," I said, taking the bait. "They might frighten one or two of your neighbors into leaving you alone. But you can't be watching all the time, so the guns wouldn't do you that much good."

"Would you try to build a steel net of some sort and hang it over your roof?"

"Sounds expensive. Besides, it might not work against small rocks or pellets," I said. I wondered where the wunderkind was going, so decided to continue playing the straight man. "I assume all these correspond to military or diplomatic options of some sort."[31]

"They do," said Rodrigo, smiling broadly. "But let's go on. Would you talk with your neighbors and try to scare them into being good, telling them that if they threw a rock your way you'd bomb them into oblivion?"

"Not unless I was in a very bad mood," I said. "Or thought they would be easily cowed for some reason."

"Might you form a defensive alliance with all the owners of glass houses in the neighborhood, so that anyone who lobbed a rock at any one of you would face the alliance's full wrath?"

"That could have a little weight," I said, uncomfortable with my answer because I knew that on some level something was wrong with it.

"The association would be better if it included all the people, including the ones in the stone houses, especially the ones who have children," said Teresa. "That way, the people in the glass houses would have less to fear."

"Now that's an approach I hadn't thought of," said Rodrigo.

"What's the one you had in mind, Rodrigo? Obviously, you've been trying to pull something out of us."

"It's nothing out of the ordinary. It's simply to make friends with your neighbors if you haven't done so already."

"Make friends with them?" I asked. I didn't know if I was incredulous or disappointed. Then, the full meaning of Rodrigo's suggestion hit me. "Hmmm," I said. "I think I'm beginning to catch your drift."

Rodrigo didn't wait for me to fumble my way through. Instead, he asked: "Professor, do you know your neighbors?"

"Sure," I said. "I knew them even better when my late wife and I lived in our house together. We were there for nearly twenty years. I've been living in a university apartment since then. But I know most of my neighbors almost as well as I did back in the old neighborhood."

"And are you afraid of any of them?" Rodrigo asked. "Worried that they might break into your house or throw a rock through your front window?"

"No, of course not. Although about ten years ago, a child of one of our neighbors threw a baseball through one of our side windows by mistake. He was tremendously apologetic and agreed to pay for it out of his allowance."

"And if you don't mind my asking, why is it that you don't fear them?"

"That's an interesting question. I've never really thought about it. I suppose it's because I know them. Our kids have played together. When Harry is away, I pick up his paper for him. When Jewel and I went out of town on short trips, their son would mow our lawn and feed our cat. I suppose theoretically, one of our neighbors could have woken up one morning a psychotic killer and come to our house and mowed us down. But the possibility never really occurred to us. Even though we live in a crime- infested society, we just didn't have that much fear of our neighbors. Even if we could hear them arguing among themselves sometimes. Or spanking their kids more loudly than we would have."

"With globalization, the world is beginning to seem more like a neighborhood," said Teresa.

"Which, if I read him correctly, is exactly what your son- in-law is driving at," I said. "We are more interrelated than ever before. Trade, products, TV images, money, and people cross borders constantly. A recession in Japan affects markets worldwide. Poverty in an Eastern European or Central American nation increases immigration to the United States or Germany."[32]

"So the easiest way to see to our collective security is simply to make friends with each other," Teresa said. "Just as the United States has nothing to fear from England or Canada or Australia, the idea that any pair of historic allies would invade the other or lob a few nuclear missiles their way when no one is looking is preposterous. It would be like blowing up your own garage or setting fire to your own guest apartment."

"Isn't your strategy a little, how shall I put it, idealistic for a Marxist like yourself, Rodrigo?" I asked, resolved to play devil's advocate as long as possible. I secretly thought that Rodrigo had hit upon something blindingly obvious but terribly important, and wanted to push him to flesh it out even more. "Do you think it really would have worked with the zealots who crashed into the World Trade Center towers last fall?"

"It's our only chance," Rodrigo said, speaking softly yet firmly. "If we want our children to grow up in a world where events like that are not commonplace. And yes, I think it would have worked with the zealots responsible for the events of New York. Maybe not each one of them, but enough of them to have given those plotting the terrible day pause. We abandoned the Afghan freedom fighters after they waged successful war—with our assistance—against the Soviets.[33] We support corrupt family regimes of immensely rich patriarchs in several regions of the oil-rich Arab east.[34] We don't use our influence with Israel to temper some of that country's more militaristic policies[35]—not to say that it isn't entitled to employ reasonable self-defense when attacked or threatened."

"Nor do we use our immense wealth to ameliorate the poverty that blights that region, or many others," Teresa added. "I read the other day that for only $15 billion a year, the 125 million children who never have the opportunity to go to school could do so. We spend less, per capita, on humanitarian aid than practically any other developed country."[36]

"No wonder some people feel tempted to throw a brick through our window from time to time," Giannina interjected. "I might too, and I'm a pacifist, unlike you, Rodrigo."

"And what we've said today ties in to what we were saying earlier," I said. "The idea is to avoid the sort of we-they thinking that relegates your neighbor to the moral regime we deploy, consciously or not, during wartime. The law should treat all with equal respect, even those— maybe especially, those—with whom we disagree, and who seem least like us. We should broaden our notion of neighborhood. As you said before, Rodrigo, we should learn to love those who strike us, at first glance, as most alien, most threatening. Then, you were speaking of teenage black youths, walking in groups on the sidewalk, wearing sneakers and hooded sweatshirts and looking mean. We should love even those who are beyond love. Today, you've argued that we should apply that same model to international relations."[37]

"Something like that," Rodrigo said, looking slightly embarrassed at the almost superheated language I had been using to paraphrase his theory. "I think it's just pragmatic, in a day in which it's so easy to wreak havoc against harmless office workers, to try to bring everyone up to a minimum level of comfort and security, to talk to them on occasion, and bring in their newspaper when they're out of town."

TEN DOLLARS AND THE VALUE OF SECURITY

"Pragmatic?" I said.

"Yes," Rodrigo replied. "Security is the new buzzword, the new form of wealth. But we deceive ourselves on the best way to achieve it. In the old days a rich man could spend ten dollars on security, and be more secure. Today, he'd be better off giving those same ten dollars to his poorest neighbor. The same is true of nations. The United States could spend fifty billion dollars on a missile defense system, and not be much safer."

"Because we're so interdependent, so vulnerable," Teresa said.

"Right," Rodrigo continued. "We'd be safer against a missile attack, but nothing prevents a determined adversary from using a cheap, primitive means of getting around our system."

"They might even take it as a challenge. Or be so mad at us for spending that tremendous sum of money on military hardware rather than on their starving children, that they start plotting our downfall," Teresa added.

"And so, Rodrigo, you are saying that the best thing a nation can do is give away its wealth. Not only is that the path to spiritual salvation, but to down-to-earth safety. A relatively homogeneous planet with few extremes of wealth or poverty is the safest, most stable condition and in the best interest of all, even the currently wealthiest nations," I said.

"Paradoxical," Teresa mused. "But sometimes moral truths are when you first hear them. Giving away the same amount of money to your adversary that you might spend on a weapon to protect yourself against him can actually make you more secure."

"At least, it's something we should consider," added Rodrigo. "It's like the law-and-economics analysis of railroad fires."

"You mean the rule of law that makes railroads pay for the cost of fires to Farmer Jones's crops from sparks emanating from the locomotive?" I asked.

"Right. Farmer Jones loses crops worth fifty dollars. But the liability rule forces railroads to install spark arresters that cost one hundred dollars."

"So some jurisdictions say the railroad has no liability. Otherwise, the farmer could be said to be injuring the railroad to the tune of one hundred dollars."

"The genius of the law-and-economics movement was to point out that if the railroad gives the farmer sixty dollars, both parties are better off. The farmer makes more from his land than he would have by raising crops. And the railroad avoids an expensive fix."

"Doesn't this just reward poor, backward countries for blackmailing their neighbors?" I asked.

"No, because we would offer this aid unconditionally and voluntarily," Rodrigo replied. "Besides, as the poorer nation develops and becomes more integrated into the world community, it will lose the incentive—if it ever had it—to engage in terrorist threats. It may even start picking up our newspaper for us when we're out of town. We reach a moral equilibrium in which we have no next-door neighbors who desperately envy us or feel they have a grievance against us."

"Speaking of occupants of the next room," Giannina interjected, "a certain somebody is starting to announce his presence. I'm afraid one of us needs to attend to him soon or we'll all pay the price."

Rodrigo leaped to his feet. "Allow me," he said, striding into the bedroom, a purposeful look on his face and rolling up his sleeves.

Giannina smiled and said, "Family harmony looks like it's going to reign, at least for a few minutes longer. The baby's probably wet, but it looks like Rodrigo's going to get there before he gets too unhappy."

"A metaphor for our times," I said, starting to pick up the empty cups and saucers and carry them into the kitchen where, I hoped, Teresa and I might steal a moment together before I headed home.

6

Interracial Love, Sex, and Marriage

THE TIME WAS several months later. The term had ended, and much had happened. Rodrigo and Giannina had returned home. I had finished my semester, discharged that onerous obligation the dean had imposed on me, and passed the responsibility for note-taking onto an unsuspecting senior professor, even older than I, who had come out of retirement to teach a tax course we were having trouble covering. Hee-hee, I thought—pretty clever of me to keep quiet about it until just before the faculty meeting, when I presented her with my stenographer's pad and a copy of the faculty handbook setting out how the minutes are to be recorded and distributed.

But the real news was that Teresa and I had just decided to move in together. It all happened rather suddenly. In fact, at this very moment I was rehearsing what I would say when Teresa and I faced the two youngsters who, with their now much more grown-up baby, would be calling on us in about—I looked at my watch—one hour. I was sitting in my office in the gathering dusk, looking at the pile of seminar papers I had to grade before packing up my apartment and moving in with—my God, I thought, I am a lucky man—the beauteous widow Teresa. I still could not believe my good fortune.

Knowing that Rodrigo and Giannina would have many questions, I thought back to the beginning. I remembered the time, more than a year ago, when I had first met Teresa, almost by chance. If I had not run into the vacation-bound Rodrigo in the supermarket that day, would I have even met her at all? Rodrigo did say that he had mentioned me to her, that she knew of my work, and wanted to meet me. But if it had not been for that chance meeting in the rows of cans of anchovies and refried beans, Rodrigo might not have invited me over, Teresa and I might never have met, and our lives might have been radically different, mine anyway. I remembered the pleasure and delight we each experienced in getting to know one another over the course of those meetings in her townhouse, accompanied by the young people, and finding out the many ways in which we were alike, yet also different.

I remembered our first, rather formal evenings out together, and the pleasure I took in realizing, over time, how much pleasure she, in turn, took in my company. I remembered the time I had first visited her apartment, in the company of Rodrigo and Giannina, and noticed that the photograph of her late husband had been casually rotated on the mantelpiece so that it no longer faced the entryway and, then, the time a few weeks later when it had been missing altogether. I remembered the terrible months when everything seemed to be coming apart—Rodrigo missing, Giannina reeling from the effects of a cesarean delivery, Teresa staying up half the night helping with the baby, and I struggling to hold the institute together. I recalled how, even during these dark days we had managed to steal our first kiss in the darkened entryway to her daughter's apartment, and how, earlier, she had fallen asleep in the taxi on the way back from a night at the theater, her head on my shoulder.

I remembered, as vividly as anything in my life, that first night, back in my hometown and with Teresa unpacked and ensconced in her new, permanent apartment, when she had asked me up to her place, alone. The night outside had been cold and still. We had gone to a local art house to see an Italian movie, one that turned out to have been made in her hometown in Italy. She had excitedly pointed out to me streets and piazzas near the very neighborhood in which she had grown up. Afterward, we drank espresso (the decaffeinated variety, in my case) in a local café, then walked home hand in hand through the dark streets, lit mainly by the new moon.

At the door to her apartment, she had hesitated a moment, then said, "I haven't got it quite all fixed up yet, but you're very welcome to come in." We walked up the short flight of stairs together, then she fished out the key and opened the door. "I just had the dead-bolt installed," she said. I felt strangely tongue-tied. For a law professor, I thought, you are behaving with the grace and wit of an adolescent. I helped her take off her coat, took off mine, and hung them in the hall closet where she indicated.

"I should offer you tea," she said, then took a long step toward me and closed her eyes. A split second later, we were in each other's arms. Minutes later, reminding myself to proceed slowly—this was uncharted territory for both of us—I stepped back. We both drew deep breaths, looked, in my case at least, in some confusion at the other, and Teresa said, "Excuse me a minute. I just want to do something." She then closed the living room blinds on the way to the bedroom, and closed the door. "Make yourself at home," I heard her say from behind the door.

I busied myself examining the books in her bookshelves, while remaining alert to any sound from within the bedroom. I heard none, and to this day have absolutely no memory of any of the books I opened and shut in the short interval before the door opened and Teresa stepped out. She was wearing only a white nightie with lace on it. Her body, surprisingly young-looking, shone in the light of the two bedside candles she had lit in the room beyond.

Our first night together, dear reader, was full of sweet surprises and the rapid falling away of barriers. Yes, we talked endlessly after our first lovemaking. Yes, the candles lasted the whole night. Yes, we woke up in the middle of the night—and not just, as you might suspect, from the usual old folks' complaint. Yes, we slept late the next morning, and had an even later breakfast whipped up collaboratively in Teresa's kitchen from provisions rescued from cartons and boxes she had opened just the day before and that had arrived parcel post from Florida.

Yes, that evening was followed by many more in an unending upward spiral that reminded me of one of my favorite lines from a South American poet, Ernesto Cardenal, who as luck would have it turned out to be one of Teresa's favorites, too.

> When we feel we are loved by the person we love, we love more, and nothing inflames our love so much as to know we are loved by the person we love, and being loved more makes the other love more too. When we think about the person we love, we love him more until we are nothing but one burning flame of love.

Now it was time to face reality in the form of two extremely, I imagined, inquisitive young people, who would want to know all about our plans. We awaited the ring of her doorbell, drinking tea to fortify ourselves and joking how our situation was a case of role reversal—bringing your date home to meet your kids.

Before we were really ready, the doorbell rang. We looked at each other with raised eyebrows, got up simultaneously, and walked together to the door. Teresa threw it open, revealing the familiar young couple, with a bashful-looking toddler clinging to his mother's skirt, and several suitcases next to them on the doorstep, where the taxi must have deposited them moments earlier.

Teresa said, "Welcome back," Rodrigo mumbled something, and Giannina threw her arms around my neck in a warm hug. "Welcome to the family," she said into my ear.

After a round of greetings, Teresa took orders for beverages, brought out a tray of croissants, and Giannina parked little Gus in front of the VCR, into which she had slipped an educational video of some sort. "I do this only as a last resort," she explained, "to buy us a little time until the baby-sitter arrives." When I must have looked puzzled, she said, "The teenager who lives next door. The family are friends of Teresa."

Soon we were all seated around the dining room table. An expectant silence descended. Teresa and I looked at each other, stole quick glances at our two young visitors, I cleared my throat, and began. I remember reciting the history I had just reviewed in my mind, but my voice, which began strong and determined, must have faltered once or twice, for I remember Giannina and Rodrigo smiling encouragingly at me from time to time. Teresa helped me fill in a few details—delicately leaving out that night we spent together and the many other occasions of nocturnal bliss that followed—and I soon came to the end with, "And so, we have decided to move in together. I'm clearing out of my faculty apartment next week and moving in here."

After a long silence, Rodrigo asked, "And do you have any plans for after that?"

"Rodrigo!" Giannina exclaimed. "That's none of our business."

"No, that's all right," Teresa interjected. "Gus and I have talked about that a little. We are both well past sixty and don't know how much time we have left. Nor do we want to upset anyone, much less the two of you. Things are quite comfortable as they are right now. How do the two of you feel about it?"

Now it was time for Rodrigo to clear his throat. Uncharacteristically tongue-tied he muttered something like, "It's the first time I'd really thought about it" (which I doubted was true), and just then the teenager from next door arrived, with a rustle of books, coloring materials, and stuffed animals.

Giannina announced, "This is our big chance." Rodrigo immediately seized on her cue to suggest we repair to the neighborhood café for some light lunch, and Teresa consulted quickly with the teenager who was already deep in the middle of some sort of puppet game with an enthralled Gustavo, who seemed to have gotten over his shyness in a hurry.

IN WHICH RODRIGO PUTS FORWARD A THEORY OF INTERRACIAL LOVE, SEX, AND MARRIAGE

Minutes later, we were seated in the upscale neighborhood café around the corner from Teresa's apartment. With a shock of recognition, I realized that it was patterned after one Rodrigo and I had patronized when we met at the AALS years ago. These chains are taking over everywhere, I thought.

We placed our orders, artichoke salads for the two women, a medium-rare steak for Rodrigo, and a smoked salmon plate for me. After the waiter left, I looked up at Rodrigo and Giannina and said, "Your mother and I hope our decision is not coming as too much of a shock."

"Not at all," Rodrigo replied. "We kind of hoped you might hit it off."

"Well, your judgment was certainly right," I said. "We have a lot in common."

"Despite being raised on different continents and in different cultures," Giannina added. "Gus, you're a man of color who has lived all your life, as I understand it, in the States. Mom was raised in Italy and came to North America only in midlife, when Dad died. The two of you, separately, embody the combination of genes and cultures that Rodrigo represents—his mother was Italian and his father, a black American."

"My friend Laz made the same point when I told him about the two of you," Rodrigo said. "He said to give you his best and to send him a wedding announcement, if you get around to doing that."

"Pretty brazen of him," said Giannina. "I take it the two of you haven't gotten that far?"

"We've talked about it," I said. "Do you remember my friend Yancey?"

"Is he the one who died recently?"

"Yes. I had just gone to his funeral that day we got together in your city. Just before you disappeared."

"Oh, right. The old-time, hard-line civil rights litigator. The one who was so disappointed with the direction the movement has taken lately."

"Yes, him," I replied. "He says it's as though the movement is suffering from amnesia. He actually was not that complimentary. He called it Alzheimer's disease, and was particularly scathing about Critical Race Theory and Lat-Crit Studies. I hesitated to tell you about this, because I didn't want you to think badly of him."

"I'd like to hear sometime," Rodrigo said.

"Maybe later," Giannina said, "if the baby cooperates. The babysitter has the number here. She'll call if he wakes up and she needs help."

"Yancey thought that with the turn this country has taken to the right, the left needs to increase its activism and resistance. Your institute would have appealed to him. But Critical Race Theory does not. Racism is not a theory, he snorted. Only a bunch of ivory tower academics could think it so."

"Alzheimer's disease?" Rodrigo mused. "A devastating metaphor. I assume he meant that the academic left is in danger of forgetting what it once knew and is a shadow of its past self."

"Something like that, " I said. "I'd been meaning to talk to you about memory sometime. But I keep forgetting."

Everyone laughed. "But I do want to talk about that a little. Yancey may have been more right than he knew."

We paused while the waiter brought our orders. I examined the savory plates he put down before us. "For a chain restaurant, not bad," I said.

"It's locally owned," said Teresa. "In fact the owners are the parents of the teenager who is taking care of little Gustavo right now."

"I do want to hear about the Professor's ideas on memory and forgetting," said Giannina. "But we also came to hear more about you two and your plans."

Just then a pair of diners passed by our table on the way to the cash register. After they were out of hearing range, I said, "Well, we're a couple. Despite what those two might have thought. I assume you noticed the look they gave us just now."

"No, I was facing the other way," said Teresa. "What did they do?"

"Not a hate stare exactly," I said.

"More like curiosity," said Giannina. "I noticed it too."

"I may be reading more into it than her look deserves," said Rodrigo. "But I couldn't help thinking the woman's look meant, 'she could do better.'"

"Yes, her face did seem to fall when she saw me, a very dark man of color and a little past his prime, sitting next to, and very near, a well-dressed, European-looking lady like Teresa."

"Her loss," Teresa said, giving my hand a quick squeeze under the table. "Her husband looks like a beached walrus."

"The odd thing is that my friend Yancey, who I thought would know better, gave me a hard time too. This, even though his own personal life was something of a mess—one round of women after another, no relationship lasting more than a year or two, and half a dozen children by different mothers. He was a giant in his field, but never figured out how to lead a stable home life."

"Yet he disapproved of you and Mom?" Giannana said.

"It was more a matter of body language than what he said," I replied. "In answer to his question about my social life, I had told him a little about Teresa, how she was a serious environmentalist and a lay member of the National Lawyers Guild. I told him she was your mother-in-law, which impressed him more than the other things I said. Then he asked me if she was white or one of the folks."

"Not a lot of nuance there," said Rodrigo.

"Yancey, for all his good points, was stuck in the black- white binary paradigm of race until the end of his days, I'm afraid," I said. "He never took much interest in the fortunes of Latinos, Asians, and Indians. Anyway, I told him that Teresa was Italian, and he sort of rolled his eyes and said, 'After Jewel,' as though to reprove me. My late wife, of course, was even darker than I am."[1]

Noticing a slightly apprehensive look on Teresa's sweet face, I quickly added, "Yancey and his nationalist friends can think anything they want. I know what my heart tells me."

"Mine too," Teresa said firmly. "But I'm glad you said that. I had been meaning to raise it with you sometime. What do we tell our nationalist friends—and Italy has its share of them, too?"[2]

I looked around the circle, then said, "I'd be grateful for any and all suggestions. Some of my best friends"—I saw Rodrigo and Giannina beginning to smile—"are black and brown nationalists who take the position that the first order of business for any minority group is to strengthen its own ties. That means joining community organizations, voting for black and brown candidates, and giving one's business to a minority company whenever one can. A black or Chicano nationalist, for example, would never join a white-dominated organization, such as Common Cause, over an organization of color, such as the NAACP, Jesse Jackson's Rainbow Coalition, or MALDEF, even if the two groups had very similar aims and objectives and the white one were better run and had a better record of getting its agenda passed."

"And of course such a nationalist person would never marry, or maybe even date, a member of another race," Giannina added, a slight look of concern on her pretty face.

"I guess that follows," I replied. "At least according to my friend Yancey. In the days of the civil rights movement, black leaders who consorted with white women incurred intense disapproval. You can't talk black during the day and sleep white at night, the saying went."

"And I suppose they would see me as white," Teresa said. "Despite my beliefs and lifelong record of civil rights activism."

"Your record and Italian origins might give some of them pause," Rodrigo said. "Neither you nor Giannina is exactly Aryan- looking, with your dark hair and brown skin. No one would mistake you for Farah Fawcett-Majors or any other blonde Hollywood bombshell. But as I understand it, extreme black or Latino activists would frown on someone like Gus—or maybe even me—getting together with women like you two. Dilutes the race."[3]

"And solidarity, supposedly," said Teresa. "I remember reading Huey Newton and Malcolm X, who was especially bitter about his white grandfather. Both leaders were against dating white women or even having whites in black organizations, especially in a leadership capacity."[4]

"Go on," I said, looking at all three of them. "This is proving exceedingly helpful. Teresa and I certainly are not going to do anything differently. But we do need to anticipate the criticism we might face from the American or Italian left."

"More likely it would come from the Italian right," Teresa interjected. "Remind me to tell you about our Northern League some day. One of my uncles, who is from Genoa, is a member."

"Didn't that region just elect a candidate from that party?" I asked.

"It did," Teresa replied. "And then there's Mussolini's granddaughter, who was just elected to the Italian Parliament. Italian fascism is very much alive, unfortunately."[5]

"As it is here," Rodrigo said. "Recall our discussion not long ago about justice at war."

"Maybe all societies draw together during times of threat," said Teresa. "That's certainly been true in the States recently. Recall the English-only movement and pressure to limit immigration. Nativism is on the rise, as is pro-American sentiment, misguided or genuine."[6]

"Just the other day, I read that the state legislature of Alabama referred to voters a law that would repeal the state's ban on interracial marriages. The law hadn't been enforced since 1967 when the Supreme Court, in *Loving v. Virginia*,[7] struck down prohibitions on such marriages that were in effect in many states. Come election day, over 40 percent of the electorate voted to keep the law in force."[8]

"A socioeconomic theory holds that racism increases during times of stress and economic competition,"[9] said Rodrigo. "That would explain Teresa's Northern League and the Alabama vote. But maybe the same mechanism holds true for minority groups as well. Even including your friend Yancey." He looked around the table.

"No social scientist, to my knowledge, has looked into that," I said, "although they have said some quite pungent, even irreverent, things about interracial marriage and sex. Teresa and I were talking about them the other day." (Actually, we were talking about them, and laughing playfully in her prim, but attractive, single bed one afternoon after greatly enjoying each other's company. I remembered that something I'd said struck her as so laughable that she had picked up a pillow and whacked me in the head with it, which in turn had led to a pillow fight, then—extraordinarily for people our age—yet another session of lovemaking until we were spent.)

"Hmm, I'd like to hear them sometime," said Giannina. "But I think you were telling us, Rodrigo, about a theory of minority- group behavior—solidarity, nationalism, and their opposites."

"Oh, yes," Rodrigo said. "It's not all that breathtaking. I just posit, as a hypothesis only, that minority groups behave just like majority groups, but in reverse. When they feel embattled. . . ."

"As they would when whites have the upper hand and are being mean for some reason," Teresa interjected.

"Exactly," Rodrigo continued. "It's a kind of cycle. When whites feel pushed around and sense that things are out of control, they increase nativism and other forms of resistance. Racism increases, and minorities feel themselves threatened, as well, so that they too draw together."

INTERRACIAL LOVE, SEX, AND MARRIAGE 101

"And expel the whites," Teresa said. "Well, Gus and I are having no part of that cycle. We're in it for the duration. I don't see a role for politics in interpersonal relations, especially love and marriage."

"Mom, you sound exactly like Romeo and Juliet," Giannina exclaimed. "I never knew you had such a romantic side."

"Shakespeare set that signature play in Italy amid the fortunes of two Italian families, the Montagues and the Capulets. Actually, our family, Giannina, is distantly related to one that Shakespeare is supposed to have modeled his characters on."

"Juliet's family, the Capulets, I bet," I said. "But I'm totally with Teresa. Yancey might be right or wrong regarding where you do business and whom you elect to the board of the NAACP or the Mexican American Legal Defense and Education Fund. But I'm not going to turn to him as my marriage counselor."

"Certainly not with his record," Rodrigo said. "How would you like to tell us what led to your pillow fight?"

I thought to myself: How did this young fellow know about our pillow fight? I didn't remember mentioning that detail. Was my memory failing? Did he have magic powers or read my mind? Did Teresa tell him sometime, outside my presence? I put a mental bookmark by the question for now, and instead began as follows:

"Social scientists have written quite a bit about interracial attraction and romance. Some of the writers are black, and not at all known for rabid nationalism. And some of their interpretations are quite unflattering. Are you sure you want to hear?"

"Our relationship can take it," Rodrigo grinned, elbowing Giannina good-naturedly. When she smiled back, I continued as follows:

"One school of thought holds that white women, like Giannina and Teresa, who link up with men of color do so for symbolic reasons or in the hope of finding a sympathetic soul mate."[10]

"The symbolic reasons I bet I can guess," Giannina said. "Identification with the underdog. Rebellion against your parents."

"And I bet I can guess another one," said Rodrigo. "The white woman who links up with a man of color hopes that he, being the frequent victim of racism, will empathize with what it's like being a woman. A sort of common bond. He won't be as sexist as a white man because of what he has been through."[11]

"That's what they say," I said. "Although I'm sure we can all think of many exceptions. Oh, and one thing more. Supposedly, some white women are attracted to men of color because of their image as animal-istic, primitive supermales."[12]

"Oh, right. The ever-potent big black stud," said Giannina, sup-pressing a giggle.

"Hey, you weren't supposed to laugh," said Rodrigo.

"I'm sorry," said Giannina. "You're quite exceptional in all depart-ments. I was just remembering a college roommate who went out with the captain of the football team, and came in for quite a disappointment when she learned about certain of the coach's rules for game day and the night before. Oh, forget that I said that," she said, covering her mouth and blushing.

"And what does the man of color see in the white woman, accord-ing to your social scientists?" Rodrigo queried.

"Now this is where a certain amount of dubious speculation comes in," I replied. "Some say that the white woman represents a sort of for-bidden fruit."[13]

"That's like the woman who rebels by seeking out a black boyfriend to defy convention and scandalize her parents," Giannina observed.

"It is, in a way," I agreed. "Still others write that the white woman is a prize, something the dark man seizes as revenge against white men for perpetrating acts of racial domination."[14]

Rodrigo shook his head in wonderment. "If dating across racial lines were as fraught with psychosexual complications as your social scientists say, word would get out and nobody would do it. I hate to be old-fashioned, and this may seem strange coming from the mouth of a Marxist, but I don't think the reasons are either psychoanalytic or ide-ological in most cases. Some couples may get together for those rea-sons, but I think most people fall in love for reasons no one ever knows or articulates. Small things like the way a person holds himself or her-self. Or the way he or she looks at you, laughs, or sees a certain situa-tion in common with you. If you want an explanation, I think it's bio-logical. Something in our makeup tells us that a person like this one will satisfy our longings. Trying to intellectualize it, much less make it part of your social and political agenda, is a sure way of getting into trouble."

"It certainly didn't help my friend Yancey," I said. "Much as I ad-mire what he accomplished professionally."

Just then the waiter appeared with a cell phone in hand. "It's my sister," he said.

Giannina quickly took the receiver, listened for a moment, then said, "Well, give us a call when he gets tired or hungry." Then, to us: "All's well. He woke up and they're playing shadow games. She said she'd call when he's tired and wants his parents. She says she's got all afternoon if we want."

"Do you think we should head back?" Rodrigo asked.

"No, it's good for him. Give him another half hour or so, or until Rosie calls again."

"The joys of parenthood," Rodrigo said. "It certainly makes you conscious of how you use your time. Speaking of parenthood, I don't suppose you two have any plans in that department? Adoption, for example?"

"Rodrigo!" Giannina exclaimed.

"It's okay," Teresa reassured her chastened son-in-law. "Gus and I have actually talked about it and decided not to take on any more than we can handle. We'll have our hands full with each other and helping you out with your little one. Grandchildren is just about our speed."

"I'm sure you've heard, Mom, about that lab in Italy."[15]

"We were reading about it on the internet the other day," I said. "But we both think we did it right the first time and don't want to tempt fate."

"But that laboratory uses eggs from young women, fertilizes them with the sperm of a man. . . ."

"Who can either be the partner of the woman who receives the implantation, or someone else," I said, feeling proud of my recall. Maybe it's not worsening after all, I thought. That home page I had read, over two weeks ago, contained a lot of details, some in small print.

"And so, Mom," Giannina continued. "You could use the eggs of a young Italian medical school student, a movie star, or even an ordinary person like myself."

Now that's a heavy thought, I thought, realizing the full import of what Giannina had just said. I could end up being the father, via my new wife, of a child produced with her daughter's eggs. That would make our child—let's see—both Giannina's daughter and sister.

"Not that I would ever volunteer," she quickly added, to my great relief. "Italian culture prizes families, but that's just too unorthodox for me."

"In any event, Gus and I decided the whole idea was just too unconventional," Teresa seconded.

"Maybe we're the reverse of what those social scientists write about," I said. "We're not out to scandalize our kids that much, at least."

"And I don't think I'd volunteer either, Mom. Unless you were desperate. Then, who knows?"

"It would truly be the test of the Professor's solidarity thesis," Rodrigo mused. "But, speaking of solidarity, what do you two make of Patrick Buchanan's recent book urging white people to procreate, otherwise they risk being swamped by the faster-breeding groups of color?"[16]

I looked at Teresa, who said: "I find it quite distasteful. He seems to be implying that something is wrong with nonwhite genes—either that or nonwhite culture."

"Besides," I added, "he's being alarmist in the mathematical sense. People of color won't begin to outnumber whites until halfway through the century. And, on a worldwide basis, nonwhites have outnumbered Aryans since time immemorial, without the skies falling."

"If anything, the whites have posed a greater threat to the more peace-loving nonwhites than the other way around," Teresa added. "One thinks of Indian relocation and extermination, the slave trade, the Holocaust, and a host of anti-Asian and anti-Latino laws and measures. Not to mention colonialism, imperialism, and wars of conquest."

"So how about it?" I asked. "If you two can be nosy, why not me? Are you planning to have more children? Maybe a brother or sister or two to keep Gustavus company?"

"Will you be contributing to what W. E. B. Du Bois called the Talented Tenth?"[17] Teresa seconded.

"The minority community needs all the help it can get," I added. "Not that we want to pressure you, but little Gus is certainly something special. Teresa and I have already offered to help out with baby-sitting. Especially after I retire."

Just then the waiter approached again, telephone in hand.

"Saved by the bell," said Giannina, smiling mysteriously. "But I may be making an announcement soon."

PART II

REMEMBERING AND FORGETTING

IT TURNED OUT, indeed, to be the baby-sitter, announcing that little Gus was getting fussy. After paying our bill and leaving a tip, we stood on the sidewalk outside, blinking in the bright sunshine. As we started toward Teresa's apartment, I said:

"Speaking of solidarity, I wonder if, when we get back, the three of you could indulge me something, assuming little Gustavo is not too clamorous, that is."

"Certainly," Giannina said. "What is it?"

"I've been thinking about remembering and forgetting lately. When you're my age you'll understand why. I'm still sharp enough. But every now and then I have a senior moment."

"Hah!" Rodrigo exclaimed. "That happened to me in class the other day. And I'm only in my twenties. I couldn't remember the name of a case I've taught at least three times and had to cover up. It came to me a few minutes later, but annoyed me no end at the time."

"Now that's real solidarity," I said. "Your confession, I mean. But my little episode got me thinking about Critical Race Theory and some things Yancey said. I rejected them at the time, but now think he may have been right after all."

"I for one would love to hear your thoughts," Rodrigo said. "I don't think I've told you, but Laz has been pushing me to make a break with Critical Race Theory and form my own movement. He says liberals are increasingly out of touch with their own premises, caught up in contradictions, and don't even bother to frame proposals with an eye for what the public wants or the courts will consider. He was particularly scathing about the new discourse scholarship, which is more concerned, as you put it, with the term 'race' than with race itself."

"Laz is a smart guy. Too bad he never met Yancey. They would have made quite a team," Giannina said.

I smiled at her juxtaposition—the conservative Laz and the fire-breathing litigator Yancey together in deep conversation. Now, that would have been something. But I snapped myself out of my reverie, reminding myself that it was not to be: I could have brought them together—why didn't I?—but missed my chance. Another path not taken in life. I reminded myself to make better use of my opportunities, a sermon I'd given myself dozens of times, and went on as follows:

"Yes, they would have been a sight to behold. But the four of us are quite a team too. And I'm anxious for your thoughts on what is wrong with current progressive scholarship."

7

Hate Speech, Free Speech:

Speech as Struggle

MINUTES LATER, we were back in Teresa's apartment. The baby-sitter was just picking up her equipment, and little Gustavo was in the kitchen with Giannina, having a snack of baby food and something that looked like polenta. "He'll be ready for a nap soon," said Giannina as we stood and watched. "Why don't you all go into the living room and start? I'll be there as soon as I can."

She was true to her word. On her return, Giannina explained that the baby had been tired from all the active play with Rosa.

"She's great. Has more energy than I do, especially when I've been up half the night studying for midterms. Where were we?"

"We were going to talk about memory and forgetting, and what's wrong with Critical Race Theory," Rodrigo said, gesturing toward a book that he had just brought from Teresa's bookshelf and that was lying open on the table next to him. I saw that it was Milan Kundera's *Book of Laughter and Forgetting.* "But first, I was mulling over something one of you said about children and race. And that in turn reminded me of something Giannina and I were talking about the other day."

"Oh, you mean about his coloring book prowess?" Giannina asked. "I wouldn't put too much store on that."

"I don't either," Rodrigo quickly answered. "But I wonder if I could get Gus's and Mom's reaction to the whole race-IQ question. If they're interested, that is."

Both Teresa and I nodded vigorously, and I said, "Remembering and forgetting can wait. I take my ginko biloba every day—I won't forget."

Giannina and Rodrigo looked blank, so Teresa explained what the miracle over-the-counter memory drug was. They nodded, and Rodrigo began:

"It's not all that significant. Gus was doing something precocious with his coloring book—inventing a plot with characters and adventures, linking all the pages together into a sort of child's eye novel as we went along, turning the pages and coloring. Giannina said that was something you'd only expect of a four-year-old, and Gustavo is a little less than a year old."

"You may not be impressed, but I am," I said. "I think your son is going to invent the next stage of Critical Race Theory. Storytelling analysis applied to storytelling itself. Or, meta- storytelling. He'll be in *Harvard Law Review* before we will."

"They just accepted a piece of mine," Rodrigo said. "So he'll have to hurry. But I expect he'll do things in his way. Which right now is to take a nice long nap. At any rate, Giannina and I were reflecting on the raft of recent books linking race and IQ. I think you and I talked about *The Bell Curve*[1] not too long ago, Professor."

"We did," I said. "And if my ginko biloba is working, I should be able to remember when. Yes, it was at that Ethiopian restaurant.[2] Giannina joined us a little later. We discussed some recent books on race."

"Your memory is good, Professor," Rodrigo said admiringly. "Giannina wasn't in on the whole discussion, so maybe we can summarize for her and Mom's benefit."

"I'll take a stab at it," I said. "We were talking about the end of equality and recent books by conservative figures such as Dinesh D'-Souza, Robert Bork, and Peter Brimelow."

"The neonativist who wants us to close down the border and preserve America for the Anglo-Saxons," Teresa interrupted. "I was reading him the other day."[3]

"Right," said Rodrigo. "We talked about the theory of surplus equality, my own counterpart to Marx's theory of surplus value. I used it to explain why our system is forced to coin theories of the biological inferiority of minority groups, like that of *The Bell Curve*. My theory holds that liberty and equality stand in inverse relation and that today, with the rapid expansion of free-market economies, equality theory is forced to contract just as rapidly."[4]

"I was there for that part," Giannina interjected. "You explained that our national commitment to equality, enshrined in such documents as the Declaration of Independence and the Thirteenth, Fourteenth, and Fifteenth Amendments, stands in tension with our legal system's protection of property, wealth, and laissez-faire economics. All men are supposed to be equal, but over time we see that they become less and less so in education, culture, wealth, and behavior. The only way to account for this disparity is to posit theories of biological difference. That way the two halves of our system—free-market economics in the private law, and egalitarianism and equal concern in our public law—harmonize. People can't be equal, we say, because nature deals them different hands. We've done enough when we provide basic subsistence for all. That and equality of opportunity for their children."[5]

"So that if a ghetto child just happens to come across one hundred million dollars one day lying on the sidewalk, or saves up his earnings from delivering a paper route, he too can own General Motors," I said. And then, more seriously, "But then you went on and laid out four theories for how our internally contradictory system deals with this built-in strain. By the way, is this going to be in your Harvard article?"

"It is," Rodrigo replied. "With due acknowledgment to you two, of course. What I want to run past you today is an extension of that line of analysis. If little Gustavo will indulge us by sleeping a little longer, I can do it quickly."

SMART BY LAW: IN WHICH RODRIGO POSITS THE LEGAL CONSTRUCTION OF INTELLIGENCE

He glanced at Giannina, who said, "He looked blissed out from all that playing. I'm guessing we've got about forty-five minutes. I gather what you are going to say is related to our restaurant talk?"

"Yes," said Rodrigo. "And also that coloring book conversation."

I noticed the two of them were checking in with each other in the kind of abbreviated code that married people develop over time, that Jewel and I had perfected to a high art by the time she died, and that I was looking forward with such pleasure to developing with Teresa.

"And do you remember when we talked about Ian Haney Lopez's book?"[6]

"I do," Giannina said. "Entitled *White by Law: The Social Construction of Race*, it shows how the American court system in a series of cases decided who was white and who not.[7] I went and read it afterward."

"The judiciary were obliged to do so under a federal statute that I taught," I chimed in. "When my colleague Hiroshi Hato, who teaches immigration law, had to take sick leave, I covered that very line of cases in class. Of course, I had the advantage of the Haney Lopez book, otherwise the students probably would not have believed me, knowing my liberal proclivities. But Haney Lopez shows, in black and white. . . ."

Teresa giggled at my unintentional play on words and squeezed my arm. "Shows in black and white," I continued, "how in about fifty cases decided under an eighteenth-century congressional statute that limited naturalization to free, white citizens, federal courts drew the legal boundaries of whiteness. The cases concerned Mexicans, Persians, Indians, Japanese, and other would-be citizens. Some of their petitions were approved, but many more were denied on the ground that they were not really white."[8]

"Haney Lopez posits that the law has the ability not just to draw lines and create categories," Giannina interjected. "It can change the physical traits and appearance of an entire nation, by excluding some and including others, circumscribing marital choices, and limiting who has children."[9]

"A powerful insight," Rodrigo said. "But I have a corollary."

"What is it?" I asked.

"It's that the law, just as it constructs whiteness, also constructs intelligence or IQ." Rodrigo looked around expectantly.

"That's not just a corollary to what we were saying about the social science of interracial attraction and the tension between solidarity and untrammeled love," I exclaimed. "Rodrigo, this is a major insight, not just a gloss, one that serves as an overarching construct, a kind of glue, that not only holds together the various strands of thought that we and others have put forward to understand racial mixing and separatism. It puts all of it into perspective, and shows law's role. I'm waxing almost poetic, so I will now restrain myself and let you talk about your theory, which, by the way, I think you should entitle 'Smart by Law.' I hope you write about it. It will serve as an important counterweight to the simplistic theories of the *Bell Curve* crowd."

"Gee, I didn't know you would get that excited," Rodrigo said, mildly. "I thought it was just a logical extension of Haney Lopez's constructionist ideas applied to family law and reproduction. The basic idea is that some groups of people—kids in a school system, for example—are not just naturally smart and others dumb. No one is just smart 'out there,' in some objective sense. Smart people and less smart people exist, of course. You and I, Professor, teach students for a living, after all.

And we know that some are quicker at getting the hang of legal analysis than others. But the rules of the game are not fixed. Legal systems, curriculum-setting agencies, testing organizations—which do this for a profit—and, not least of all, the legal system, decide, in most cases arbitrarily, what kind of response to deem smart and what kind not."

"Didn't Robert Hayman write a book on this subject?"

"He did. Entitled *The Smart Culture*,[10] it lays out how all this happens, and how a child who would be deemed a genius in one setting— say, Jewish working-class families—might be considered a dunce in another—say, an African village or a Chicano migrant camp in the Southwest."

"And you propose to go beyond Hayman by showing the part that law plays in this process of differentiation and grading?" Teresa asked.

"Exactly. Giannina and I have talked about coauthoring something next summer, if she doesn't get that internship with the state supreme court. We'd look at a series of court cases having to do with mental retardation, competency to stand trial, and challenges to standardized testing. We'd look at the raft of new state laws requiring testing before students advance from one level to the next, and at various quasi-official genius designations, such as the MacArthur awards, National Merit scholarships, and the multibillion-dollar-a-year testing industry."

"Aren't some of those entirely private?" I asked. "How do you get state action?"

"Easy," Rodrigo said. "The Law School Admission Test, for example, is administered by the Law School Admissions Council, which is a counterpart to the College Board. Like the Board, it is composed of schools—namely, all the accredited law schools in the country. Many of them are public, and all of them use the LSAT in their admissions process. You can't go to a public law school unless you are officially deemed intelligent by the test."[11]

"I took the LSAT not that long ago," Giannina said. "I resented all the time I spent preparing for it. I did well and got into top schools, but the range of skills it tested struck me as exceedingly narrow. I don't know what sentence completions, verbal analogies, logical riddles, and games have to do with being a good lawyer."

"Maybe the ability to complete sentences for others is a requirement for being a male lawyer," Teresa said, looking over at Giannina, who smiled broadly. Then, "Not that you do this, Gus. You're a model of nonsexism, so far as I can tell."

"Wait until I slip a ring on that little finger," I said. "Heh Heh."

"Seriously, though," Teresa went on. "I very much hope the two of you do write about law's role in the construction of intelligence. I can even think of a few more topics you might want to consider, including the law's treatment of abortion[12] and abortion funding,[13] family caps for welfare recipients,[14] truth- in-testing legislation,[15] and, above all, statutes that in almost half the states allow authorities to order the sterilization of persons found to be feeble-minded or likely to pass on deleterious genes.[16] Then you have bans against intermarriage, which I understand stood on the books untouched until years after *Brown v. Board of Education*,[17] not to mention recent cutbacks on affirmative action, which until recently allowed at least a few black, brown, Asian, and Indian kids to get a college education.[18] Republicans are on the warpath against unwed black mothers and anxious to cut them off from welfare, HeadStart for their children, and practically every other kind of public program that enabled them to keep things together. You could even delve into academic research, some at top universities, aimed at showing that children of color have lower IQs than their white counterparts and are incapable of benefiting from education beyond a certain point."[19]

"That sounds like Shockley and Jensen," I said.

"Them and others," Teresa continued. "As a former community college instructor, I still follow the writing of this coterie of pseudoscientists, some of whom have websites where they propagate their peculiar theories. I'm sure you know of William Shockley's bonus plan that would offer cash incentives for poor black women with IQs below a certain point willing to be sterilized."[20]

"And I was reading, just the other day, a writer who urged that states require couples planning to marry to pass a parenting test. If they couldn't produce a certain score on an exam normed, no doubt, on white middle-class values, they couldn't get married,"[21] I added.

"Well, Rodrigo, you've got your work cut out for you," Teresa said. "But if we're all as smart as we think we are, we might be wise to turn to Gus's topic—memory and forgetting—while the baby is asleep, that is."

"I'd love your comments," I said. "Like you two, I might write about this one day."

IN WHICH THE PROFESSOR AND HIS FRIENDS
DISCUSS THE HATE SPEECH DEBATE AND A LOST ALLY

"By all means," I heard from one of my young interlocutors. So, taking a deep breath, I began:

"Earlier, we were saying how Critical Race Theory has become estranged from its materialist roots."

"Right," Giannina said. "All the writing these days is about discourse. It's as though our once-radical friends had tired of writing about the world and decided instead to write about how people speak about the world."

"It's certainly easier," I said dryly. "One doesn't have to come to grips with the twists and turns of racial history, the vexed interaction of groups of color with each other, and the economic side of racial exploitation. One doesn't have to deal with these new, ferocious, in-your-face conservatives who accuse *you* of being racist because of some slight departure from perfect color blindness. One just talks about terms and categories, like the census. Or other people's writing."[22]

"Like a village that wants to make a living by taking in each other's washing," Teresa said.

"Exactly," I agreed. "Early CRT writing fell squarely in the materialist, or real-world, vein. In a famous article, Derrick Bell showed how interest-convergence—the self-interest of white elites—explained much of the ebb and flow of black racial fortunes."[23]

"Including, as I recall, *Brown v. Board of Education*,"[24] Teresa said.

"Exactly," I replied. "He also showed how class divisions within the black community would sometimes set litigators from the NAACP and other progressive organizations on one side, and the black community on the other. The black community wanted better schools, the litigators wanted integration—wanted to establish a new legal principle.[25] Alan Freeman and Girardeau Spann examined the Supreme Court's role in the development of civil rights law, showing that that Court's leadership has been, at best, faltering.[26] Spann even urged that black lawyers abandon the court system and instead engage in pure politics, by which he meant street demonstrations, electing black candidates, and neighborhood organizing."[27]

"And you think we've gotten away from that kind of writing?" Rodrigo asked.

"In many ways, yes," I replied. "Examining hate speech, media images, census categories, and intersectionality—people who fit into two legal or social categories, like black women, gay black males, or single black working mothers—is interesting, and even important. It helps us understand how we think and how others think about us. But the world of events and actions has a logic of its own, which we ignore at our peril."

"Could you give me an example?" Giannina asked.

"Sure," I said. "Suppose the United States suddenly begins cracking down on immigration from Latin America. A discourse theorist would likely explain that in terms of prevailing social attitudes toward brown people. He or she would examine recent texts on Latinos and Latinas and look for evidence of stereotypes and images."

"While a materialist," Rodrigo said, completing my thought, "would look at it in terms of shifts in the job market, or tipping points in the country's demography, so that whites start to feel that they are hearing too much Spanish spoken on the streets, or seeing too many Latino kids in school requiring special attention from the teacher."[28]

"Or demanding affirmative action in college admissions, so that white students from good homes are sometimes turned down by their top choice schools,"[29] said Giannina.

"Exactly," I said. "And that's why analysis of racial phenomena in terms of ideas, words, and images is ultimately an evasion. To understand our predicament, we need to know not just the language in which people describe that predicament, but the forces that produce it.[30] The same is true of hate speech."

"You know, I've never heard it explained that way before, but it's considerations like those that prompted Giannina and me to set up the institute almost a year ago."

Giannina, who had just tiptoed back from the bedroom for a peek at the baby, announced, "He's starting to stir. That usually means we have about fifteen minutes before he announces in no uncertain terms that he's awake. Gus, if you are going to tell us about your hate-speech example, now's the time to do it."

FIRST AMENDMENT LEGAL FORMALISM AND
A PROGRESSIVE ORGANIZATION THAT
LOST TOUCH WITH ITS ROOTS

"Let's see how far we can get," I began. "Anyone need a refill first?" I took orders, Teresa and I made a quick trip to the kitchen to get coffee and tea started, then dashed back to the living room.

"Where were we?" I asked. "Oh, yes. That disease whose name I can never recall. My thesis is that it's not just Critical Race Theory that has forgotten what it stands for. Forgetting and evasion are rife in progressive circles. One mechanism I've been thinking about is formalism, which enables you to ignore substantive values like justice—the reason why you went into law in the first place—and live instead in a world of procedure and rights."[31]

"While sleeping well at night," Rodrigo added.

"Right. Although it's a natural human response—because it allows you to think you've tamed an unruly reality—formalism flattens out the range of possibilities you consider and prevents you from seeing the full panoply of forces confronting your constituents. A little form is not a bad thing, as every law professor who has graded a blue book knows. But it can contribute to serious injustice. Remind me sometime to tell you my Nuremberg story. But, in addition to First Amendment legal formalism, we might consider some other mechanisms. For example, I was just reading Stanley Fish on principle,[32] which suggested a second one. Then, there's a third kind of displacement that takes place when the leftist forgets what made her upset in the first place and takes on a different target.[33] A fourth is a kind of bribery in which the establishment buys off black protest.[34] And a final one comes from wearing a certain type of blinders and seeing only the struggles of your own racial minority group.[35] I call this exceptionalism, and it's related to the black-white binary of race that you and I were talking about once, Rodrigo. We could address each of these in separate sessions."

"Good plan, Professor," said Giannina. "But please start on the first one. I want to hear your analysis of hate speech and the ACLU before a certain toddler exercises his own free speech rights."

"My insight, such as it is," I began, "is that you start by asking yourself about the role speech has played in reform movements in this country."

"Professors Charles Lawrence and Nadine Strossen, the national president of the ACLU, debated an aspect of that very question in the pages of *Duke Law Journal*,"[36] Giannina said. "My reading group was discussing it the other day. Strossen argued that speech was vital to social reform; Lawrence, that marches, protests, and sit-ins were much more instrumental."[37]

"That was, indeed, a foundational exchange," I said. "But a second, more recent one shed further light on that very same issue. This one featured a different critical race theorist debating the same Nadine Strossen at a conference convened by the Bancroft Library. The event commemorated the opening of an archive of the Free Speech Movement (FSM), one of the Berkeley campus's more colorful chapters. I was lucky enough to be there."

"I may have seen a flyer," Teresa said, "on the bulletin board at the Wilderness Federation, where I volunteer three days a week. The event featured over a dozen sociologists, historians, political scientists, and law professors, as well as student activists from those cataclysmic days. The two law professors spoke on the closing panel, if I'm not mistaken."[38]

"Your memory is good, Teresa," I said.

"And I bet I can guess the ACLU speaker's position," Rodrigo interjected. "An absolutist one with no room for regulation, even of hate speech and hard-core pornography. And I bet she argued that unbridled speech was best for minorities."

"Exactly right," I said. "Even though we may not know it. And of course the critical race theorist argued the opposite. Juxtaposing the two, I've concluded one can look at movements like the FSM in at least two different ways. At the Berkeley event some of the audience seemed to hear the historians describe how the early feminist movement led to the civil rights uprising of the sixties, and that in turn led to the antiwar movement that shook America—all in terms of an underlying value, namely, speech—the unquenchable desire of human beings to speak out."

"And I bet the other half, represented by Delgado and maybe some of the more activist speakers . . ." Rodrigo began.

"And some feminists too, I would bet," added Giannina.

"Right. I would bet that the other half interpreted those great events in terms of a different value—struggle," Rodrigo hazarded.

"You read my mind," I said. "They saw those very same events as illustrating an equally unquenchable human impulse—the desire to live in a better, freer world. Both groups, the free speech and the struggle camp, share many of the same values and objectives, of course. But one's choice of variable—speech or struggle—can make a big difference."

"Can you explain how?" said Teresa. "I'm having trouble seeing how they wouldn't come down to the same thing."

"I think I can see what Gus is driving at," said Giannina. "For example, if you're in the speech camp, like Professor Strossen, and the next case that comes along concerns pornography[39] or the rights of neo-Nazis to march in Skokie or burn crosses on the lawns of black people,[40] that may strike you as a good opportunity to expand your favorite value, speech. But imagine that a different case comes your way, say, one presenting an issue of environmental justice or gay liberation. That may not present such clear-cut opportunities to expand the contested field of speech. Perhaps the movement is at an incipient stage, and nobody is trying to silence it right then. But if you are in the struggle camp, that case may be right up your alley."

"I see what you mean," said Teresa.

"The two camps may be coming closer together," I added. "A new book by Steve Shiffrin[41] proposes a dissent view of free speech. According to him, we should see the First Amendment as intended mainly to protect dissenting speech, speech that challenges orthodoxy or the actions of the government. Under this view, we would give little protection to obscenity or hate speech, because they do not constitute dissent, but a great deal to movements like the FSM or Chicano liberation."[42]

"Now I see where you are going," said Rodrigo. "You're going to argue for the primacy of struggle, so that First Amendment legal formalism—the idea that the system of free speech exists to protect regressive, hateful, racist speech just as much as the other kind—is a kind of evasion, a form of forgetting. This I want to hear. Give me fifteen seconds."

Rodrigo tiptoed quickly to the bedroom, looked inside and returned quietly. "He's dead to the world," he said. "Go on."

"I come by my views honestly," I said. "Despite the mighty First Amendment, I have seen indigenous women I championed turned down for tenure for speaking out against institutional racism, seen fellow critical race theorists lose out on job chances for writing in favor of affirmative action or against hate speech. . . ."

"Ironic!" exclaimed Teresa.

"I have also seen outstanding women, like Catharine MacKinnon, one of the brightest lights on the academic scene, relegated to a nomadic existence for years, because no law school would hire her—all this despite our vaunted system of free expression."[43]

"I can see why you might see the First Amendment as something less than a magic talisman," said Giannina. "But can you explain why you see it as a formalistic device? I thought I knew what legal formalism is, but I'm not sure I see the connection between it and free speech."

"Let me try," Rodrigo said, giving me a break in the long exposition. "I'm sure you know, Giannina, how in the early years of the twentieth century, law schools had just set up shop on American campuses.[44] Today, law schools like yours and mine are parts of universities, like the department of English, or political science where Teresa taught before she retired. But this was not always so. Before that time, aspiring lawyers learned their craft by the apprenticeship method, by reading the law, as Abraham Lincoln did, at the feet of some local lawyer who agreed to take them on."[45]

"And then, early in the century, things changed?" Giannina asked.

"They did," Rodrigo answered. "The new departments needed to put as much distance as possible between themselves and the old trade school, apprenticeship approach. Right around that time, a Harvard law professor named Christopher Columbus Langdell discovered. . . ."

"Not America, I gather," Teresa cracked.

"No, but the famous case method," Rodrigo said, smiling. "But it was just as useful to the aspiring legal academicians as a new continent, because it enabled them to claim intellectual terrain that was recognizable to their faculty peers. In the new method, professors grilled students on their casebooks—collections of reported decisions organized by subject matter—and demanded that they distill out general principles of law. The discipline emerged as a branch of empirical science, something one learned, like physics, through the inductive, scientific method—something you could then test by an examination geared to seeing what your students had learned."[46]

"Instant credibility," Teresa said.

"That approach, known as formalism or mechanical jurisprudence, remained unchallenged for three decades, long enough for law professors to learn to hold their heads up high at the faculty club. Under it, the job of students was to study judicial opinions and derive general principles; that of judges, to apply those principles to new cases that came before them. Over time, the body of legal principles would grow and become ever more detailed, covering every eventuality."[47]

"But we all know that didn't happen," Giannina said. "Even in the first year of law school, by the end of the first semester my classmates were talking about how even the cases printed in the casebooks are inconsistent. Sometimes back-to-back cases can't be squared with each other. The professors push you to find some higher level at which they can be reconciled. In class, we try to play the game, but outside some of us whisper that the emperor has no clothes."

"Well, you have good company," I said. "A school came along, one with some of the greatest names in U.S. legal history—Holmes, Brandeis, Cohen, Llewellyn—that showed, through just the sort of examination you and your classmates conducted, that every case does not have a single right answer, that most can be argued either way.[48] The realists wrote that to get cases right, judges not only had to pay attention to the law on the books, so as to choose one of the alternatives that was genuinely plausible. But in choosing among them, they needed to know human behavior, social organization, economics, and politics.[49] They also needed to know enough about the science of persuasion and rhetoric to enable them to make their opinions persuasive to the disappointed party."

"That movement swept the land," Rodrigo continued, "leading to law and society, critical legal studies, radical feminism, and Critical Race Theory, disciplines that, in one way or another, take the political dimension of law seriously, operating in the intellectual spaces that legal realism opened up. These movements cast aside tired maxims, overbroad certitudes, and rules riddled with exceptions, in favor of an examination of the way law actually functioned."[50]

"But what about the First Amendment?" Teresa asked.

"I was just coming to that," I said. "Want me to check the baby first?"

Giannina shook her head. "When he wakes up, he'll let us know. Go on."

"Okay. It's an interesting story. The legal-realist revolution swept the law, casting aside easy generalizations and rules riddled with exceptions, in every area except one—the First Amendment, where thought-ending clichés and per se rules . . ."

"Like no content regulation, or the best cure for bad speech is more speech," Rodrigo chimed in.

"Exactly, held sway until recently.[51] They were the ACLU's stock-in-trade, because they usually favored the speech- protective position while sounding vaguely progressive. But in the last few years, under pressure from minorities and women, that old, formalistic approach has been giving way in favor of a more nuanced one that tries to understand how speech really works, how it sometimes can conflict with other values, and that sees speech as one value among many."[52]

When I fell silent, Giannina spoke up. "Thanks, Gus, that helps me understand some things I had been trying to sort out. And I gather your main point is that the ACLU style of First Amendment formalism, under which minorities and women were supposed to grin and bear it when subjected to racial abuse or a gauntlet of sexual innuendos and pinup posters at work, no longer serves society."

"It never did, really," I said. "Whenever the law ran across a powerful value that conflicted with one of the broad First Amendment doctrines, such as no viewpoint discrimination, it simply coined a new exception."

"It's like having an organization devoted to free vegetables, that adopted the rule that all vegetables were good for you and should be distributed by the government free of charge to everybody. Then, it turns out that some vegetables are poisonous, that others are expensive and hard to grow, that you need to eat other things than vegetables to be healthy. And so, the American Vegetable Liberties Union tolerates all these exceptions while staunchly defending the idea that every child should be forced to eat his vegetables, and to shut up and stop resisting."

"I'm sure they would reject the analogy, amusing as it is," I said. "But it does point up the illogic of absolutist ideology. Which reminds me of a competition that took place recently at my own university. It asked contestants to write about how free speech helped make America great. One or two of my students entered it, although one of them told me he had doubts about the premise. Later, I ran across the head judge, a member of the English department, and asked her how she thought the panel would have reacted had one of the entrants argued that it is not so much the system of free speech, but the exceptions to it, that made America great. She hesitated, then replied that the judges would have found it an interesting answer."[53]

"I'm not sure I follow you," Rodrigo confessed. "In what sense was it the exceptions to the First Amendment that made America great?"

"Let me explain," I said. "Consider how the United States stands unquestionably at the head of the world in precisely two respects—military might and economic production. But these areas flourish precisely because of the protection we afford official and commercial secrets and patent and copyright protection for inventors and authors.[54] These are of course areas in which speech is not free. By the same token, hate speech, media stereotypes, and pornography, under current doctrine, are free. Lacking their own exception, these types of speech are responsible for much misery in minority communities."[55]

"You're starting to sound like one of those idealists," Rodrigo pointed out.

"Well, er, I hope not," I said. "Merely because one points out that speech can stigmatize and hurt. . . ."

"That words can wound, as one author put it,"[56] interjected Giannina.

"Right," I said. "Merely because one wishes that speech doctrine were more sensitive to its impact on marginalized groups, it does not follow that one is according speech and images more weight than they deserve. Bad speech is just one of many disadvantaging conditions that the civil rights community faces. And when it tries to do something about it, it always finds the ACLU on the other side."

"On the side of the pornographers, skinheads, neo-Nazis, and bigots writing books about our innate, biological inferiority," Rodrigo added. "Pornography is a billion-dollar-a-year industry, and I was just reading that it contributes lavishly to the ACLU."[57]

"It stands to reason that it would," Giannina said. "And one of the advantages of Gus's neorealist First Amendment approach, it seems to me, is that it enables one to ask the who-benefits question. You get to look at the way people with no genuine commitment to free inquiry, dissent, robust discussion, or any of the other First Amendment values that John Locke and Alexander Hamilton wrote about hide under the cloak of this great liberty. First Amendment legal realism lets us start to ask the right questions."[58]

"It also allows us to look at certain statistics in a new light," I said. "These other categories of free speech—pornography, hate speech, invidious media stereotypes of people of color—may well be responsible for the main areas where America is not great. This has been a great mystery to some. The United States today ranks low—as low as twentieth among industrialized nations, according to figures I have read—in longevity, health, mental health, incarceration, and school completion for minority populations, and lower still in terms of income and quality-of-life disparities between the well-off and the rest. These figures, which organizations like the UN and Amnesty International have been pointing out, are sources of national embarrassment. Hate speech and abuse may account for some of them."[59]

"Now I see what you were saying earlier," Teresa said. "Speech helps make America great because of the exceptions—because of the areas in which we suppress it, quietly and without making a fuss. Of course, there would be an exception for military secrets or for industrial formulas or for an inventor's or author's work product, we say. But for some of the most vulnerable people in our society. . . ."

"Like eighteen-year-old black undergraduates attacked by abusive loudmouths late at night while walking home from the campus library," Rodrigo added.

"Precisely," Giannina continued. "Someone like that Berkeley crit or Charles Lawrence proposes a mild-mannered campus rule punishing campus racism, and our friends in the ACLU get quite excited."

"The First Amendment must be a seamless web, they say, ignoring all those exceptions for the military, defamation, copyright, plagiarism, words of threat, and dozens more," I added.[60] "There, speech is unfree because some powerful group, such as consumers, has decided that false advertising, for example, cannot be tolerated.[61] That is why America is great. In the areas where it manifestly is not great, speech is free—hate speech and pornography, which demoralize minorities and women."

"Reminds me of a speech that Thurgood Marshall gave just before he died,"[62] Rodrigo said. "It was in the middle of the Bicentennial celebrations. He pointed out that in the parties and celebrations that were ringing out across the land, relatively few African Americans could be found.[63] He pointed out that the Constitution expressly protected the institution of slavery in no fewer than six places . . ."[64]

"Which are still there today," Giannina added.

"They have never been expunged," Rodrigo observed.

"Marshall pointed out that the Constitution, as drafted, was radically imperfect, requiring a host of amendments, a bloody Civil War, and much struggle before it would emerge as the document it is today,"[65] I concluded.

"And I suppose you want us to consider what he would say, if he were alive, of the ACLU's absolutist view of the First Amendment," Teresa said.

"I think I know," Giannina volunteered. "He might have pointed out that this mighty guarantee of liberty coexisted comfortably with slavery for one hundred years,[66] that during the civil rights-era of the sixties, when blacks made the greatest gains, civil rights demonstrators marched, were arrested, and convicted. They sat in, were arrested, and convicted; picketed, were arrested, and convicted. Spoke on courthouse steps, were arrested, and convicted. True, every now and then their convictions would be reversed on appeal. . . ."[67]

"After the expenditure of thousands of dollars and hundreds of hours of gallant lawyering," Rodrigo added.

"Our system of free speech, at least as currently understood, provided little protection. Their speech was always too disruptive, too loud, not prayerful and mannerly enough, or uttered in the wrong time and place."

"Or without asking permission first," Teresa added. "I'm not a lawyer but I read about a case in which a court upheld the conviction of Martin Luther King for leading a march in a Southern city on the ground that he didn't first challenge the injunction the city had obtained against him."[68]

"The injunction was patently overbroad and unconstitutional," Rodrigo said.

"Yet the court held he had no business violating it. He was required to have gone, hat in hand, to the Southern judge who had issued it, asked him to rescind it, appealed all the way up the ladder, and then, perhaps, he could have marched,"[69] Giannina concluded, shaking her head in disbelief.

"Of course, by then the moment would have passed," Rodrigo pointed out. "His followers would have long since gone home."

"So, what you and Gus are saying is that the system of free expression has not been anything like minorities' best friend. The ACLU keeps insisting that we are benighted souls who, if we knew better, would stop clamoring for protection from hate speech and minor inconveniences like that," Teresa summarized.

"But my First Amendment legal realism lets you see how they could come to think so. It explains what Jack Balkin calls ideological drift—the process by which a principle or rallying cry dear to the left, over time becomes a tool of the right.[70] Everyone knows how conservatives today love to quote Martin Luther King. In similar fashion, free speech has become a favorite tool of pornographers, purveyors of hate speech, and white supremacists. Left-leaning civil liberties organizations that once defended writers, socialists, and labor organizers today make common cause with the libertarians of the Cato Institute and the cigarette industry, anxious to have cigarette advertising and smoking in public spaces declared constitutional rights."[71]

"Dinesh D'Souza and his crowd, who monitor campuses for the least display of political correctness, also love the First Amendment,"[72] said Rodrigo. "I've heard activists of color say that the First Amendment today is the white people's amendment. They have the First, we have the Fourteenth."

"Or whatever is left of it," Teresa cracked. "The Supreme Court has been steadily dismantling it under the banner of color blindness. Which strikes me as clear-cut a case of formalistic perversity as you could find."[73]

"I agree," I said. "A friend of mine—actually, someone I ran into at Yancey's funeral—who specializes in law and development tells me that even in the most totalitarian countries, freedom has a way of growing in niches and cracks, until one day it rises up and challenges the totalitarian order.[74] Unfortunately, the same may hold true in reverse. Ideological drift allows our liberties, including speech, to be taken over by scoundrels and profiteers hiding under their banners and using them for ignoble ends."

"Our system of free speech also allows someone to convert what ought to be substantive controversy into a procedural one," added Giannina, "becoming a martyr at the same time.[75] A character like David Horowitz places an ad saying something outrageous, such as that blacks don't deserve reparations for slavery because that institution did them a favor.[76] A campus editor refuses to run the ad, and guess what happens?"

"He hollers that his precious First Amendment rights have been violated," Teresa replied. "Free speech allows someone to deflect attention from what should be the real question—whether what someone said is progressive or not—and instead to focus on whether he had a right to say it. The speaker now becomes a hero for standing up to orthodoxy and saying something unpopular, such as that blacks are stupid or needed slavery to remove them from the Dark Continent to this wonderful, enlightened land."[77]

"With its First Amendment," I added.

"Which never protects what we really want to say, when we really need it," Rodrigo recalled.

"The Berkeley student activists called their movement the Free Speech Movement at first. But they soon dropped it, realizing that their real targets were the war, racism, and impersonal, bureaucratic education,"[78] I mused.

"I am beginning to see your point, Professor," Rodrigo said, leaning forward in his chair. "Most ACLU members start out liberal. They have the right instincts. They want to help minorities and preserve human dignity and freedom. But First Amendment formalism causes them to seize on a single principle and look at the entire world through that lens alone. They end up ignoring nuance, history, and a host of evidence showing that speech alone doesn't guarantee fairness."

"They start out knowing that," Giannina added. "I have a friend in my study group who said that in some ways, law school is making her stupider. You forget things you once knew. As the Professor put it, formalism flattens out knowledge. It's a kind of forgetting. The formalist is like an Alzheimer's patient. He has lost access to things he once knew."

"He's like Kundera's character Mirek in that book over there," Teresa said, gesturing toward the volume Rodrigo had open next to him. "A classic formalist, he writes everything down to avoid forgetting anything important."

"He wants to be responsible," Rodrigo went on. "But his friends warn him he is being just the opposite. And his carelessness has consequences; his friends are right. The government finds his notes and arrests him."

"He ends up betraying his friends and himself," Teresa added.

"And do you think that, in similar fashion, the First Amendment can do positive harm—not just cause you to overlook important aspects of your situation?"

"I do," she replied. "Consider how the reigning First Amendment metaphor, the marketplace of ideas, subtly disadvantages reformers.[79] You see, if the marketplace of ideas is really free, then the ideas of the outsider group. . . ."

"For example, that affirmative action is good, that a bicultural/bilingual educational system is better than the present kind, and that ethnic studies is a worthwhile subject—all these lost out in free competition. It was a fair fight. Bush won. Christopher Columbus beat the natives. Dinesh D'Souza gets larger advances for his books than leftists do for theirs. The West has indoor plumbing," Giannina added.

"Exactly," her mother continued. "But of course it was not a fair fight. The minority view starts out at a disadvantage, because everyone has been indoctrinated in the opposite starting from early grades. Plus, it costs money to rent a microphone, buy a TV spot, or lobby Congress or a school board for one's position.[80] That's what I mean when I say that free speech is not just a type of formalism that limits your imagination. It makes you and your society resist change. It helps condemn and marginalize what lies outside the canon, while everyone feels comfortable with that state of affairs."[81]

"In that sense, First Amendment absolutism doesn't just cause you to forget things you once knew. It places whole realms of experience beyond reach, officially devalued. Why should anyone look into them—they lost out in the footrace," Rodrigo summarized.

"What a paradox," Giannina said quietly.

"First Amendment realism suffers yet another drawback—in addition to its apologetic aspect, I mean. Would you like to hear it?" I asked.

My young interlocutors nodded enthusiastically, and seeing that Teresa appeared to be going strong, I began as follows: "Getting real about the First Amendment allows you to look beyond the bland assertion of a thriving marketplace of ideas, in which supposedly the best idea wins and artists are free to express themselves, and see what our system of free expression really consists of."

"I bet you're going to say a lot of pulp novels and sitcoms. The sort of thing my students read outside class, supposedly for comic relief," Rodrigo said wryly.

"You read my mind," I replied. "Only 6 percent of our fellow citizens read a single book a year.[82] Nearly all of them receive their ideas from TV, which glows for fifty hours a week in the average household, talk radio, or the internet.[83] Publishing houses are constantly merging so that the market for serious books decreases every year.[84] Six best-selling authors, including Stephen King, account for over 60 percent of all books sold, with self-help books making up most of the rest.[85] A quarter of e-mail messages are spam.[86] Many children can't find the United States on a map of the world.[87] Seventy percent of Americans believe in angels, but very few have any idea how much of their lives is controlled by corporations.[88] Only 2 percent of teenagers could name the chief justice of the Supreme Court."[89]

"Although 59 percent could name the Three Stooges," Rodrigo interjected. "I saw that same article."[90]

"Campus bookstores are a lost cause," Giannina said. "Most of them sell required texts, crib sheets, coffee mugs, stuffed animals, sweatshirts bearing the team's logo, and little else.[91] The state has little need to censor anything because most of the books say the same thing. All this happened in the last fifty years or so."

"At a time when First Amendment advocacy was reaching its peak," I observed. "But speaking of state power, classic free speech theorists like John Locke and John Stuart Mill wrote at a time when society was relatively homogeneous and the main threat to liberty was the state—official power, official censorship, the king. But today it is the collective aspect of private speech, like water dripping on sandstone, that constitutes the main challenge to freedom.[92] An upcoming book by Alexander Tsesis shows that in every case of mass atrocity, on every continent, the perpetrators first demonized their victims through a campaign of vilification."[93]

"An interesting reversal, Professor," said Rodrigo. "You're saying that just as when we study discrimination, we can't limit ourselves to the old intentional, dominative kind, but must also take into account unconscious, structural, or institutional racism, we need to expand our free-speech paradigm beyond King John-style censors with pairs of scissors to include the tacitly coordinated set of social scripts, narratives, invective, and stories that render minority people one-down, on the defensive, second-class citizens."

"That silences them," Teresa added. "So that the social dialog ends up containing less, not more, speech."[94]

"A further irony to add to the one Giannina pointed out earlier," I said, "First Amendment doctrine is at war with itself."

"Incoherent, perhaps. But not entirely useless," Giannina observed. "We were talking in my constitutional law class the other day about *New York Times v. Sullivan.*"[95]

"The most celebrated First Amendment case in history," her husband clarified. "It held that a public figure, in that case a Southern sheriff, has to plead and prove actual malice to recover from a newspaper for defamation. The case was heralded as a great victory for freedom of the press."

"As indeed it was," Giannina said. "But it may also have been an interest-convergence case, as Derrick Bell argued *Brown v. Board of Education* was. Consider: Transistors had just been invented. Policy makers, including Supreme Court justices, must have been able to foresee a future economy based on information transfer and technology. Protecting media giants like the *New York Times. . . .*"

"Or, in today's world, AOL or a giant website," Rodrigo added.

"Exactly," Giannina agreed. "Protecting them from libel suits by small-time Southern sheriffs or disaffected individuals who believe their reputations have been sullied by something carried on the internet, must have been seen as a first order of business. Insulating the liberal *New York Times* from suit by a redneck sheriff was the perfect vehicle for enhancing protection for messages of all kinds, including the myriad bits of information that now stream through fiberoptic networks and are the mainstay of our economy."[96]

"Not just ours," Teresa said. "Think of ads selling American jeans in Beijing or Pepsi Cola and weight loss programs in remote Fiji villages, so that native girls for the first time suffer bulimia and anorexia. How else would they learn they are expected to vomit and die to be thin?"[97]

We looked around at each other, having all heard a telltale rustling sound from the other room.

"Oops," said Rodrigo. "Well, Gus, if I can summarize, you've shown that it's vital not to romanticize speech. Also that First Amendment formalism does violence to other values, which it causes you to forget and put out of mind. You made a case for speech as struggle, and for understanding movements like the FSM not as aimed at expanding what you can say, but as challenging an unjust war and exposing connections between the university and the defense industry. You've shown that the role of the courts and free speech in these movements is easily overstated, and that free speech doctrine was as often an obstacle to social progress as an ally and friend."

"Even in Berkeley, the justice system did the students little good. The California governor sent the attorney general of the state, a former law professor, to Berkeley to make sure every last one of the free speech leaders was arrested and sent to jail," I recalled.

"And the supposedly neutral press fell right into line," Teresa added, getting up to help Giannina with the baby. "They depicted the Berkeley students as drug-addled, sex-crazed bums with nothing better to do than rebel against their parents and hate America.[98] The very instrument they invoked—free speech—was turned against them."

"The more things change, the more they stay the same," I concluded. "We need to keep our memories sharp and remember our histories and our own values. Otherwise, the great stone wheel will just keep right on turning."

"Free speech does not exist, yet is the new orthodoxy, the new authoritarianism," said Rodrigo. "If what we've said today offers a moral, it's that we should fight for what we believe, hold on to what we know, remember where justice lies, and know that complex issues cannot be captured by a single formula. We should place only as much faith in the system of free expression as it deserves. And now that I've had my memory refreshed about California history—remember, much of that happened before I was born—I'll end with a vow. I bet I speak for Giannina too, and for little Gus when he gets a bit older."

"What's the vow?" I asked.

"It's that I'll see all of you again, if not before, on the Sproul Hall steps when it's time to get rid of Proposition 209."[99]

"I'll be there too," I said.

8

The Trouble with Principle

ALTHOUGH WE CONTINUED to exchange letters and cards, I did not see Rodrigo nor his family for several weeks. They returned home shortly after our conversation in Teresa's apartment, and Rodrigo's letters spoke about the myriad details of resuming his teaching career, Giannina's summer plans—it turns out that she was, indeed, selected for that coveted supreme court internship—and the precocious baby's accomplishments. (One grainy photograph even showed him proudly displaying his first tooth!)

Then, late one afternoon, while I was performing a most mundane function—washing my hands in a men's room at Gatwick airport, where I was to be picked up by a delegation of black lawyers—I heard a familiar voice. Looking around I saw Rodrigo's lanky figure entering the bathroom with the equally tall, pale figure of Laz. They were talking animatedly.

"Rodrigo!" I exclaimed. "And Laz! I thought I heard two American voices. What are you two doing here?"

"Gus! How incredible! We had heard you might be on the program tomorrow, but when we saw the draft they sent us, you weren't on it. So we assumed you weren't coming."

"I'm the evening keynote speaker. So technically, I suppose I'm not on the program," I said. "What a coincidence. We do seem to meet up in the most unlikely places."

"I bet they're picking you up. You're a VIP."

"They said they would. But my flight is almost an hour early. If you don't mind waiting, I'm sure they can give you a ride too. They said something about a van."

Rodrigo looked at Laz, and when he nodded emphatically, said, "We'll take our chances. Besides, we're starved. The breakfast on the plane was mainly meat, so my vegetarian friend here couldn't eat anything. I sat it out too, out of misguided solidarity."

"Traveling isn't what it used to be," I said. "Let me buy the two of you some breakfast."

Minutes later, we were seated in a comfortable airport restaurant, a soccer match blaring away on a TV in the corner. We ordered—the oatmeal he had missed on the plane for Laz, eggs and bangers for Rodrigo ("I'm not quite sure what they are, but I'll try anything"), and a light cheese omelet for me, my stomach still churning from a bumpy descent a few minutes ago.

"What panel are you two on?" I asked.

"Critical Race Theory," Laz replied. "Rodrigo is supposed to introduce the main themes, while I'm supposed to give a critique of some sort, although as you know I'm quite sympathetic. My parents were poor immigrants from Poland, and the main problem I have with the movement lies in its failure to include a class component."

"What about you, Gus? What's your keynote speech about? Or do you prefer to keep it to yourself until you deliver it, as many speakers do?"

"I don't mind," I said. "Although it's not quite finished yet. I'll have to spend a little time on it tonight in the hotel. I brought along this little baby. Have you seen it?" I showed my two young friends my new laptop computer, of which I was quite proud.

"Not bad," said Rodrigo. "I remember not too long ago you were resisting the new technology."

"I use it mainly for word processing. That and e-mail."

"A mixed blessing, I bet," said Laz. "You're so eminent I bet you receive dozens of requests a day from people wanting a favor of some kind—a letter of recommendation, a manuscript to critique, a tenure file to evaluate."

"I have a love-hate relationship with it," I acknowledged. "But I've learned to put an intercept message on that says when I'll be traveling or otherwise incommunicado. Then, when I come back and turn the thing on, hardly any messages await me. People seem to learn to live without me. It's a little deflating."

When my two young companions kept looking at me expectantly, I said, with a start, "Oh, sorry. My mind must be more jet-lagged than I realize. I'm speaking about Stanley Fish's latest book, *The Trouble with Principle*.[1] The organizers asked me to talk about something broader than race, so I picked this."

"How about that?" said my two friends at the same time, then cracked up. Rodrigo rummaged inside the lightweight carry-on bag on the chair next to him, then triumphantly held up a copy of the very book I had mentioned. "I finished it on the plane. Laz told me I had to read it."

"Oh, oh," I said. "Now I'm not going to be able to get away with anything. At least two people in the audience will know the book as well as I do."

"We promise not to give you a hard time," said Laz. "I read the book kind of fast. Enrique opened a new show last week, so our home life was pandemonium. What's your thesis?"

"It's a spin-off of something Rodrigo, Giannina, and Teresa and I were talking about: remembering and forgetting. This may actually be something you two can use on your panel."

Just then the waiter arrived with our plates. "Oh, that's what bangers are," Rodrigo said, picking one up on his fork and examining it with interest.

"Not my cup of tea," I'm afraid, said Laz. "I think I'm going to be eating a lot of Indian food while I'm here. But you were starting to tell us your thoughts on Fish."

"I'd love your feedback," I said. "I'm going to argue that legal arguments from principle are, as Fish says, indeterminate and self-deceiving. They have an unearned good reputation. We feel good and virtuous when we profess to be arguing for a particular policy, such as bombing Afghanistan or adopting a mandatory grading curve in law school, on the basis of principle. We think we have risen above parochial self-interest. Then, I'll show how the problem he identifies is part of a more general malaise."

"Sounds interesting," Rodrigo said.

"I'm anxious to hear more," Laz said. He took one last spoonful of his oatmeal, buttered a slice of toast, and said, "Ready when you are."

THE TROUBLE WITH PRINCIPLE

"Fish, whose previous work addressed such issues as meaning, communication, and interpretation, takes on another of law's basic premises, namely, that legal reasoning can ever attain a degree of certainty greater than that with which someone began.[2] The structure of legal argument is irreducibly rhetorical. Appeals to principle only serve as disguises for the speaker's personal commitments."

"I remember one of his examples," Laz said. "Suppose someone begins an argument by saying, 'Let's be fair.' That sounds fine, but the listener has no idea what the speaker means by fairness until he gets further along in his analysis. The same is true for appeals to consistency, free speech, equality, or any other principle: We don't get to understand what they mean until the speaker puts his cards on the table and tells us the cash value of his favorite platitude. Often it turns out not to be what *we* mean by equality, fairness, and the like, at all."[3]

"In other words, it's Fish continuing his anti- foundationalist project," Rodrigo said. "One he began with books like *Doing What Comes Naturally,*[4] *Is There a Text in This Class?,*[5] and *There's No Such Thing as Free Speech.*"[6]

"Do you remember his passages on hate speech, affirmative action, academic freedom, and religion?"[7] I asked. "He shows how speakers, especially ones who profess to be driven by principle, commit mistake after mistake, assuming the conclusion, overlooking the lessons of history, adopting transparently result-oriented tactics, and so on."

"Instead of elevating discourse, principles seem to lower it. We would do better by arguing for our preferences directly," Rodrigo observed.

"Not only that, principles are easily co-opted," I continued. "Suppose that civil rights activists demand that the state of South Carolina stop flying the Confederate flag over the statehouse, because it insults African Americans by gratuitously recalling the institution of slavery. As soon as they do that, what happens? South Carolina citizens declare that the flag has nothing to do with slavery but merely symbolizes regional pride and tradition. The very same principle—respect for history and the feelings of a small group—is marshaled on both sides of the controversy. Fish shows how paying attention to the way language works in controversies like these allows us to avoid getting caught up in traps of our own making."[8]

"He also shows," Rodrigo chimed in, "how we can avoid having principles we hold up on one occasion used against us on another."

"Indeed," I said. "Principles rarely guide us in the abstract—only in their use. Always stated at such a high level of generality that a speaker can use them to arrive at whatever conclusion he wants, their very point is to make that conclusion appear inevitable and the route used to get there high-minded.[9] If we had the courage of our convictions, we would do away with much of the overlay of principle that clutters our conversation and amounts to little more than noise."[10]

"But if moral commitments are all we know, and principles only help partisan agents attach an honorific vocabulary to their agendas. . . ."[11]

"Which may be good or bad," Laz interjected.

"How, then, are we to choose?" Rodrigo continued. "I don't remember how Fish solves this quandary."

"I don't know if he even tries," I said. "Perhaps we need to realize we are thrown back on our own resources, must keep our basic values and commitments in mind, and refuse to be swept up by an adversary's earnest platitudes. The idea, according to Fish, is to advance one's cause or provide a judge a reason for ruling in one's favor. Some of the worst cruelty in the world has been waged in the name of principle—eugenics, Indian removal, Manifest Destiny, converting souls to Catholicism. You can't avoid occasionally resorting to arguments from principle.[12] But be clear to yourself what you are doing—trying to win in a good cause."

"I remember one of his examples," Laz said. "When Justice Brown in *Plessy v. Ferguson* approved a railroad's separate but equal law that consigned blacks to one railroad car and whites to another, on the ground that it treated the races *the same*, he detached a rule—equal treatment—from its historical setting, the one source that could give it any meaning. The nondiscrimination principle became an empty vessel into which he could pour anything he wanted. And he wanted to uphold separation of the races, although any ordinary citizen could have told him that the social meaning of the railroad's policy was intensely degrading to black riders."[13]

"So, even principles that you and I approve of, like the equality principle, mean nothing. They can just as easily be used against as for us," Rodrigo summarized.

"Not only that. Neutral principles disable you from perceiving differences that really matter, such as between pornography and Leonardo da Vinci, or Martin Luther King and a neo-Nazi advocating racial cleansing,"[14] I said. "After *Brown v. Board of Education* was decided, a famous scholar worried that the case was unprincipled because it seemingly traded the right of blacks to associate with whites for the right of whites *not* to associate with blacks.[15] But that approach empties the issue of any historical content and equalizes two options that are far from morally equivalent. One that helps a disadvantaged group is far different from one that allows white males to sue them. Neutral principles cannot tell us this, but morality, history, and our own intuitions do,"[16] I said.

"Do you remember the part where Fish takes nine arguments against affirmative action. . . ."

"Each impeccably principled," Laz interjected.

"Indeed," said Rodrigo. "He then shows that each one collapses on examination, exposing the narrowness and meanness of their proponents."[17]

"A remarkable *tour de force*," I said. "But Fish is an equal- opportunity trasher. He takes on some of the pompous certitudes of the left as well, including cultural relativism, religious toleration, and free speech. Speech is always coercive, he points out. You go to the trouble of saying something because some other person has said something else, wants to make a point you disagree with. One speaks not to encourage other people to speak, but to change something in the world, to bind others to your agenda.[18] All speech is action. The way to resolve most speech controversies is to consider your basic commitments and apply common sense."

"Now I'd like an example," Laz said.

"Okay," I said. "What's the difference between inviting Marxists and bigots to speak on campus? Easy—Marxists are educationally useful, bigots are not.[19] What about a law prohibiting demonstrators from hassling women at abortion clinics versus a hunters' rights bill that penalizes animal rights activists who close in on hunters and hold up picket signs? Easy—history shows no great need to protect hunters, but over a thousand acts of violence at abortion clinics make a protective bill for women clients imperative."[20]

"Or," Rodrigo chimed in, "what's the difference between early civil rights laws and recent race-conscious efforts to ease college admissions for blacks and Hispanics? Nothing. The early bills were not aimed at producing a color-blind society but at improving conditions for blacks and Latinos denied opportunities for upward mobility."[21]

We finished our breakfasts in silence. "So that's the general outline of my talk. The first part, anyway."

"But you said there was a second portion—about Fish seeing only part of the story," Rodrigo prompted.

"You never let me get away with anything," I said in mock complaint.

"If you'd rather save it for your talk, we'll understand," Laz said. "But I'd love to hear."

"Especially if you connect it with remembering and forgetting," Rodrigo said.

I looked at my watch. "Let's start," I said, "and see how far we get."

THE BODY OF LAW AS PROPRIOCEPTIVELY DERANGED

"Let me begin with a medical analogy," I said.

"To illuminate a sickness in the law, I bet," Laz interjected.

"Precisely. Have you two read Oliver Sacks?"

"The neurologist who writes about patients with strange disorders, split brains, and so on?" Laz asked.

"Right. And do you remember the chapter in his book, *The Man Who Mistook His Wife for a Hat*,[22] where he describes a patient named Christina, the disembodied lady?" I began.

"I do," Laz replied. "She's the one who lost her proprioceptive faculty, if that's the right name for it."[23]

"It is," I said. "Christina, who had been a robust young computer programmer who liked outdoor sports, was admitted to the hospital for a routine gall bladder operation. But something went wrong. On the day of her operation, perhaps as a reaction to medication, Christina had a disturbing dream. In it, she was swaying uncontrollably, could not feel the ground under her feet, and kept dropping things because she could hardly feel anything in her hands. A doctor described her as suffering preoperative anxiety—something they see all the time—but that very day, Christina's dream, unfortunately, came true. She found herself unsteady on her feet and unable to control objects in her hands, because they wandered all over unless she kept her eyes on them."[24]

"A Kafkaesque predicament," Rodrigo said.

"She never regained her position sense," I continued. "On testing, it turned out her parietal lobes were working, but had nothing to work with. Her muscles, tendons, and neuroskeletal system had simply stopped communicating with the rest of her. No longer able to feel anything, she had become, as she put it, a wraith, a pithed, disembodied ghost of her former self."[25]

"Sacks took to showing her home movies of herself with her children, taken just before the advent of her condition. They just caused her more pain,"[26] Laz said.

"And you believe her condition is a metaphor of some sort?" Rodrigo asked.

"Right. My thesis is that law—not just critique—but law in general, has become proprioceptively deranged."

"Lost touch with its body," said Rodrigo.

"Like Christina," Laz added. "Become a stumbling, half-blind patient who no longer knows where her limbs are without looking."[27]

"Bodiless, a wraith," I went on. "The trouble that Fish identifies with principle is, in a sense, a form of proprioceptive damage, a loss of positional sense. One who habitually argues from principle suffers a fate even worse than that of Christina, who merely needed to open her eyes to see where her hands were. One who places his faith in principle sees an infinitude of hands, with no way of knowing which one is his. Like a pithed patient, he is fated to inhabit a body of law filled with myriad, often contradictory maxims, tenets, doctrines, and principles, all with a seemingly equal claim to his allegiance and pointing in different directions."[28]

"Does Fish offer any way out?" Laz asked. "I skimmed the last part of his book in order to pass it on to Rodrigo."

"Only a brief suggestion that we give up principle and rely instead on the structure of the Constitution."[29]

"I wondered about that passage," Rodrigo said. "He means our system of separation of powers, which supposedly neutralizes governmental might and provides some semblance of balance in lawmaking."[30]

"I'm afraid that's about the best Fish was able to offer, at least on this occasion," I said.

"Me too."

"Then he's got his work cut out for him," Rodrigo said. "Because separation of powers only contributes to the very type of disconnection that your metaphor highlights."

"Contributes to it?" I asked.

"Right," Rodrigo said. "Government has even fewer scruples than individual actors do. Indeed, the hope that it will restrain itself for moral reasons is probably the most classic category mistake of all. Even more than individual actors, governments have readily accessible a panoply of principles—sovereignty, national interest, free trade, manifest destiny, even human rights—to rationalize what they really want to do."

Rodrigo continued, "Fish believes that, even if government is inclined to act badly, our system of checks and balances will guard against overreaching. But consider how readily we find ways around that system. Congress is supposed to be the only branch of government able to declare war. Yet, as commander-in-chief of the armed forces, the president is able to deploy troops practically at will, circumventing Congress's authority. Indeed, most recent wars have been undeclared."

"Hmm," I said. "That reminds me of some of his executive orders in the recent war on terror.[31] That's something I can use."

"Or, consider the Plenary Power doctrine, Professor, under which the judiciary declines to review matters having to do with immigration, even ones presenting clear-cut equal protection issues, or the myriad of related doctrines, including abstention, mootness, and political questions that enable judges to avoid deciding issues that might require politically sensitive interference with another branch of government," Rodrigo said.

"Not to mention the way well-funded interest groups and corporations ensure that all three branches of government favor policies they want, nullifying any hope that one will act as a check against the others. Sometimes when citizen groups want immediate results, they simply short-circuit the political process by financing referenda and initiative campaigns," Laz added. "Neatly cutting all three branches out of the equation."

"Separation of powers offers little protection against governmental overreaching, then," I agreed. "It's even less of a brake than principle."

"Not only that," Laz added. "Someone who is looking for derangement needs to look at the private side of law, as well—the body of nonconstitutional law that we use to regulate social and business transactions."

"You mean areas like family and contract law," Rodrigo said. "Property and real estate law."

"And tax and trusts and estates," I added. "And certainly torts—the body of law that governs redress for injuries and accidents. It has little constitutional dimension, but instead developed as a congeries of common-law rules governing duties of care, defenses such as contributory negligence, and the law of damages."

"That's my bailiwick," said Laz. "As you know, I'm more interested in law and economics than the sort of broad-brush areas the two of you deal with, such as antidiscrimination and social regulation."

"And I gather you are saying, Laz, that our private law of enterprises and accidents is just as incoherent as the public law that Fish took as his target?"

"I can spell it out a little more, if you like," Laz offered. When we both nodded vigorously, he said: "Let's pay our bill first, so that we don't hang up our hosts when they arrive."

DISCONNECT: HOW PUBLIC AND PRIVATE LAW INCREASINGLY FUNCTION AT CROSS-PURPOSES

"Good idea," I said, fishing out my credit card. The waiter materialized as though by magic, took it, and departed.

"I'm sure the two of you have noticed how our system of public and private law suffers from a serious disjunction," Laz began.

"You mean between a system of private law governed by free- market principles and a public law full of lofty democratic precepts and aspirations?" Rodrigo replied. "I've often wondered about that. No one seems to write about it."[32]

"Although the four of us mentioned it briefly once, at Teresa's apartment. The idea is that the large concepts underlying public law—administrative regularity, the equality of all citizens as moral agents, due process, dialog as a way of reaching consensus—stand in tension. . . ."

"Largely unarticulated," Rodrigo exclaimed. "That's where the Professor's proprioceptive derangement enters in."

"You read my mind. These lofty public-law ideas stand in tension with the rules governing private law—free accumulation of wealth, protection of settled interests, liberty of contract, and the right to leave it all to your children, even if they are no good. Our system is a hydra, a creature with two heads."

"Which promises radical democracy in the public sphere and individualistic, dog-eat-dog capitalism in the private one," I added, getting excited over the picture Laz was painting for us. "This I definitely can use in my talk."

"In a sense, the system has always been on a collision course with itself," Laz continued. "Until recently, the public side has managed to counter some of the excesses of aggressive capitalism by ensuring that at least a few of the working class rose and assumed places in government, academia, and public life. The private and public spheres, in short, were at cross-purposes but not radically so."[33]

"But you think that this is ending?" I asked, anxious to hear where Rodrigo's conservative colleague was going.

"I do," Laz said. "Globalism and the advent of an economy based on information . . . ."

"Courtesy of that prescient First Amendment case we mentioned earlier," Rodrigo interjected.

"Right," Laz said. "Current trends are concentrating wealth so rapidly that the uneasy truce that allowed the two-headed system to work is starting to break down.[34] Already the United States is the most economically stratified country in the developed world."[35]

"We just passed Great Britain, a country with a history of official stratification, including kings, a royal family, and nobility. We had prided ourselves on being different," I observed.

"A land of opportunity," Rodrigo seconded.

"Public education, historically, has been our means of guaranteeing that poor but bright children, like my own brothers and sisters, could rise, assume offices in the public sector, and wield influence beyond their clan, neighborhood, or factory. It allowed us to maintain the fiction that democracy and capitalism were compatible,"[36] Laz continued.

"But now that avenue is narrowing," Rodrigo interjected. "Underfunded schools send very few ghetto kids to Harvard's Kennedy School of Government. No president in U.S. history has been black or, in recent times, from a truly poor family. Your right-wing buddies, Laz, resist funding inner-city schools, attack teachers' unions, and would rather offer vouchers for a few to escape failing schools than bring them all up to a uniform standard of excellence."

"We'll have to talk about that sometime," Laz retorted firmly. "You can't solve a problem by throwing money at it. But I am concerned about bad schools."

When Rodrigo nodded, I continued: "You mentioned presidents. It occurs to me that much the same is going on in the realm of election law.

The Supreme Court tolerates few restrictions on campaign contributions, so that wealthy candidates or ones whose platforms are congenial to corporations start out at an enormous advantage. It resists redistricting to increase the chances of minority candidates. And the recent scandal in Florida shows that poor districts have the worst voting machines, lowest turnouts, and highest rates of graft, discrimination by voting officials, and police hassling of people on their way to the ballot box."[37]

"Our public and private systems of law do contain devices to control distortions of various types," Laz conceded. "But generally only within each system. It's like a split-brain patient, each of whose halves functions relatively well but without any coordination between them. Public law, for example, contains strict scrutiny, which enables courts to review under a stringent standard any governmental action that infringes on the rights of minorities or abridges a right guaranteed under the Constitution.[38] Legislators may not accept bribes,[39] while on the other side of the line, our private law contains a different set of guarantees."

"I can think of some," Rodrigo said. "Antitrust law, unfair competition statutes, laws against misleading advertising."[40]

"As well as rules regulating corporate directors and insider trading,"[41] I chimed in. "Even fair weights and measures law, which guarantees that merchants sell you a pound of beef weighing sixteen ounces."

"Yuck," said the vegetarian Laz. "I prefer one that punishes merchants who sell bright-red apples that turn out to be mushy. But we've captured my general idea, which is that our system proceeds like a hydra-headed monster, with one head consisting of a highly idealized set of public law, and another of a less idealized private law governing the way we make profits and earn livings, but little to mediate between the two.[42] Our system of dual public-private law is as disconnected as any of Oliver Sacks's patients. And Fish's solution, that we look to the structure of the Constitution for help simply leads into that blind alley the Professor mentioned. The structure of the Constitution is the problem, not the solution."[43]

The waiter returned with our bill. I grabbed it before Laz and Rodrigo could, and, despite their protestations, signed and handed it back. "You two have given me much grist for my mill. I think I'm going to get not just an after-dinner speech but a law review article out of this."

"Maybe even a chapter in a book," grinned Laz.

"Maybe so," I said. "Certainly our predicament is deeper than the one Fish so brilliantly . . ."

"Not to mention implacably," one of my young interlocutors interjected.

"Depicts," I continued. Principle will rarely stop a determined adversary versed in rhetorical tricks. It can even leave you confused about what you really believe, looking around like Christina. . . ."

"Or certain former liberals we could name," Rodrigo added.

"Indeed," I said. "Constitutional separation of powers never stopped a determined president, a power-mad Congress, or a Supreme Court out to impose its will. Our public and private law function like two-headed beasts or patients with split brains. Three-quarters of our population are effectively insulated from any impact on public policy at all. We are left, then, with our own intuitions. . . ."

"Fish is right about that," Laz agreed. "Although mine, as a conservative law-and-economist might be different from his . . ."

"With our own intuitions, to the extent we don't forget them," I continued. "Those and the resources we bring to any encounter: honesty, good rhetoric, and the persuasiveness of an argument that resonates with history, context, and the common store of narratives we all believe in."

"To believe that we command any more is a dangerous illusion. That's what Fish is saying," Rodrigo added.

"With a little help from his friends," I said, smiling. "And, speaking of friends, I think that other group is here."

Four well-dressed, pinstripe-wearing black men, one of them holding up a placard with my name on it (preceded, mistakenly, by the title "Doctor") had just entered the restaurant and were looking around. We picked up our carry-on baggage, waved at our welcoming committee, and strode off in their direction, vowing to get together, as the conference wound down, for a cup of coffee and a further conversation.

9

On Causation and Displaced Rage

Forgetting What Provoked
Your Indignation in the First Place

THE CONFERENCE WENT WELL. My dinner speech, fortified by a few choice ideas from that airport talk, received a standing ovation. I ran into several old friends from the States, a few classmates from my own law school days, and even Laz late one afternoon in a near-deserted corridor in the giant conference hotel. We talked for a few minutes about whether a follower of Fish could condemn without absolutes,[1] and I called in his promise to tell me his views, as a conservative, on legal formalism, which he did. Laz and Rodrigo's panel session went well, so far as I could tell, although it was conducted almost entirely in high-Crit talk and was so far over my head that I felt like a first-year student.

We never made good on our promise to get together during the conference. Once or twice I saw Laz and Rodrigo walking around together talking animatedly, or having a snack with others at the hotel cafeteria. But I decided not to interrupt, and once or twice when I spied them I was with someone else, such as a former student anxious to tell me about his latest big case.

The conference ended without our having that promised meeting. Thus it was with excitement that I saw a neatly folded piece of paper with my name printed on it on the message board on my way to my room after the closing panel. Written by Rodrigo, it invited me to give them a call. It explained that they were going to have a quick bite with a colleague to plan next year's conference. After that, if I was free, we could have dessert in the cafeteria about nine. I immediately left a message on their room phones and arranged a quiet dinner with an old friend I had not seen in years.

On arriving at my hotel room, I found a spray of flowers and a note from Teresa, back home in the United States and delivered by a local florist. (I considered reprinting her love note for you here, but modesty prevailed.)

When I arrived at the cafeteria a little before nine, in a very good mood, my two young friends were just saying goodbye to their colleague. They motioned me to sit down.

"You two have had a busy conference," I said. "I thought your panel went extremely well, from what I understood of it. And I had no idea you two were organizing next year's event. That's a big job."

"Sheila, the woman you just saw, is in charge of the program. Laz and I are responsible for local arrangements," Rodrigo said. "How would you like to give a lunchtime talk? I know Sheila would be honored to have you."

"Let someone else do it," I said. "This year's keynote was enough for me, and probably my fans as well. But I'll attend, God willing. Maybe Teresa will come this time."

"Giannina is planning to come," Rodrigo replied.
"We'll have a reunion," I said, "Maybe Laz can join us."

Laz nodded vigorously. Just then, we all started at the strains of Vivaldi emanating from somewhere under the cafeteria table.

"Excuse me. That's my cell phone," said Laz. "Actually, Enrique's." He fished it out of a green bookbag from underneath the table and put the receiver to his ear. "That's wonderful," he said. Then, after a pause, "I can't wait to hear more. I'm in a cafeteria with Rodrigo and Gus. Call you when I get back to my room."

"The reviews of his new play are in. Looks like he's got a hit. Where were we?"

"Next year's conference. Give him our congratulations," I said. Rodrigo echoed my sentiments, then continued as follows:

"We're glad we were able to get together, Professor. Earlier, you promised to tell us about a second feature by which the left forgets what it stands for. Laz and I were trying to recall what it was. I thought it had something to do with indignation."

"And you, Laz?" I prompted.

"I thought it had to do with racial exceptionalism."

"As it so happens, I mentioned both. It's late, though, and at my age, I need my sleep. What if we take on the shorter of the two—indignation—and leave racial exceptionalism for another time?"

Both my young companions nodded eagerly. After placing our dessert orders, a double serving of ice cream for my rail-thin friend Rodrigo, apple pie for the conservative Laz, and a mild flan for me, I took a drink from my water glass and began:

THE MYTH OF LAMPETIA

"Are the two of you familiar with the myth of Lampetia?"

When they looked dubious, I explained: "In a classic tale, Apollo's daughter is left to guard her father's sacred cattle on the island of Thrinacia, where Odysseus and his sailors land one day. Although Odysseus warns his men to leave the cattle alone, some of them carry away and kill some of the magic beasts. But their hides walk about, the roasting flesh bellows, and the island reverberates with loud lowing. On learning of the sacrilege, Lampetia informs her father, who waits until the men sail away. He then summons up a terrible storm, which kills not only the men who actually did the poaching, but the entire crew. Odysseus escapes by holding onto the broken mast."[2]

"It's coming back. We studied it in one of my classics courses at Bologna," Rodrigo said. "What made you think of it right now?"

"An article I read by someone I greatly respect. Written by one of the founding figures of the Critical Race movement, it discusses causation in American tort theory.[3] The author proposes that we broaden the notion of fault, if not as drastically as Lampetia and her dad did, at least in ways that gave me pause."

"Lampetia and her father held everyone on the scene responsible for the lost cattle, even though only some of the men took part in the heist," Laz recalled. "Hah! I bet I know the article you are talking about. It was in the *Columbia Law Review*. Right?" When I nodded, he continued: "The author suggests two versions of broadened causation rules. In the first, we would expand responsibility to the agent who is next-nearest in the chain of causation when the most proximately responsible one is judgment proof or otherwise beyond the law's reach.[4] For example, if an impoverished drug addict allows a child to obtain a gun and the child takes it to school and shoots a classmate, we would hold the addict liable."

"And if he can't pay, then we'd go after the gun manufacturer," Rodrigo added. "I remember that part."

"The author says we should take the harm and figure out who is in the best position to prevent it,"[5] Laz went on. "Every act has multiple causes. If placing the blame at the hands of the most likely candidate doesn't work, just try another."[6]

"And do the two of you remember her second proposal?" I asked.

"I seem to remember something even more utopian," Laz said, furrowing his brow.

"It was," Rodrigo said. "She urged that we hold our collective selves responsible for any harm that befalls another human being. If you or I were to step over an unconscious derelict on the way to work, and the man later died, we would hold ourselves responsible. And the same goes for neglected children and victims of poverty, illness, plant closings, and other misfortunes stemming from broad social conditions."[7]

"Particularly ones from which we derive a benefit," I added. "The gulf between the rich and the poor in this country loads the gun as clearly as any human hand does,[8] she writes. So, every member of a society that tolerates great disparities in wealth is responsible for the bitterness, crime, and early deaths that proceed. 'Cause is a web, a circle, the well from which we all drink,'[9] she holds. Anyone who poisons that well or takes all the water for himself should be held accountable."

"And why does this article strike you as a case of misplaced indignation?" Rodrigo asked. "It seems to me more like an object lesson in getting out ahead of the social consensus. Society is simply not ready for the sweeping reforms she proposes, appealing as they may sound to liberal ears like ours."

"Speak for yourself," said Laz. "I don't find them appealing at all."

"Let me begin by means of a story," I continued. "One she herself tells. An Indian veteran fell into a stuporous depression on returning from Vietnam. Worried that he would end his days in a VA hospital, his family called on a practitioner of traditional tribal medicine. The folk doctor asks his patient if he has killed someone; in Indian culture this requires a form of atonement. The veteran replies that he does not know—that was the kind of war Vietnam was. The medicine man is stymied, his curative power blocked by such a strange thing."[10]

"And the moral of the story is . . . ?" Rodrigo prompted.

"It's that spiritual angst afflicts many of us, not only foot soldiers like the Indian who shot blindly into the jungle. Even dot-com millionaires experience unaddressed pain if they adopt policies, such as work-place rules, that injure their employees or fail to take an active role in addressing poverty at large."[11]

"So, Professor," Laz said, leaning forward. "Broader causation rules would promote mental and spiritual health. They also would provide recompense for victims who might otherwise go without. Does she make the case on those grounds alone? For if so, I see lots wrong with her proposal on straight economic- efficiency grounds."

"She has one or two more up her sleeve," I replied. "Broader rules would strengthen social ties and cohesion.[12] They would help deter an-tisocial, uncaring conduct. They would reinforce John Donne's maxim."

"That no man is an island. The bell tolls for all of us,"[13] Rodrigo added. "In some ways, it's an attractive notion. If you're going to find fault with it, I may come to her defense. I'd like to hear your critique first. Laz's too."

MISPLACED ANGER

"I don't think there's anything wrong with her proposal per se," I said. "Although I'm sure Laz would take it to task for saddling entrepreneurs with a crushing load of liability, punishing productive conduct, and for getting ahead of the curve, as you put it."

"Then your criticism must be that it amounts to a kind of forgetting. But it can't be that, for she is assuming the role of moral prophet, call-ing us to a form of duty few of us consider," said Rodrigo.

"It does represent a kind of forgetting," I said. "Let me explain."

At this point, the waiter appeared to ask if we would like anything more to eat. He asked the question in a perfunctory way. We all pre-dictably said no, and he left.

"Not very solicitous," Rodrigo said.

"Or entrepreneurial," the law-and-economics devotee, Laz, added. "Not a good way to get a big tip."

"If we give him a small one, it'll just reinforce his belief that men of color are stingy tippers," I said. "A recurring predicament."

"White folks act on a stereotype, we respond in kind, and the stereotype etches in a little deeper. Maybe your author is right, after all," Rodrigo posited. "Cause is multifactorial and full of ripple effects."

"I have no problem with her general project," I said a little defensively. "It's certainly good to be alert to the many factors that can enter into producing a certain untoward result. But I do think she misconceives her target. Unless the waiter turns out the lights and chases us away, I'd like to explain."

Rodrigo said, "In that case, I'm going to order a second helping of ice cream. I'm still hungry from traipsing around this giant hotel, not to mention talking with you and Laz half the night. Waiter?"

Not too enthusiastically, the waiter took Rodrigo's order. "We're closing in fifteen minutes," he said coldly. As he walked away, Laz cracked, "The sign said ten o'clock. Maybe he's in a hurry to go to the closing session. Well, I for one would like to hear what a pair of liberals like you see wrong in a plan to make everybody feel guilty for poverty. Here comes Rodrigo's ice cream." Looking at his watch, Laz said, "I figure you've got until it melts."

"As you know," I began, "the law already has been moving in the direction of recognizing group harms. In that sense, it has begun imposing collective responsibility through measures like class actions[14] and liberalized joinder rules.[15] On the substantive side, modern decisions have been affording remedies for loss of a chance[16] and for harms to a determinate, known plaintiff who has suffered an injury at the hands of multiple defendants, such as two hunters both of whom shot negligently in his direction, even though only one bullet hit."[17]

"Recent cases have extended that principle to marketers of defective pharmaceuticals," Rodrigo added, "even if they proceeded according to an industry-wide formula. In *Sindell v. Abbott Laboratories*,[18] a young woman sued nine drug companies for a form of cancer characteristic of DES after her mother took the drugs over twenty years ago when pregnant with her. Since her mother had no way of proving which company's medication she had taken, under ordinary tort law her daughter's claim would fail for lack of proof of causation."

"I remember that case," Laz said. "The court allowed the woman to shift the onus onto each of the nine companies to prove it did *not* manufacture the pills the mother had taken. When none could, it made them all responsible for the daughter's damages in proportion to their share of the DES market."[19]

"It's sometimes called market-share liability," I added. "The case your conservative allies in the law-and-economics movement love to hate, Laz."

"I don't hate it," Laz said mildly. "It distributes blame according to risk and punishes only actors who were negligent in the first place. That comports just fine with my conservative principles."

"You may be an exception," I said. "The real test will come when the reverse-*Sindell* situation[20] starts to arrive with increasing frequency. Are you familiar with that term?"

When Laz looked uncertain, I explained: "It's one a critical race theorist—not the one we've been talking about—coined. It refers to situations in which a single defendant has exposed a number of individuals to a risk of some sort. All of them are now sick, only some of them so as a result of the exposure."[21]

"In other words, a case of mixed causation," Laz said.

"Yes. In an actual case, the government, which was conducting nuclear testing aboveground, negligently exposed the residents of a small region of Utah to high levels of fallout, then lied to them about the dangers. Many years later, they started to show an increased incidence of a type of cancer associated with radiation exposure."[22]

"But it wasn't a signature disease—like asbestosis or DES- induced cancer—associated with only one cause," Rodrigo added. "I think I know the case you are talking about. It's a Ninth Circuit decision litigated by a famous environmental lawyer."

"That's the one," I replied. "*United States v. Allen*. The difficulty was that cancers of the sort that increased in the region also occur naturally, so each plaintiff could not be sure his or her case was caused by the government's testing program. It might have occurred as a result of bad luck, bad genes, or just being in the way of too much ultraviolet radiation during a Girl Scout hike ten years ago."[23]

"How did the court handle the situation?" Rodrigo asked.

"By apportioning responsibility, so that the government was held responsible for all the damage attributable to its negligence. All the excess cases, in other words—the ones representing an increase above the usual background level. Then it divided those damages among the plaintiffs, so that each recovered a portion of his or her expenses."[24]

"Including those who would have gotten the disease anyway," Laz added. "That *is* likely to drive my law-and-economics friends nuts." Then, after a moment, he added, "But of course, there was no way of knowing. I see the rub. Maybe the court did do a form of rough justice after all."

"As did the court in a second case. In *In re Agent Orange*,[25] a single supplier of a chemical defoliant used in Vietnam to kill trees failed to warn users of its dangers. After the war, hundreds of soldiers began experiencing neurological symptoms of the very kind that the chemical causes in humans. The problem is that those same symptoms also occur naturally."

"And did this one come out the same way?"

"It did. A famous federal judge approved a class-action settlement. In his memo justifying that settlement, he wrote that developments have been moving in the direction of recognizing recoveries for indeterminate plaintiffs. In other words, extending *Sindell* to the situation of a victim who does not even know for sure that he is one."[26]

"It does have a certain sort of weird logic. If you're a liberal, I suppose," said Laz. "Yet you two draw the line at your friend's suggestions. Why?"

"They're too broad," I said. "Conservatives—no offense to you, Laz, you're as fair-minded as they come—could seek to hold welfare mothers responsible for the actions of their children.[27] Manufacturers of defective tires or automobiles could seek to hold their unions responsible for creating a climate in which the workers cared more about their benefits than product safety.[28] Right-wing ideologues could place the blame for failing schools on progressive educators who teach multicultural knowledge."[29]

"So that once you thrown causation wide open, you can't be sure that fault will end up resting on the actors that the reformers have in mind. An aspect of the indeterminacy thesis you lefties love," Laz concluded.

"In a way, it is," I admitted. "Our author knows very well that not every case has one right answer. Judges apply a host of factors, not just precedent, on their way to a decision—something that should not be regretted at all. In similar fashion, expansion of tort and criminal liability rules will prove to be just as difficult to control. Just because we open the doors to broader liability, it does not follow that anyone's favorite villains will end up saddled with it."

"Do you recall," Rodrigo said, "how in the wake of Columbine, commentators rushed to put forward a host of theories for why it happened? Society was responsible.[30] Lax school discipline was at fault.[31] The police were, for not following up leads.[32] The gun industry was the prime actor.[33] Bullying in the hallways was.[34] Violent teenage music and video games set the stage.[35] In some sense, all these factors played a part—if society had no guns, exercised complete control over the entertainment industry, and schools maintained prison-style security, the disaster perhaps would not have happened."

"But then, we would have had a different society," Laz said.

"With the simplistic and ideology-driven causation stories that Rodrigo just mentioned, it's easy to see what's wrong," I said. "But they do help me put my finger on what troubles me about our writer's proposal. Consider how, under the new rules, judges . . ."

"Who are socialized in widely shared, majoritarian norms," Rodrigo interjected.

"Precisely. Judges are apt to fasten blame on the same actors as before. They may even use their broader discretion to fasten liability on actors they do not like—rebels, malcontents, long-haired individuals, or persons leading lifestyles they disapprove of," I said.

"At least with individualistic approaches," Laz pointed out, "the range of options is finite—either actor A, B, or C did it. If all three did it, we can apportion responsibility. But with collectivities, the range of possibilities increases enormously: Society at large? This leader? This village council? This manufacturing association? Conservatives for shredding the safety net of welfare programs?[36] The black community for not taking responsibility for its own children?[37] Liberals for coddling black crime?"[38]

The waiter came to take away Rodrigo's dish and looked meaningfully at his watch. After he left, Laz said, "I think he's not bucking for a big tip. Reminds me of one of our earlier conversations on whether free-market incentives are likely to drive out racism.[39] Maybe the answer is no, after all."

"So let me conclude," I said, picking up the conference papers on the table next to me. "Our author's intention is admirable. She wants society to feel more responsible for the poverty, homelessness, and desperation of its poorest members. But her remedy, broadened tort liability rules, advances that goal only crudely and indirectly. It suffers from indeterminacy even more than most legal rules do. It invites judges to select defendants they dislike. And if it carries over to the criminal realm, it will simply increase the number of black and brown men in prison."

"She should proceed more straightforwardly," Laz added. "If she wants gun manufacturers to stop making Saturday-night specials, she should use the substantive law of crime to effect that aim. Make it a crime to make cheap guns whose only possible use is to kill people at close range . . ."

"Rather than let them make the guns and then stretch causation rules to find them liable when somebody gets killed," Rodrigo went on. "Rather than hold a harried businessman who hurries past a derelict in the park responsible when the man dies, why not tax all of society to provide shelters for the homeless?"

"So, your point, Professor, is not so much that our progressive friend has forgotten her ideals, values, and intuitions. She simply has misplaced her anger, allowed it to get channeled off into a highly formalistic avenue—causation rules. She is doing indirectly what she should be doing directly."

"You said it better than I could have myself," I said. "Collectivizing responsibility through social insurance and programs eliminates the need for many torts suits and is far superior to broadened tort rules that judges will bend to their own purposes."

"It will strengthen social bonds," Rodrigo added, "will do everything your author called for, but without the need for lawyers. It will bring the United States into conformity with the many Western industrialized nations that take seriously their obligations to their poor, sick, unemployed, and elderly. It will spread the burden of social support equitably. It will reduce the number of desperate, destitute people and miseducated children, and promote social stability and peace."

"The social stability part I agree with. The rest I'm not so sure about. You liberals do talk a good line, though," Laz said with a look of grudging respect.

"If I follow you, Rodrigo," I said, standing up from my chair and stretching. "Our Indian veteran who shot blindly into the jungle, under the broadened rules our author urges,[40] could be sued by any villager or innocent bystander who was hit by a bullet. Paradoxically, this would absolve the society that waged an unjust and undeclared war. It could blur, not sharpen, group causation and reduce the incentive to consider reparations for groupwide injury, something the author and others like her champion on other occasions.[41] Declaring a war an evil, warranting reparations, a Saturday-night special a crime, or marketing drugs known to be dangerous without labeling them so actionable are much more straightforward ways of advancing social justice than broadening the notion of causation."

"The Indian in her example is guilt-ridden enough already," Rodrigo concluded, leaving a small tip and standing up. "The problem lies with the rest of us who are not. We refuse to accept responsibility for Vietnam, too readily absolve a senator who ordered his troops to fire into a village knowing that the main occupants were women and children.[42] The country owes a debt to the citizens of the war-ravaged nation of Vietnam, just as it will do to the citizens of Afghanistan when we are through there, and does today to our own homeless, uninsured poor, and children in underfunded inner-city schools. But searching for a hapless foot soldier or fledgling teacher whose students can't pass a standardized exam based on middle-class norms merely postpones the time when we address problems of human need and injustice."

"I'm going to have to think about it," Laz said, as the waiter pounced on our now-evacuated table and started clearing things away. "I agree with the forgetfulness part of your thesis, Professor. But the notion that liberals should stop being angry and just tax everyone heavily gives me pause. Maybe a little indignation over social misfortunes is not a bad thing, and taxation is."

"Maybe there's a role for each," Rodrigo said, with a yawn. "Like that waiter, I think I'm ready for bed. "What time is your flight tomorrow, Professor. Do you have time for a bite of breakfast with us before hopping on your plane?"

10

Selling Short

The Rise and Fall of African American Fortunes

WHEN I EASED into the breakfast line in the hotel cafeteria early the next morning, at least half the guests were wearing some type of exercise outfit. It came as no surprise, then, when I spied my two young friends, a little ahead of me in line, wearing running gear and conversing animatedly as they picked out their breakfast food. I selected mine—my usual oatmeal with raisins and low-fat milk—and followed them to an empty table.

"We've decided to give you a break," Rodrigo said, picking up his plates, heaped high with scrambled eggs, coffee, and toast, and setting the tray on a nearby empty table.

"Yes," said Laz. "While we were out running, we thought of a new example of forgetting for your collection. Actually, Rodrigo thought of it, but I love making liberals uncomfortable, so I chimed in too. Want to hear it?"

"Sure," I said, depositing my own breakfast on the tabletop and easing myself into a cafeteria chair. "What time is your flight? Mine's at eleven."

"Eleven-thirty," Rodrigo said. "But I don't mind going early. Want to share a cab?"

I nodded, and Rodrigo began. "The idea came to us after reflecting on something you had said the other day about liberals being ready to abandon their ideology when a new fad—or funding source—comes along. One year they're all working on world hunger. Then it's racism. Then the Peace Corps."[1]

"Conservatives, if I may say so myself, are much more focused," Laz said. "We devise a simple program and stick to it. We develop our own funding sources if they're not in place already. We work on one thing until it's accomplished, then move on to something new."

"And so, Rodrigo, you think that progressives are too scattered and swayed by monetary considerations? I thought conservatives were the ones motivated by economics."

"I know it sounds paradoxical, Professor. Have you heard of Jimmy Wilson?"

I racked my brain, but all I could think of was a jazz musician. But I doubted he was who Rodrigo had in mind, so I shook my head, feeling reassured that Laz was looking blank too.

"He was a black handyman a 1948 Alabama court sentenced to die for the crime of stealing two dollars.[2] Mary Dudziak writes about him in her new book, *Cold War Civil Rights*."[3]

"I know her law review article,[4] and have been meaning to look at that book," I said. "As I understand it, it develops Derrick Bell's insight about *Brown v. Board of Education* and interest-convergence[5] even further."

"Exactly," Rodrigo replied. "Laz lent me his copy, which I finished last week. It's worth reading."

"And it begins with the Jimmy Wilson story?" I prompted.

"No, but she mentions it as an example of her thesis. When the world press trumpeted the story, an embarrassed Secretary of State John Foster Dulles intervened and succeeded in overturning the man's sentence. Dudziak's book argues that the Wilson case was not an isolated event but one of many in which concern for international relations drove domestic policy during this period."[6]

When Rodrigo stopped for a swig of coffee, I added: "As anyone who has followed African American fortunes knows, progress has traced a zigzag path, with periods of great gains followed by ones of retrenchment.[7] During Reconstruction, blacks made huge strides. But the advances of the 1870s were met by violence, terror, lynching, and the Black Codes, which swallowed up black gains.[8] *Plessy v. Ferguson*[9] was a further setback, but fifty years later fortune smiled a second time with *Brown v. Board of Education*[10] and the civil-rights era."

"Which, in turn, came to a screeching halt with the Burger Court, two Republican presidencies, and a climate that today seems tired of minorities and worships color blindness instead," said Laz.[11]

"That's what Laz and I were talking about during our morning run—this rise and fall of racial fortunes. And what accounts for it," Rodrigo said.

"And some further ideas on forgetting," Laz chipped in. "Eat your food, and we'll tell you about them."

I looked down at my oatmeal, stirred it, and took a big spoonful. "I'm all ears," I said.

"I'll start," said Laz. "We all know that two schools of thought offer competing explanations for civil rights history. One, an idealist school, holds that race is a social construction,[12] so that racial setbacks and reverses are attributable, basically, to erroneous thoughts. For this group, blacks and other groups of color are racialized by a system of thoughts, words, messages, narrative, and scripts that implant in the minds of the American public indelible stereotypes of their inferiority.[13] The way to overcome racism is to speak out against it and to teach equality and fairness in the schools."[14]

"For this school of thought," Rodrigo picked up, "the key targets are hate speech,[15] media images of black criminals, and a school curriculum that excludes minorities' accomplishments. Social images and ideas drive social fortunes, and the way to change those fortunes is to change the way the American people think about race."[16]

"A competing view," Laz continued, "acknowledges that race and racism do include ideas and are, in that sense, under our control. But they hold that material factors, including competition for jobs, spaces in universities, and the class interest of elite whites, play an even larger role.[17] Writers in this group include Derrick Bell, who highlights how racism reinforces material and psychic advantages for the dominant group.[18] Critical Race Theory was dominated by materialists like Bell and Alan Freeman[19] in its early years, but recently, the discourse theorists have been moving to the fore."[20]

"And this is where the new Dudziak book comes in," Rodrigo said excitedly. "And that in turn spurred the two of us to think of a way to extend her and Bell's thesis."

"To account for the end of the civil-rights era, some fifteen years after *Brown* sparked it off," Laz added.

"You've certainly got your work cut out for you," I said. "But I'm anxious to hear what you have to say, especially if it adds to my list of mechanisms of forgetting."

"We suspect you've got a book in you on this subject," said Laz. "Rodrigo, why don't you go on?"

"As Laz was saying, the Dudziak book seems to herald a return to the powerful insights of Critical Race Theory's founding figures. In it, she expands on a theme she first articulated in an influential 1994 *Stanford Law Review* article.[21] That piece, in turn, built on Bell's interest-convergence article, in which he hypothesized that gains for blacks co-incide with periods of white self-interest, and that racism serves such powerful economic and psychic interests that only equally strong coun-tervailing forces can hold it in abeyance."[22]

"I'm familiar with that hypothesis," I said. "What does Dudziak add?"

"A couple of things," Rodrigo said. "You recall how Bell used the example of *Brown v. Board of Education*, theorizing that this remarkable decision came about through the interplay of Cold War politics. He in-vited his readers to consider how the NAACP Legal Defense Fund had been litigating desegregation cases for decades in the South, usually losing, or winning at most narrow victories.[23]

"Then, in 1954, the skies opened and the Supreme Court, for the first time, held that separate was no longer equal.[24] Repudiating the rule of *Plessy v. Ferguson*—the separate-but-equal case—the Court held that segregated schooling is inherently unequal and stigmatizing. Why just then? Pointing out that the United States had just ended a bloody world war against Germany and Japan, during which many black servicemen and women served gallantly, Bell surmised that racial unrest would have broken out had the country tried to usher them back to the old, prewar regime of servile labor and yes-sir, no-sir."[25]

"At the same time," Laz added, "we were in the early stages of a Cold War against the forces of godless communism, competing for the loyalties of the uncommitted third world, much of which was black, brown, or Asian.[26] Incidents like the murder of Emmitt Till or the death sentence of Jimmy Wilson, splashed across the pages of the world press, weakened our position."[27]

"And that's where Dudziak comes in," Rodrigo said excitedly. "She documents what he hypothesized. After perusing thousands of pages of columns and releases from the world press, and examining hundreds of documents in the files of the Department of State and other federal agencies, she shows that *Brown v. Board of Education* and the softening of racial attitudes that it heralded were very much prompted by Cold War considerations. Memo after memo, release after release, converge on the same conclusion—the United States needed to do something dramatic for blacks to fortify its position on the world stage."[28]

"So Bell was right," I said. "Bull Connor, police dogs, Emmitt Till, and Jimmy Wilson brought about *Brown v. Board of Education* and the 1964 Civil Rights Act."

"The State Department implored the Justice Department to start intervening on the side of the NAACP.[29] Several justices of the Supreme Court who decided *Brown* were expressly guided by international-appearances considerations,"[30] Laz added. "A stronger case for a materialist explanation would be hard to find."

I must have looked skeptical, for Rodrigo said, "Wait. I've got a quote for you right here." Rummaging in the shapeless duffel bag he had stowed under the table, he triumphantly pulled out a red, white, and black book with a picture of civil rights protesters on the cover. Turning to one of dozens of torn strips of paper marking passages, he said, "Here's one of fifty. It's a memorandum that Secretary of State Dean Acheson sent to the chairman of the Fair Employment Practices Commission right around the time of *Brown*:

> The existence of discrimination against minority groups in this country has an adverse effect upon our relations with other countries. We are reminded over and over by some foreign newspapers and spokesmen that our treatment of various minorities leaves much to be desired. . . . Frequently we find it next to impossible to (respond) to our critics in other countries.[31]

"Here's another," he said, opening to another bookmark:

> A year, a month, or even a week in Asia is enough to convince any perceptive American that the colored peoples of Asia and Africa, who total two-thirds of the world's population, seldom think about the United States without considering the limitations under which our 13 million Negroes are living.[32]

"That's from a 1952 speech by Chester Bowles, U.S. ambassador to India. Dudziak has a tremendous amount of stuff. Foreign press releases. Propaganda from *Pravda*. Memos by U.S. officials from the National Archives. Items in special collections, like the Harry S. Truman Library in Independence, Missouri, federal hearing reports, and even government amicus curiae briefs in civil rights cases," Rodrigo concluded.

"She seems to have missed nothing," I said. "But I think you said that you have thought of a way to go beyond her insight, to explain the next step in civil rights evolution."

SELLING YOUR SOUL FOR A FORD FOUNDATION GRANT: HOW THE CIVIL-RIGHTS ERA ENDED

"Dudziak should be commended for documenting an impressive insight," Laz said. "But her main tool—interest- convergence—explains not only how the civil-rights era came into being. It can also explain what happened, a decade later, when that heady era came to an end."

"This I'd like to hear," I said. "I haven't seen this anywhere in the literature. You two are on virgin ground."

"I wouldn't be surprised if it's occurred to somebody," Rodrigo said modestly. "One corollary of the softening of domestic attitudes exemplified by *Brown* and the 1964 Civil Rights Act was the expectation, on the part of the establishment, that African Americans would do their part to combat communism.[33] The implicit bargain was that African Americans, in return for civil rights gains, would demonstrate loyalty to America and hostility toward communism. They were expected to purge their ranks of communists and support foreign wars, such as Korea and Vietnam."[34]

"Dudziak's own data support this implicit bargain," Laz added. "In the opening pages of her book, she points out how the establishment cracked down on early figures like Paul Robeson,[35] Josephine Baker,[36] and W. E. B. Du Bois[37] who flirted with communism during the thirties or criticized the country's racial policies, especially overseas. The black press generally fell right into line."

"And what happened later is even more telling," Rodrigo said animatedly. "Although you have to go outside her book to prove this, my research shows that the traumatic events of the late sixties and early seventies may also have been cases of interest- convergence, but in the reverse direction."

"What do you mean?" I asked.

"Recall how during this time, Black and Chicano Power appeared on the scene.[38] Panthers began reading and quoting from Marx and Engels. Others read Che Guevara and Frantz Fanon.[39] Malcolm X called white people satanic and America the devil."[40]

"Then what happened?"

"With the implicit bargain breaking down, elite groups did two things. They cracked down on the Panthers with lethal force.[41] And to ensure that leaders of color were indebted to the establishment, they instituted the War on Poverty and enlisted many of them, including Denver's Corky Gonzalez, in it, giving them grants, jobs, and other forms of patronage that they could hand out to their friends.[42] The Ford Foundation also poured millions of dollars into the black community at this time."[43]

"That does sound familiar," I said. "And your interpretation is . . . ?"

"Simply that black well-being surged a second time, but incipient black radicalism was lost, not to return for a long time."

"Do you mean in the form of Critical Race Theory?" I asked.

"Precisely," Rodrigo replied. "A much milder version of what was developing back then. The opportunity to develop a far- ranging critique of American social institutions was lost. The most promising generation of civil rights leaders was ostracized, exiled in foreign countries, or bought off."

I remained silent, absorbing the bleak picture Rodrigo had drawn. Then I snapped out of my reverie and said:

"You two may be onto something. I'll definitely add your hypothesis about the loss of black leadership and the end of the civil-rights era to my list of structures for losing touch with what one is about. If you're right, the very premises that enable Bell and Dudziak to show how the United States came to tolerate civil-rights gains for blacks in the early civil-rights era also explain how that impressive period came to an end. An implicit part of the bargain that America's power brokers offered blacks, in return for largely symbolic gains, was that they distance themselves from communism, socialism, radicalism, and agree not to criticize the government too loudly. Early visionaries such as Robeson, DuBois, and Baker were marginalized and their careers destroyed, sometimes with the acquiescence of the black press and community. Later, when sixties-era black leaders took a more militant stance, the government, acting in concert with major philanthropies, offered an irresistible combination: lethal force for Panthers and other recalcitrants, and lucrative grants for leaders who agreed to fit in."

After a pause, Laz reflected: "Makes you wonder what's in store for today. With early rumblings of discontent over America's domestic policies and growing diffidence toward antipoverty measures, what will the next manifestation of majoritarian self-interest be?"

"Will the establishment insist on Americanism and toeing the line in the war on terrorism, and demand that minorities demonstrate loyalty, in return for a symbolic concession or two?" Rodrigo mused. "Will it choose one minority group for favored treatment, in the hope of keeping the others in line?"

"With the demise of the Soviet Union and absence of any international competitor, the United States may lack the incentive to consider the legitimate demands of minority groups," Laz observed.

"Or will global capitalism provide the opportunity for U.S. minorities of color to form coalitions with groups overseas in combating practices that oppress them all?" Rodrigo asked.

"It seems to me," I said, "that if Dudziak's book teaches any lesson, it is that progress for marginalized groups comes most easily when a strategic concession benefits powerful groups in government and business. Without an alignment of interests, change is slow in coming. In the seventies, we had no such alignment—indeed, the vectors were pointing in the opposite direction. To preserve momentum, we sacrificed our brightest minds. Some of them sacrificed themselves, to be sure, for comfortable jobs and grants. Today is no different. The mood of the country favors business and wartime industries. Minorities are divided and lack leaders. My friend Yancey was right—the times are bleak."

"If there's any ray of hope," Rodrigo said, catching a quick look at his watch, "it's that the internet offers a way by which large numbers of discontented people may nurse common grievances, while the demonstrations that broke out in Seattle, Chiang Mai, Toronto, Prague, and Genoa show that protest is still capable of generating a hearing for new ideas."[44]

"As the country and world continue to diversify, and the gap between the wealthy and the poor widens, the threat of disruption may come to haunt the consciousness of ruling elites sufficiently that change may once again come, however slowly and haltingly," I said. "Do you two need to change clothes and check out before we head for the airport?"

"We do," my two companions said, rising. "What if we meet you at the concierge's desk in fifteen minutes?"

11

Black Exceptionalism

Two Mistakes

I WAS SITTING in a booth in the basement coffee shop of the giant hotel where the AALS annual meeting was being held, eyeing a small pot of tea steeping on the small round formica table in front of me. I had gone there to calm my nerves after what seemed like an unending three-day round of thirty-second conversations with wired law professors, mostly younger than I, and a series of panel discussions and talks conducted in a form of high-Crit academic language, full of terms like "reification," "hypostosizing," and "hegemony" that I had trouble following. Maybe I'm too old for these things, I thought to myself. They never seem to have anything to do with the world I was raised in or the imperatives that brought me to the profession of law nearly half a century ago during the heyday of civil-rights activism. Do I need a refresher course on Derrida and Foucault? Should I think about that phased retirement option my university was offering and that the dean had, gratuitously I thought, reannounced at the beginning of the last faculty meeting back home?

I poured my tea, drank some, and my nerves had just stopped jangling when I heard a familiar voice from behind me.

"Professor, is that you?"

"Rodrigo! You're here after all. I've been looking for you all conference long. You weren't at the minorities section luncheon."

"I was seeing Laz off to the airport. He had to return early for a meeting with his publisher. Did I tell you he's editing a book on the economic origins of the Constitution?"

"Sounds like him, all right," I said. "Care to join me? I was exhausted just now and taking a break. But now that you're here I'm feeling better."

Rodrigo looked at his watch. "Sure. I've got until the afternoon session on comparative law. I'm moderating, but my remarks are all prepared." He patted some papers in his breast pocket. "I could use a bite myself."

Minutes later, he was back from the cafeteria line, his tray loaded with a bright red apple, a yellow banana, and a leafy sandwich of some kind. "What was the luncheon program about?" he asked, setting his plates on the table and sliding the empty tray onto a rack nearby.

"Reparations," I said. "For racial harms. The program was supposed to include Native American, Japanese, and Mexican American land claims. But except for an occasional reference, it was mostly about blacks."

"I'm not surprised," Rodrigo said. "That's where all the action is these days. Was the event crowded?"

"Not particularly," I said. "The room wasn't as full as it was last year for the program on immigration. The press was out in force, though, with a TV crew interviewing some of the speakers afterward. They set up lights in the corridor and chased everyone else away."

"I think I caught a glimpse of it on the evening news," Rodrigo said. "At the airport, after I dropped off Laz. The interviewer was a white man in a blue blazer interviewing two of the speakers, who were black. A large potted tree of some kind stood in the background."

"That's the very same interview I saw," I said. "Even though four panelists spoke, the reporter was interviewing just the two who were black."

"An unintentional but perfect recapitulation of the black- white binary paradigm of race," Rodrigo said, mirroring my own thoughts.

"Although I'm sure the TV crew would say they were just doing what they could with limited time," I said. "It's surprising how all the news, from the census and elsewhere, about the growth of Latinos and Asians and the increasing complexity of the U.S. racial scene has not filtered down to reporters on the street."

"Or even to a lot of our liberal friends," Rodrigo added. "We talked about this once before."[1]

"And since we did, a number of authors—including Cynthia Kwan Lee,[2] Elizabeth Martinez,[3] Vine Deloria,[4] and Juan Perea[5]—have been writing and speaking about that binary, calling attention to the way U.S. racial law and thought incorporate an implicit black-white binary paradigm. . . ."[6]

"Which often—not always—causes a lot of mischief," Rodrigo added.

"Indeed," I agreed. "In that paradigm, two races, and two only, the black and the white, define the parameters of discussion, constituting both the objects of and the terms within which courts and scholars consider matters of racial justice. Our shared understandings of what is important arise from the experiences blacks and whites have had with each other since the country's early years."[7]

"Hi, you two," said a familiar friendly voice. We both looked up.

"Giannina!" I exclaimed. "I didn't know you were here. Have a seat. Did you two come together?"

"We did. My sister's looking after the baby. I'm here for the law students section. It's on the role of the LSAT. It just wound up. I spoke on abolition."

"Of the test, I assume?" I asked.

"You bet," she said. "What have you two been talking about?"

"The black-white binary," Rodrigo said. "Gus just came back from the luncheon."

"It was about reparations," I added.

"And where had you left off?" Giannina asked, looking around to see what the cafeteria line offered.

"I was just explaining some thoughts on black exceptionalism," I said. "Even though I look black and most people take me as such, the exclusiveness of some of the discussion these days disturbs me. The luncheon program and the CNN version of it got me going. Why don't you grab a bite and join us?"

"I'd love to," Giannina said, setting down her conference bookbag with the AALS logo on it. "I've got about half an hour before I have to meet with Professor Yen. Don't start without me."

THE BLACK-WHITE BINARY OF RACE

Moments later, she was back with a tiny cup of espresso and a giant bagel with cream cheese. "Where were we?" she asked.

"The Professor had just said that the binary draws on one set of experiences as emblematic of the whole. It highlights one set of problems and issues; others enter only secondarily or by way of analogy to those

affecting the two primary groups—whites and blacks
reproduce this paradigm when they write about
groups of color as though Native Americans, Asians
adequately be taken into account if you only really
their history, and struggles."[9]

"Early critics," I continued, "focused on the work of progressive
writers such as Andrew Hacker,[10] Cornel West,[11] Joe Feagin,[12] and Joel
Kovel,[13] showing how the black-white framework that those otherwise
fine writers were caught up in obscured the realities facing nonblack
minority groups, rendering the forms of racism they face virtually invisible."[14]

"Not only that," Rodrigo added, "it reduced the potentially powerful insights of the differential racialization hypothesis—which holds
that different racial groups have been racialized in different ways at different times, in response to different social conditions—to mere side-
lights."[15]

"And it introduces tangible results," Giannina added. "I was reading a case the other day of a civil rights plaintiff—I think a Filipino—
who sued for discrimination based on accent . . ."[16]

"Although it could have been for perceived foreign origin, religion,
or a nonblack stereotype, such as the model minority myth for Asians,"
Rodrigo interjected.

"The plaintiff lost because American civil-rights law developed
with African Americans in mind. She was not able to analogize her
treatment to one that black-coined body of law covered. African Americans born here are not mocked for a foreign-sounding accent. No statutory or case law supported her, so she lost." Giannina concluded: "The
law in that area needs developing."[17]

"As any Latino would tell you, as well," Rodrigo said. "My Latino
friends are constantly telling me about friends with advanced degrees
and exemplary credentials who are turned down for jobs. The employer
won't hire them because of the stereotype that equates any trace of accent with incompetence."

"And have the two of you noticed how the critique of the black-
white binary, explosively controversial in its early years, has taken a
historical turn? Writers have been showing how its narrow framework obscures the checkerboard of racial progress and retrenchment."[18]

"I have seen writing in that vein," Rodrigo acknowledged.

"Me too," said Giannina.

"It also renders minorities overly dependent on whites,[19] while impairing interracial coalition among outgroups,"[20] I added.

"That I hadn't heard, but it stands to reason," Giannina said.

"I can fill you in later, if you like," I said. "But what I really would like is your thoughts on a recent turn that scholarship and even popular thought on the black-white binary have taken."

"And that is . . . ?" Rodrigo coaxed.

"You know how controversial the idea of the binary proved to be when Juan Perea and others first began writing about it." My two young friends nodded. "Some, especially in the black community, denied that any such binary existed.[21] Others conceded that it did, but said whites invented it.[22] Still others conceded its existence, but insisted that the black-white binary paradigm of race is justified by reason of blacks' unique history."[23]

"That's what you mean by exceptionalism, right?" Giannina asked.

"Yes," I said. "It holds that placing blacks at the center of analysis is warranted by their distinctive role in American legal history.[24] No other group has endured slavery and Jim Crow laws, the argument goes, nor been so instrumental in the development of such American milestones as *Brown v. Board of Education*[25] or the 1964 Civil Rights Act."[26]

"It seems to me," Rodrigo added, "that exceptionalism is both an accompaniment of the black-white binary of race and a defense, or justification, of it. It accompanies binary thinking because any approach that considers two groups constitutive of racial discourse is apt to lavish a great deal of attention on issues facing the nonwhite group paired with the dominant one."

"And it is a justification of that binary because it holds that this state of affairs is as it should be," Giannina continued. "I suppose the two of you have a thesis of some sort?"

Rodrigo and I looked at each other. "I'll take a stab at it," he said. "Gus may disagree, but I think that exceptionalism of any kind—black, brown, Indian, or Asian—is conceptually problematic. All the groups are exceptional, although in different ways, and nothing allows us confidently to declare one ground of exceptionalism more compelling than any other. Second, exceptionalism, just like the various binaries it often accompanies, harms even the groups that it ostensibly privileges by placing in the center."

"As we were saying, early critiques drew on examples from history or literature,"[27] I observed. "I think this may have been because of the somewhat frontal nature of the challenge. . . ."

"Which asserts that nothing special marks a group that another speaker has been in the habit of championing," Giannina interjected.

"Exactly. But, if we have time, I'd like to introduce two contemporary manifestations of the black-white binary and racial exceptionalism. First, though, we might want to bring ourselves up-to-date by summarizing the critique of the black-white binary."

Both my friends agreed, so, by tacit decision, we got up for refills of our beverages, paid the cashier, and returned to our table. "You seem to have been reading up on the binary, Rodrigo," I said. "Why don't you begin?"

BINARIES AND PARTIAL KNOWLEDGE

"Okay," my friend said good-naturedly. "One recent critique has to do with the way the black-white binary of race obscures knowledge that minorities need to know—about their situation, history, and the operation of white privilege."

"I could use an example," Giannina said.

"Well, the history of U.S. racial groups shows that when one is progressing, another is often losing ground. For example, in the mid-1950s, *Brown v. Board of Education*[28] ushered in a period of great gains for blacks. . . ."

"Which, as we know, didn't last long," I said, recalling our recent conversation on this subject.

"To be sure," Rodrigo conceded. "But my point is that the same period also witnessed Operation Wetback, a congressionally- sponsored program under which 1.3 million Mexicans and Mexican Americans were deported."[29]

"You're right," said Giannina. "Those happened almost exactly at the same time. The United States was nice to one group when it was being really mean to another."

"Not only that," Rodrigo continued. "Earlier, the North fought a gallant and bloody war with the South, ostensibly to free the slaves.[30] Yet, only a short time earlier, the nation had fought a bloodthirsty, imperialist war against Mexico in which it seized nearly one-half of that nation's land. Later, Anglo land agents, surveyors, and crooked lawyers colluded with land-hungry Anglos to steal the lands of Mexicans who opted to remain in the United States under the Treaty of Guadalupe Hidalgo."[31]

"By the same token," I continued, "Reconstruction ushered in great advances for blacks—slavery was disbanded, civil rights amendments enacted, and laws passed providing for black suffrage.[32] Yet, around this very time, Congress enacted legislation depriving Native American tribes of sovereignty and the right to enter into treaties with the United States, while California amended its constitution to make it illegal for any corporation to hire a Chinese.[33] In 1913, the same state passed the Alien Land Law, which made it a crime for Japanese to farm land for longer than three years.[34] Yet, a few years later Congress eased restrictions on immigration of Mexicans who by then were needed to work on California's farms."[35]

"You really know your Asian American history," Rodrigo said admiringly.

"Well, I did teach immigration law that one semester when my colleague Hiroshi Hato was sick," I explained. "Half of the law in that field seems to have been made at the expense of that poor group."

"I can think of respects in which the same patchwork of progress for one group, accompanied by retrenchment for another, continues," Giannina said. "Today, litigators have been winning breakthroughs on behalf of Indian tribes cheated of trust fund money,[36] enlarging the right to offer casino gambling,[37] and requiring the return of native artifacts lodged in museums and private collections[38]—all at a time when many states have been enacting English-only[39] or anti-immigrant measures aimed at Latinos and Asians."[40]

BINARIES AND POWER

"I think you were saying that racial binaries impair reform in a number of ways," I prompted. "What are some of the others?"

"They don't just prevent minorities from knowing things about their histories, they conceal the way white power shapes those histories. One way is by pitting one group against another," said Rodrigo.

"Or against itself," Giannina chimed in. "I was reading the other day that during slavery, plantation owners often assigned lighter-skinned blacks to work in the houses or as supervisors of the field hands. They were expected to spy on them and report to the master any rumblings of discontent or plans for escape."[41]

"And, as Gus mentioned earlier, during many periods American employers replaced one minority group with another to suit shifting tides of opinion and changes in the labor market. Even today, backers of Proposition 187 in California sought support from black voters by appealing to fears that Mexicans were taking black jobs,"[42] Rodrigo continued. "Even venerated Chicano activist George Sanchez exhorted his fellow Mexican Americans to support tough immigration measures on the ground that new immigrants hurt the chances of Mexican Americans already here.[43] I've been studying Chicano history recently, because my father's family immigrated here from the Caribbean and spoke perfect Spanish."

"I wish I had," Giannina said. "It would have come in handy when you were missing in Mexico back then."

"Although if you had found me too soon, I don't know what would have happened," Rodrigo replied.

"You had to rely instead on a scout, or detective," I said. "Which reminds me of the role of the Buffalo Soldiers. Immediately after the Civil War, the U.S. Army recruited newly freed blacks to help in putting down Indian rebellions."[44]

"The Indians detested them," Giannina said. "They expected solidarity, but got trained killers."

"And while we're on the subject of power, consider how the binary confers on the group paired with whites the ability to rule by analogy. Please bear with me, Gus—I know you hate this high-Crit talk, but I can explain."

"I doubt it," I grumbled. "But go ahead and try. I've spent the whole conference wishing for a glossary of European philosophy. I might as well endure it from my own protégé."

Rodrigo's face reddened slightly, but he quickly recovered. "Recall the case of the Asian or Latino attempting to redress a wrong for which no counterpart exists in the case of blacks."

"Accent discrimination, or the kind based on national origin, for example," Giannina posited.

"Those and others," Rodrigo continued. "The experiences, needs, agenda, and wrongs of this group, once placed at the center, limit consideration for other groups to situations where they can analogize themselves to blacks. Sometimes this feature works in reverse. Recall, for example, the model minority myth coined by neoconservative whites.[45] It challenges blacks and Latinos to compare themselves with supposedly high-achieving Asians. In the first situation, minorities become complicit in the oppression of other minorities. In the second, whites control them through the same mechanism. . . ."

"Namely, analogy," said Giannina.

"Yes, but wielded in the opposite direction," I said.

"Binary thinking also prevents the favored group from appreciating the compromises it makes in return for center stage. For example, we recently noted how much black progress during the *Brown v. Board of Education*[46] era was the product of a momentary alignment of white and black interests, not some moral or legal breakthrough on the part of whites.[47] Later, when the Black Panthers, Malcolm X, and a few student groups broke with nonviolence, questioned participation in foreign wars, and began quoting Marx, Mao, Lenin, and Fanon, the implicit bargain in which black advances were permitted in return for Americanism and support against communism was broken,"[48] Rodrigo recalled.

"Right," I said. "American power cracked down with lethal force—as well as foundation and government money for minority leaders who went along.[49] The minority community acquiesced, so that domestic radicalism in the tradition of W. E. B. Du Bois, Paul Robeson, and Cesar Chavez ended, not to return until recently."[50]

"When a mild version, Critical Race Theory, sprang up," Rodrigo said. "In other words, us."

BINARIES AND LOST COALITION

"A heavy thought," Giannina commented. "But I can think of yet another way that binary-type nationalistic thinking injures the very groups it ostensibly privileges. Would you like to hear?"

"I have all the time in the world," I said. "I was just unwinding before going to bed."

"It impairs the ability to unite with others. Groups that know or understand little about each other are apt to be suspicious of them. Not only that, other groups may sense their diffidence and confuse it with disrespect.[51] Unaware of cases where interracial coalitions worked, they may neglect to look for opportunities today."[52]

"Can you give us an example?" Rodrigo asked.

Giannina was silent a moment. Then: "I can. Maybe the two of you can use this in your teaching. Our study group happened on it the other day. Have you heard of *Westminster School District v. Mendez?*"[53]

"The early school desegregation case from somewhere out West?" I asked.

"Exactly," Giannina said. "Filed some ten years before *Brown*, it arose when a group of Mexican American parents sued certain Southern California school districts for segregating Mexican American schoolchildren, not because a state statute required it but because Anglo parents did not like their children attending school with Mexican boys and girls.[54] When the federal court found for the plaintiffs on the ground that, in the absence of a statute, the *Plessy* doctrine of separate-but-equal[55] did not apply and that sound educational reasons did not support segregation, as the school boards had maintained,[56] the district appealed."

"While the case was pending," Giannina continued, "it came to the attention of the NAACP, which, realizing that the Mexicans were pursuing legal objectives very similar to their own, filed an amicus brief.[57] The NAACP brief, written by Robert Carter, put forward many of the arguments the lawyers for the Mexican parents had made, but added a new one—that forced separation of the races demoralized the minority community, led to poor citizenship, and hurt education for all schoolchildren because few districts could afford the cost of a dual system of schools and would inevitably cut corners with the ones serving the minority kids."[58]

"That brief had overtones of the approach the NAACP took years later in *Brown*," I observed.

"It certainly did," Giannina seconded. "But a second brief filed by a group of progressive social scientists, including Carey McWilliams . . ."

"Who was also a lawyer," I added.

"I didn't know that," Giannina admitted. "He was quite a figure. At any rate, his and the social scientists' brief went even further. Citing studies of the effects of separate schooling, the social scientists argued that minority schoolchildren were especially vulnerable to messages of their own inferiority, and that segregation in separate schools drove home that message in devastating fashion.[59] Those two arguments, especially the second, more focused one, were incorporated successfully by the NAACP in *Brown v. Board of Education*.[60]

"The California litigators, appreciating their argument's potential, sent briefs of the case to William Hastie, one of the principal architects of the NAACP campaign that was leading up to *Brown*.[61] Appreciating its significance, he related it to Thurgood Marshall, who assigned a young staff member, Annette H. Peyser, with training in social science, to develop the psychological argument so as to have it ready when one of the Fund's cases reached the Supreme Court."[62]

When Giannina paused and looked around at us, I said, "What you are saying is that *Mendez* shows how openness to one group's struggles can sometimes redound to the great benefit of another. Had the NAACP not taken note of the Mexican case moving up the appellate ladder in California, the road to *Brown* would have been longer and harder."

JUSTIFYING THE BLACK-WHITE BINARY: BLACK EXCEPTIONALISM

"What about racial exceptionalism?" Rodrigo asked. "We may have developed a devastating critique of the black-white binary, but to a person deeply entrenched in that binary, racial exceptionalism trumps everything we've said. If blacks, say, are truly unique, then they deserve to be seen through a unique lens. And if that way of regarding them introduces problems of its own, one just has to cope with them as they come up."

"We can say, for a start," I began, "that exceptionalism—the notion that binary thinking is justified because the group one champions is genuinely central to analysis—raises many of the same concerns that racial binaries do. It obscures broad patterns of racial history, including the way elite forces pit subordinate groups against each other. It encourages dependence on whites, since only you and they are important. It ends up limiting discourse, imagination, and knowledge that struggling minority groups need to understand their situation."

"But you said it also introduces problems of its own," said Rodrigo. (He never lets me get away with a thing, I thought. But I took a deep breath, drained my teacup, and proceeded as follows:)

"I thought I was going to get off. Well, okay. It interferes with a group's forming coalitions with others even more than the black-white binary does. It's not merely that the racial exceptionalist neglects to consider racial groups other than his or her own; he affirmatively sees their concerns as of lesser interest and importance. This is scarcely calculated to endear him to other groups."

"I also had a second argument: it can blind you to compromises you have been making in order to reap white beneficence. Recall our discussion of the unraveling of the civil-rights era and the way the black community sacrificed black radicals for a few OEO grants and patronage jobs."

When I was silent, Giannina piped up. "I can think of one last argument. Too bad Laz is not here, for I am sure he would enjoy making it himself."

"What is it?" I asked.

"It's that exceptionalism and black-white binary thinking forfeit the chance to forge what I might call a secondary market of racial exchanges.[63] Instead of constantly approaching whites, hat in hand, minorities should consider approaching each other. For example, a black community organization anxious to have a city or state increase affirmative action hiring for firefighter jobs might approach Asians with an offer to support their demands for bilingual education in public schools. They could approach Latinos, offering to temper their objection to immigration in return for solidarity on the firefighter issue or opposition to racial profiling, and so on."[64]

"I like that idea," Rodrigo said. "Laz would probably go on to point out that many situations might turn out to be polycentric, so that people of color can find ways to work together for win-win solutions that better everyone."

"It will also reduce the need constantly to beseech the power structure," I said. "And when it is necessary to bargain with whites, you get to do so in full force and with a complement of friends at your side."

BLACK EXCEPTIONALISM: RECENT MISTAKES

Giannina looked at her watch. "Time passes fast. . . ."

"When you're having fun," Rodrigo completed her thought. "What time is your appointment with Sien-Ho?"

"In about ten minutes," she said. "But Gus said he had some contemporary examples where black exceptionalism hurt that very group. I'd love to hear them."

I paused to collect my thoughts. Then: "The first example is the campaign to rescue small black family farms. The second is the one for black reparations. I've been reading about the first recently, and of course the second has been in the headlines of every newspaper for the last year."

"What's going on with black farms?" Rodrigo asked. "I've only heard a little about that."

"A number of federal reports,[65] a book,[66] and a law review article,"[67] I began, "focus on the plight of that endangered institution. The law review article is by a young black scholar I met once. Do you know Thomas W. Mitchell?"

"Only by reputation," Rodrigo replied.

"It's a good article. Like the other authors, he points out how, at the end of the Civil War, blacks owned very little farmland.[68] Before then, the slaves had worked the land, of course, and were intimately familiar with the techniques of farming. But black ownership of farmland was practically nonexistent. Then, beginning with the broken promise of forty acres and a mule and the disappointing performance of the Freedman's Bureau, black farmers clawed their way into possession of nearly fifteen million acres of land in the half century following Emancipation."[69]

"Then what happened?" Giannina asked.

"That's the question," I replied. "Today, this acreage barely exceeds three million.[70] Mitchell set out to find out why, focusing on one aspect of Southern land tenure law that falls heavily on poor, subsistence-level farmers, black and white alike—the tenancy in common."[71]

"I think I understand how that works," Giannina said. "We studied it in property law. When an owner of such an estate dies intestate, as many do, his or her share passes to each of his heirs. Over time, ownership fragments."[72]

"Exactly," I said. "And that's the source of Mitchell's problem. Eventually, some of the blacks will leave the family farm for life in the city, where they and their successors may be unaware, until reminded by an outsider, that they still own a one-sixty-fourth share of the family farm back home in Mississippi."[73]

"Sounds unwieldy," Rodrigo ventured.

"Not only that," I said. "It meshes poorly with modern business practice. With dominion scattered among many titleholders, it's hard to obtain a mortgage, make repairs, or use the land as collateral. Farms pass on from one generation to the next in near-feudal, economically marginal conditions."[74]

"I bet I can guess what happens next," Giannina said. "An absentee part-owner petitions for a partition sale. A greedy investor, developer, or farm conglomerate puts him up to it. The sale forces the family back home to bid against United Fruit for their own farm. You can guess who wins."

"Mitchell offers some ways out of this predicament," I said. "Including consolidation of titles, placement of black farms in a trust, establishment of rural legal services, and limited liability companies, all aimed at stemming the tide."[75]

"Hmm," Rodrigo said. "If Laz were here, he would probably question the choice of those strategies. Cooperative ownership predated capitalism and the industrial age, and is still practiced in parts of the world today.[76] Many minority communities prefer communal arrangements in child care, oversight of the police, rent parties, and a dozen other areas."

"Besides," Giannina continued, "Ownership in common would seem, to me at least, to stand nowhere near the top of forces contributing to the loss of black land. Historically, violence, terror—remember *Mississippi Burning*?—and discrimination in mortgage and credit transactions. . . ."[77]

"Not to mention large-scale transformations in the way farming is conducted,"[78] I added.

"Maybe you can tell us about that, Gus. But I'd say that tinkering with the form of ownership is at best an indirect way of safeguarding black farms," Giannina concluded.

"You may be right," Rodrigo said. "It occurs to me that many other minority communities suffered fates similar to that of the black farmers. In early times, alien land laws deprived Japanese immigrants of the chance to gain a toehold in California.[79] Later, some of them did, only to lose those farms and businesses to World War II internment."[80]

"And recall the Mexican American farm holders in the Southwest. After the War with Mexico ended with the Treaty of 1848, Mexicans living in the newly conquered territory were guaranteed the right to retain their lands.[81] In one of the shadiest chapters in legal history, sharp lawyers and land surveyors stole the Mexicans' lands for their Anglo clients," I added.[82]

"And everyone knows about the poor Indians," Giannina said. "When the Europeans arrived, they occupied the entire continent. This was inconvenient, so settlers and judges coined theories such as the doctrine of discovery and Manifest Destiny that made short shrift of them."[83]

"So, what are we to make of all this?" Rodrigo asked.

THE ICEBERG AND THE CALF

"One way to look at it is to consider what the experiences of these groups had in common. Some held their land communally, but others did not. Yet they all fell prey to Western expansion. I thought of a metaphor for their fate."

"I love metaphors," Giannina said. "What is it?"

"It's the iceberg," I said. "Navigators of shipping lines that ply northern waters know that these huge masses of floating ice that form lethal obstacles to ships sometimes throw off calves, smaller versions that separate from the parent mass and proceed along their separate courses. Sailors must be alert not only to the iceberg, but the smaller off-spring as well."

"So, you're saying that theft of minority and Indian land is a recurrent phenomenon, like the calves of an iceberg," Rodrigo exclaimed.

"Aspects of a single generative structure, racism. So, instead of fixating on the legal form of black ownership and proposing changes aimed at making it marginally more resilient, authors like Mitchell should name and identify the iceberg—the source of the danger to black farming. If you look at the experience of other, nonblack minority groups, you may be less prone to blame a form of ownership—the tenancy in common—that may seem quite familiar and natural to some black farmers," Giannina said.

"Precisely," I said. "If Western expansion always finds some way to divest minority communities of their lands, pointing the finger at black farmers for their communal practices and refusal to make wills may deflect attention from social practices and large-scale changes in the way farming is conducted."

"And that will continue to grind away at black farmers even if stop-gap measures, such as more legal aid for rural residents, are put in place," Rodrigo added.

"To see this, consider the fate of a second group of farmers in another rich agricultural region, California," I said.

THE ICE FLOE

"You've mentioned Japanese. So I assume you now plan to talk about Chicanos, the other large group of farmers in that state," Rodrigo hazarded.

"You took the words right out of my mouth," I said. "Although I doubt you are familiar with the case I have in mind. It did not go up very high on appeal, so isn't in any of the casebooks. It's *California Agrarian Action Project v. Regents of the University of California.*"[84] I waited for a reaction, heard none, so went on:

"I had a feeling even well-read young people like you wouldn't have heard about it. What happened is that in 1979, California Rural Legal Assistance (CRLA) . . ."

"Them I have heard of. They're famous," Giannina interjected. "I have a classmate, Leticia Ontiveros, who's dying to go to work for them."

"CRLA filed suit," I continued, "on behalf of the Agrarian Action Project, an association of small farmers and migrant workers, against six regents, three UC administrators, and a number of researchers at the big agriculture school at UC-Davis, alleging improprieties in the way that campus carried out agricultural research. The charges included conflict of interest stemming from connections between high university officials and California agribusiness."[85]

"And all these practices fell heavily on small family farms and migrant workers, I bet," said Giannina.

"Exactly. Their complaint alleged that the university's research undermined farm unionization and contributed to the production of inferior but high-priced produce. It charged that the university was spending public money to confer private benefits on large farm operations in violation of the California constitution and a number of federal statutes."[86]

"Did the case go to trial?" Rodrigo asked, leaning forward intently. "I can't wait to tell Laz about this."

"It did," I said. "Witnesses testified how corporate influence caused the university to select research priorities that included large, expensive farm machines, harvesters, and crop varieties suitable for use only by very large farms. These economies of scale reduced the number of workers needed to operate a farm, shut down smaller operations, and endangered family farming as a way of life."[87]

"What sort of relief did they ask for?" Giannina asked.

"Several kinds," I said, "including a requirement that the university produce a *social impact statement* that would assess the consequences of every program of agricultural research on small farmers, consumers, and the citizens of the state."[88]

"I seem to recall some books on the subject," Rodrigo ventured.

"The lawyers built on research by agricultural economists in works such as *Harvest of Shame*, *The Dirt on California*,[89] and *Dollar Harvest*.[90] Some of them recounted the development of square tomatoes and mechanical pickers designed just for them."[91]

"How did the case come out?"

"CRLA won a narrow victory in trial court," I said, "but the court of appeals reversed, finding that nothing in the California constitution nor any federal statute imposed a duty on the university to operate its research program so as to not injure small farmers or consumers.[92] Publicity from the suit, however, coming on the heels of pressure from citizen groups, prompted the university to modify its practices in the directions CRLA had highlighted."[93]

"I see why you chose that example," Giannina said. "If official funding of pesticides, insecticides, genetically engineered crops, and new expensive farm machinery is everywhere rendering small farms uneconomical, marginal improvements in the way black farmers hold their land and pass it on from generation to generation will do little to stem the tide.[94] Someone who believes in the value of small family farms must confront the ice floe—the slow, grinding force that is rendering them obsolete."

"Otherwise they will become nonviable no matter how well we protect them from partition actions brought by disaffected family members," Rodrigo summarized.

"You have captured my thought exactly," I said. "Are you ready for my second example?"

THE CASE FOR BLACK REPARATIONS

Giannina looked quickly at her watch and nodded. Rodrigo, too, seemed to be going strong. So I said:

"A second setting where black exceptionalism plays a prominent role is the campaign for black reparations. Did either of you attend the minority section program? I think you said you didn't, Rodrigo." Rodrigo nodded and mentioned the need to get Laz to the airport. "How about you, Giannina?"

"I couldn't either," she said. "The previous program ran late, and I didn't want to barge in in the middle. But I've been reading about reparations in the news. And one of my professors talked about it the other day in class."

"So you must know that the roots of the movement go back to the famous book by Boris Bittker . . ."

"*The Case for Black Reparations?*"[95] Rodrigo hazarded.

"Right," I said. "And even earlier.[96] Still, it's only been in recent months that a high-profile campaign has gotten off the ground. A group of prominent lawyers is considering filing a class action.[97] Editorial writers are urging that society in general, or particular social institutions that benefited from the slave trade, make amends.[98] In the 1960s, James Forman made a famous demand. . . ."

"At New York's Riverside Church," Rodrigo interjected.

"Exactly," I said. "For $500,000,000 from organized religion for its role in slavery and black subjugation."[99]

"The state of Florida recently voted reparations to the survivors of Rosewood,"[100] Giannina added.

"And don't forget the controversy that broke out when President Clinton, near the end of his term, considered making an apology to blacks for slavery,"[101] Rodrigo added.

"The theory of reparations is, legally speaking, fairly simple. Proponents argue that American society achieved wealth through forced black labor," I said. "They also point out that the United States was slower than many other developed countries to repudiate slavery, and that the country has already made reparations to certain Indian tribes and Japanese Americans interned during World War II.[102] Germany made reparations for the Holocaust."[103]

"Reparations to blacks could help right a serious moral wrong," Rodrigo said, "while the money would go some way toward enabling them to recapture the wealth that would have been theirs had their ancestors not been enslaved."

"Proponents point out that President Andrew Johnson thwarted efforts by General Sherman and Thaddeus Stevens to distribute confiscated Southern land to the freed slaves,"[104] I added. "Early in this century, Cornelius Jones unsuccessfully sought damages from the Department of the Treasury for taxes collected on cotton produced by slave labor.[105] And for the past dozen years, Rep. John Conyers has introduced a bill to similar effect. It hasn't yet left committee, but he has secured apologies by companies such as Aetna and the *Hartford Courant* that profited from the slave trade."[106]

"Didn't I just read about a study that indicted Yale University—long heralded as a staunch opponent of slavery—for accepting benefits from it?" Giannina asked.

"It did. Yale apparently used slave money for professorships, scholarships, and the library. Many campus buildings bear the names of notorious slave traders."[107]

`   "What are some of the legal grounds for redress?" Rodrigo asked.

"They vary," I said. "One is for the harm of slavery itself. Another is the destruction of self-esteem and self-worth stemming from the continuing discrimination that followed, including state-endorsed school segregation, housing covenants, and redlining.[108] A final ground is the financial gains pocketed by white America."[109]

"Quantum meruit,"[110] said Giannina.

"That plus violation of several treaties to which the United States is a party," I added.

GOING IT ALONE

After a brief silence, Giannina spoke up. "But I gather you mentioned all this as a preface to a point about political strategies."

"Oh yes," I said, snapping myself to. "I wanted to make a point about black exceptionalism. Most of the proponents of black reparations seem to be going it alone. Robert Westley, whom you two know, posits that granting reparations to African Americans might help other groups obtain them at some later, unspecified date.[111] Anthony Cook reminds his readers that Martin Luther King advocated compensation for blacks alone. But he does go on to add that discussing reparations may help society learn to think outside the box, leading to successful efforts on behalf of other groups in the future.[112] Aside from that, most black activists have elected to fight for reparations for their group alone."

"A Lone Ranger effort," Rodrigo observed.

"Afraid so," I said. "For some, this may have been an oversight or something to be gotten around to later. For others, blacks seem to be the only—or the main—group deserving compensation."[113]

"To play devil's advocate for just a minute, what's wrong with that?" Giannina asked. "Feminists often ask for measures that will benefit only, or mainly, women."

"A unified campaign could be much stronger," I replied. "For example, Native Americans and Hawaiians also seek reparations for loss of their lands. Latinos have begun to discuss this among themselves, as well.[114] Combining forces increases the likelihood that all the groups will realize some benefit, while pursuing separate courses exposes each to the risk that the dominant class will play them against each other and avoid sharing the wealth."

"As we discussed before. In fact, I seem to recall one or two conservative commentators who took advantage of just that opportunity," Rodrigo interjected. "John Skrentny[115] and Charles Krauthammer[116] both urged that society consider granting concessions to blacks in return for ending affirmative action for all other groups."

"Some blacks wanted to take them up on it, as I recall," Giannina said.

"Right. For them, forgoing affirmative action is an acceptable price in return for compensation for past harms," I said.

"Krauthammer presented reparations as an opportunity for a clean start—a one-time cash payment in return for a new regime of irrevocable color blindness,[117] as he put it," Rodrigo went on.

"Of course, nonblack minority groups will receive nothing. But they will lose the meager benefits of affirmative action," Giannina pointed out.

"Black reparation's boosters sometimes speak as though blacks are the only victimized minorities. This, too, plays right into the hands of Krauthammer. He favors reparations for blacks precisely because other, supposedly less worthy, groups have been coming in under the banner of affirmative action, which he would like to see stopped,"[118] Rodrigo explained.

"So the danger is twofold," I summarized. "Without the participation of other groups, African Americans risk worsening their plight by validating the belief that they are not really oppressed.[119] This not only trivializes the real, if different, problems these other groups encounter, it engenders distrust among the groups, making it easier for society to enact English- only laws,[120] tougher immigration quotas, or further welfare cuts . . ."

"Not to mention reluctance to grant reparations to other groups in the future," Rodrigo added. "The question is not whether reparations are owed African Americans for the unspeakable evils of slavery and discrimination."

"Nor whether they have suffered greater harms than other groups," Giannina interjected.

"Rather, it's whether justice for all Americans can be realized without a concerted effort," Rodrigo said.

Giannina glanced at her watch and then looked up. "I'm afraid I've got to be going, so let me see if I've got the main points. We pointed out how the master narrative—the black-white binary of race—narrows the range of thought, obscures the way white elites manipulate breakthroughs for one group at the expense of another, and impairs racial coalitions."

"While its companion structure, black exceptionalism, does all that and more," Rodrigo added. "Exceptionalism of any kind is almost always undertheorized. Buying into it deprives you of allies with whom you might form a secondary market of racial exchanges, renders you overly dependent on white largesse, and obscures compromises you make on your way to what you think is your favored position."

"Previous work has exposed the frailties of the black-white binary and exceptionalist thinking by employing examples drawn from history or literature," I continued. "Although that choice might have been justified diplomatically, it lacks immediacy. It can give the impression that the black-white binary and racial exceptionalism are mere discourse defects lacking real-world consequences. But we have examined two contemporary examples of one type of exceptionalism . . ."

"The black variety," Rodrigo said.

"Although we could just as easily have found examples of Chicano, Asian, or Native American nationalism," Giannina added. "Every group succumbs at times to the impulse to go it alone."

"And our two examples," I continued, "show that narrow exceptionalist thinking leads to errors of conception and strategy. We discussed a campaign to rescue black farms and the push for black reparations. In each case, narrow exceptionalist thinking led to errors and oversights, prevented the proponents from seeing broad patterns in the forces arrayed against them, and left them open to clever counteroffers by neoconservative whites who may not have their interest—or that of any group of color—at heart."

"These are not easy topics, Professor," Rodrigo lamented. "Addressing interminority group relations is a tense subject. Yet, doing so is necessary for subordinate groups to understand their histories, each other, and the role white power plays in their changing fortunes. It lets you see what's behind the checkerboard of racial progress and retrenchment without becoming captive to it. And it enables disempowered groups to form coalitions on terms that provide opportunities for all."

"So that even after the current alignment of interests shifts, a new generation of reformers, like you young people, is able to start from a higher plateau than the one we reached and, with luck, achieve a higher one still," I concluded.

"I would like to think that," Giannina said, picking up her bookbag. "Now, I must go."

Epilogue

THE NEXT DAY, on the plane back to home and Teresa, I reflected on the many conversations I had had with Rodrigo and his friends since his miraculous return from exile off the coast of Baja. I recalled our discussions of justice at war, and Rodrigo's startling but well documented assertion that conflict is the usual state of affairs in American law and politics, and that war only seems like an exception to those whose lives do not constantly bump up against our legal system. I recalled his suggestion, impressive for a young Marxist, that the solution to the problem of international terrorism is to imagine that one lives in a glass house and strive to make one's neighborhood a safer, friendlier place.

I recalled vividly our discussion of interracial sex and marriage, prompted by that rather formal, somewhat stilted occasion when Teresa and I disclosed our plans to get together to the young people. Most of all, I reflected on our series of recent conversations on forgetting—a subject dear to my aging professor's heart—and the way Rodrigo and I developed it as a metaphor for the shortcomings of the contemporary left.

I wondered what the future held for my young protégé and his equally brilliant wife and child. Would the patriotic, close- the-ranks quality of American public life these days find no place for talented gadflies like him? His institute seemed to be flourishing. Would the grant money keep rolling in? Teresa and I had discussed making a large contribution, which was tax deductible, but we knew we both had to conserve our resources for retirement, which in my case seemed imminent if my dean had her way.

Would the next generation contain any Rodrigos—audacious, original thinkers, educated abroad or at least in unorthodox settings, capable of seeing the world with new eyes? Once, when Rodrigo had been missing and feared dead, I had wondered whether a bright, young bilingual detective, who expressed interest in law school, could turn out to be the next Rodrigo. But then Rodrigo himself returned and I had no further contact with the young Mexican operative.

Then too, any new Rodrigos would need mentors and straight persons, like myself, to push them to develop their ideas, caution them against their own excesses, and encourage them to persevere even though, as I once put it, the road is long and the night dark. Where would these come from? I did not want to flatter myself that I was unique, but many of my once-liberal friends seemed discouraged and apathetic. Those who were still writing were caught up in the new discourse analysis and seemed to have little heart for tackling the real-world problems of poverty, racism, and injustice. Was I becoming a curmudgeon, mired in a past seen through rose-colored glasses? I thought with quiet satisfaction about Teresa and the fine role she had played, raising such an outstanding daughter as Giannina and doing her part to encourage and nurture Rodrigo. Perhaps the future of progressive politics lay with women like those two, I thought, just as a previous generation of male figures like Derrick Bell, Oscar "Zeta" Acosta, and Martin Luther King had acquitted themselves so gallantly.

Just then, the pilot's voice over the intercom interrupted my reverie by announcing the beginning of our descent. I looked forward to seeing Teresa's sweet face waiting for me at the airport and driving home together in the little compact car ("we must buy it, Gus, it gets great mileage") we had recently bought together. I looked forward, with less pleasure, to the appointment that the dean had scheduled with me the following day. Would she pressure me to retire, as I feared? When I had last called Teresa from the conference hotel just before leaving, she had casually mentioned hearing about something good in the offing at the law school. I wondered what it was.

With a bump, the plane landed. The brakes set up a deafening clatter for a few seconds, then the pilot's voice—a woman's this time—came on, welcoming us to our destination. Hoping it was an omen, I gathered up my things and prepared to make my way, with the long line of passengers ahead of me, to the deplaning gateway.

Notes

NOTES TO CHAPTER 1

1. The State of Black America (Lee A. Daniels ed., National Urban League 1998).

2. Terry Eastland, Ending Affirmative Action: The Case for Colorblind Justice (1996).

3. William G. Bowen & Derek Bok, The Shape of the River: Long-Term Consequences of Considering Race in College and University Admissions (1998).

4. Paul M. Barrett, The Good Black: A True Story of Race in America (1999).

5. A Civil Action (Touchstone Pictures 1998).

6. National Urban League, *supra.*

7. *See id.* at 37–51.

8. *See id.* at 15–36.

9. *See id.* at 37–51, 89–105.

10. *See id.* at 195–227 (showing how low technology and factory jobs have disappeared with the advent of an economy based on information and computers).

11. *See id.* at 53–69, 89–105, 195–207 (detailing devastation wrought by joblessness).

12. *See id.* at 37–51, 89–105 (showing impact of unemployment on the black family and other social institutions).

13. *See id.*

14. *See id.* at 109–60.

15. *See id.* at 109–227.

16. *See id.* at 247–90.

17. Eastland, *supra.*

18. *See id.* at 9, 21–38, 59, 76, 85, 90, 141, 195–200.

19. *See, e.g.,* Ruth Colker, *Anti-Subordination above All: Sex, Race, and Equal Protection,* 61 N.Y.U. L. Rev. 1003 (1986) (arguing that the purpose of civil rights statutes should not be the policing of color-blind neutrality, but the removal of subordination).

20. *See* Eastland, *supra*, at 21–38, 199–200.

21. *See* Derrick A. Bell, Jr., Race, Racism, and American Law 27–28 (3d ed. 1992) (noting four clauses whose purpose or effect was to protect the institution of slavery).

22. *See* Eastland, *supra*, at 2–8, 17, 76, 152 (rejecting imposition of costs of racial remedies on whites who were not responsible for racial sins).

23. Bowen & Bok, *supra*.

24. *See id.* at 53–192, 336–49 (notes on methodology and statistical strength of outcomes).

25. *See id.* at 53–90, 91–192, 277–80, 353–58.

26. *See id.* at 281–82, 284–86.

27. *See id.* at 280–82, 284–86 (displacement on order of 1.5 percent).

28. Barrett, *supra* (detailing the story of Larry Mungin, an African American lawyer, written by his one-time school roommate, Paul Barrett).

29. *Id.* at 23–28; *see also id.* at 41, 64, 65, 66, 68, 78 (ignoring slights such as "nigger" and keeping his feelings bottled up), 166.

30. *See id.* at 80–91, 97–99, 113–22, 180.

31. *See id.* at 24,117–80, 238–39, 248–51, 271.

32. *See* S. James Anaya, *The Native Hawaiian People and International Human Rights Law: Toward a Remedy for Past and Continuing Wrongs*, 28 Ga. L. Rev. 309, 336–60 (1994); Robert A. Williams, Jr., *Encounters on the Frontiers of International Human Rights Law: Redefining the Terms of Indigenous Peoples' Survival in the World*, 1990 Duke L.J. 660, 701–3.

33. *See* William Raspberry, *Human Rights Abuses, Not Abroad, but at Home*, Wash. Post, Oct. 12, 1998, at A21; Amnesty International, Recommendations to the United States Government to Address Human Rights Violations in the USA.

34. *See* David Mechanic, *Professional Judgment and the Rationing of Medical Care*, 140 U. Pa. L. Rev. 1713, 1738 (1992); Avram Goldstein, *GU Study Finds Disparity in Heart Care*, Wash. Post, Feb. 25, 1999, at A3; Brigid Schulte, *Unequal Care for Minorities—Even the Rich, Educated, Insured—Prospect of Healthy Life Less Sure*, Detroit Free Press, Aug. 3, 1998, at 1A; Jack E. White, *Prejudice? Perish the Thought*, Time, Mar. 8, 1999, at 36.

35. *See* Leon Forer, *Low Marks for Health Care*, Newsday, Dec. 7, 1991, at 16; Schulte, *supra*.

36. *See* Christine Russell, *How Goes the War on Cancer? Cancer Gaining on Heart Disease as Number One Killer*, Wash. Post, Feb. 14, 1995, at Z12; Schulte, *supra*, at 1A.

37. *See* Melvin Oliver & Thomas Shapiro, Black Wealth/White Wealth: A New Perspective on Racial Inequality (1995); Allen S. Hammond, IV, *Universal Access to Infrastructure and Information*, 45 Depaul L. Rev. 1067, 1091 n.80 (1991); *Setting the Record Straight on the State of Black Inequality in the United States*, J. Blacks in Higher Ed., Autumn 1998, at 46.

38. *See* Christopher D. Pixley, *The Next Frontier in Public School Finance Reform: A Policy and Constitutional Analysis of School Choice Legislation,* 24 J. Legis. 21, 31 (1998); Sarah Wyatt, *U.S. Lagging on Graduation Rates: International Group Ranks American Eighth Graders Low in Math,* Boulder Daily Camera, Nov. 24, 1998, at 7A.

39. *See* Letters, Faxes & E-mail: *Let Parents Decide,* Denv. Post, Sept. 27, 1998, at K2; Wyatt, *supra,* at 7A.

40. *See* Derrick A. Bell, Jr., Brown v. Board of Education *and the Interest-Convergence Dilemma,* 93 Harv. L. Rev. 518, 524 (1980) (noting that the NAACP and federal government in Brown argued that desegregation would help the United States compete with the Soviet Union for alliances with third world countries).

41. *See id.* at 524.

42. *See* Paul Butler, *Racially Based Jury Nullification: Black Power in the Criminal Justice System,* 105 Yale L. J. 677 (1995) (urging that black jurors nullify prosecutions whose basic fairness they doubt).

43. *Id.* at 434.

44. *See* Robert H. Aronson, Professional Responsibility in a Nutshell 478–83 (2d ed. 1991).

45. *See id.*

46. *See Race Factored into Sentence,* Nat'l L.J., Dec. 28–Jan. 4, 1999, at A8; Law. Wkly. USA, Jan. 25, 1999, at 7.

47. Barrett, *supra,* at 276.

48. *See id.* at 238–39, 248–50, 271.

49. *See generally* Richard D. Kahlenberg, The Remedy: Class, Race, and Affirmative Action (1996) (urging shift away from race- to class-based affirmative action).

50. *See* Cal. Const. art. 1, § 31 (codifying 1995 California Civil Rights Initiative).

51. *See* Heath Foster, *Affirmative Action Rules Tossed Out by State Voters,* Seattle Post-Intelligencer, Nov. 4, 1998, at A1.

52. *See* Jean Stefancic & Richard Delgado, No Mercy: How Conservative Think Tanks and Foundations Changed America's Social Agenda 45–81 (1997).

53. *See id.*

54. *See* Dinesh D'Souza, Illiberal Education 251–53 (1991); Kahlenberg, *supra,* at 83–120; William J. Wilson, The Truly Disadvantaged: The Inner City, The Underclass, and Public Policy 112–18, 146–47 (1987); Mickey Kaus, *Class Is In,* New Republic, Mar. 27, 1995, at 6; Michael Kinsley, *Class Not Race,* New Republic, Aug. 19, 1991, at 4.

55. Hopwood v. Texas, 78 F.3d 932 (5th Cir. 1996) (striking down any consideration of race in university admissions in three states).

56. Deborah C. Malamud, *Affirmative Action, Diversity, and the Black Middle Class*, 68 U. Colo. L. Rev. 939, 995 (1997) (noting how admissions officers compete for the top rung of candidates from the diversity pool).

57. *See* Richard Delgado, *1998 Hugo L. Black Lecture: Ten Arguments against Affirmative Action—How Valid?* 50 Ala. L. Rev. 135, 152 (1998) (describing likely consequences of shift to privilege-based programs).

58. 438 U.S. 265 (1978).

59. *See* 438 U.S. at 314; *see also* Richard Delgado & Jean Stefancic, *Home-Grown Racism: Colorado's Historic Embrace—and Denial—of Higher Education Equal Opportunity*, 70 U. Colo. L. Rev. 703, 703–704, 710–14 (1999).

60. In other words, privileged children (such as those from wealthy families) who take for granted their status and the advantages it brings, and who do not work hard to achieve their full potential, are given negative marks when compared to underprivileged children, who even though they do not have many advantages, work hard and achieve.

61. The movement was named and launched by Rev. Benjamin Chavis in the wake of a report by the United Church of Christ that examined inequities in the siting of biohazards. *See* Luke Cole & Sheila Foster, From the Ground Up: Environmental Racism and the Rise of the Environmental Justice Movement (2000); Sheila Foster, *Race(ial) Matters: The Quest for Environmental Justice*, 20 Ecology L.Q. 721, 722–23 (1993). On the movement and its development, see Robert D. Bullard, *Environmental Justice for All: It's the Right Thing to Do*, 9 J. Envtl. L. & Litig. 281 (1994); Robert D. Bullard, *Environmental Racism and Invisible Communities*, 96 W. Va. L. Rev. 1037 (1994); Robert D. Bullard, *The Legacy of American Apartheid and Environmental Racism*, 9 St. John's J. Legal Comment. 445 (1994); Luke W. Cole, *Empowerment as the Key to Environmental Protection: The Need for Environmental Poverty Law*, 19 Ecology L.Q. 619 (1992); Luke W. Cole, *Remedies for Environmental Racism: A View from the Field*, 90 Mich. L. Rev. 1991 (1992); Luke W. Cole, *The Struggle of Kettleman City: Lessons for the Movement*, 5 Md. J. Contemp. Legal Issues 67 (1993/94); Robert W. Collin & Robin Morris Collin, *Equity as the Basis of Implementing Sustainability: An Exploratory Essay*, 96 W. VA. L. REV. 1173 (1994); Richard J. Lazarus, *Pursuing "Environmental Justice": The Distributional Effects of Environmental Protection*, 87 Nw. U. L. Rev. 787 (1993).

62. *See* Robert Gottlieb & Peter Dreier, *Environmentalists Torn between Elitism and Justice*, Hous. Chron., Mar. 5, 1998, at A31 (describing similar debate in Sierra Club membership).

Teresa's organization's interest may have been triggered by a presidential directive ordering agencies of the federal government to develop strategies to minimize inequity in the distribution of environmental hazards. *See* Exec. Order No. 12,898, 3 C.F.R. 859 (1994), reprinted in 42 U.S.C. § 4321 (1994).

63. *See, e.g.*, R.I.S.E., Inc. v. Kay, 768 F. Supp. 1144, 1150 (E.D. Va. 1991), *aff'd*, 977 F.2d 573 (4th Cir. 1992); East Bibb Twiggs Neighborhood Ass'n v. Macon-

Bibb County Planning Comm'n, 706 F. Supp. 880, 887 (M.D. Ga. 1989), *aff'd*, 896 F.2d 1264 (11th Cir. 1989) (both requiring that intent to discriminate be shown before equal protection action would lie).

64. *See, e.g.*, R.I.S.E., 768 F. Supp. at 1149–50; Jill E. Evans, *Challenging the Racism in Environmental Racism: Redefining the Concept of Intent*, 40 Ariz. L. Rev. 1219, 1277 (1998).

65. *See, e.g.*, El Pueblo para el Aire y Agua Limpio v. County of Kings, 22 Envtl. L. Rep. 20,357 (Cal. Super. Ct. 1991).

66. *See id.* at 20,359.

67. Endangered Species Act of 1973 (ESA), 16 U.S.C. § 1531 (1995); *see also* Jim Chen, *Diversity in a Different Dimension: Evolutionary Theory and Affirmative Action's Destiny*, 59 Ohio St. L.J. 811, 811 (1998) (rejecting affirmative action as "banal" because comparison to "a series of elaborate legal analogies," including laws protecting biological species, demonstrates that the need for ethnic minorities in workplaces is slight).

68. *See* Christopher Stone, *Should Trees Have Standing?—Toward Legal Rights for Natural Objects*, 45 S. Cal. L. Rev. 450, 456 & n.26, 464–67 (1972) (urging that trees, rocks, rivers, and other "non-animal but natural objects" be permitted to sue—with the aid of a guardian ad litem, to be sure—in their own right for injuries they have sustained at human hands). My two protégés' proposal would, similarly, allow humans to benefit from laws and procedures originally designed with animals in mind.

69. *See* Cuthair v. Montezuma-Cortez, Colo. Sch. Dist. No. RE-1, 7 F. Supp. 2d 1152, 1155–56 (1998).

70. *See* Nancy Ehrenreich, *The Colonization of the Womb*, 43 Duke L.J. 492, 514–52 nn.70–74 (1993).

71. 437 U.S. 153 (1978).

72. *Id.* at 188 n.34.

73. *See, e.g.*, Chen, *supra* at 852–53 (praising ESA for its power and sweep); John Andrew Zuccotti, Note, *A Native Returns: The Endangered Species Act and Wolf Reintroduction to the Northern Rocky Mountains*, 20 Colum. J. Envtl. L. 329, 333 (1995); *see also* Tennessee Valley Authority v. Hill, 437 U.S. at 174–76 (describing extraordinary sweeping powers of the ESA). International treaties also protect biodiversity, but in less categorical terms. *See, e.g.*, Multilateral Convention on International Trade in Endangered Species of Wild Fauna and Flora, Mar. 3, 1973, 27 U.S.T. 1087.

74. Hill, 437 U.S. at 173 (quoting 16 U.S.C. § 1536 (1994)) (internal quotation marks and emphasis omitted).

75. *See* 16 U.S.C. § 1538 (1994).

76. *Id.*

77. 50 C.F.R. § 17.3 (1998); *see also* Babbitt v. Sweet Home Chapter of Communities for a Great Oregon, 515 U.S. 687, 697 n.9 (1995).

78. 16 U.S.C. § 1532(5)(A) (1994). "The term [']critical habitat [['] for a threatened or endangered species means—(I) the specific areas within the geographical area occupied by the species, at the time it is listed . . . on which are found those physical or biological features (I) essential to the conservation of the species and (II) which may require special management considerations or protection; and (ii) specific areas outside the geographical area occupied by the species at the time it is listed . . . upon a determination by the Secretary [of the Interior] that such areas are essential for the conservation of the species." *Id.*

79. Hill, 437 U.S. at 174.

80. *See id.*

81. 16 U.S.C. § 1532(6) (1994).

82. *Id.* at § 1532(20) (1994).

83. *See* Pub. L. No. 95–632, 92 Stat. 3752 (codified as amended, 16 U.S.C. § 1536(e)–(h) (1994)).

84. *See* Mary E. Thurston, The Lost History of the Canine Race (1995); Kelly D. Burgess, *Coping with Your Loss*, Pitt. Post- Gazette, May 12, 1996, at VE2.

85. *See* Todd A. Krichmar, *Prepayment of Funeral Expenses for Medicaid and SSI Recipients*, N.Y. St. Bar J., July–Aug. 1997, at 42 (discussing limitations on funeral arrangements for welfare recipients under pre-1997 New York state law); *County Considers Cremation Policy for Poor*, Press J. (Vero Beach, FL), Dec. 27, 1998, at A10.

86. *See* Diane Calkins, *The Ones Left Behind: Finding Pet Care Can Make, Break Vacation*, L.A. Times, June 21, 1990, San Diego County edition, at 3.

87. *See* K. C. Baker, *The Privileged Pooch*, N.Y. Daily News, Oct. 13, 1996, at 70.

88. *See* Emergency Vets (Animal Planet television broadcast, Mar. 10, 1999); *see also* Richard Quinn, *Vet Treats Exotic and Famous Animals*, Boulder Daily Camera, Mar. 13, 1999, at 8C.

89. *See* Allan Coukell, *New Zealand Group Seeks Human Rights for Apes*, Denv. Post, Mar. 16, 1999, at A16.

90. *See* Cal. Gov't Code, §§ 399–423 (West 1995) (protecting state seal, flag, and emblems); United States v. Eichman, 496 U.S. 310 (1990) (invalidating criminal punishment for flag- burning); Texas v. Johnson, 491 U.S. 397 (1989).

91. *See* Cal. Gov't Code § 421 (West 1995) (protecting poppy).

92. David J. Bederman, *Symposium: Limitations on Commercial Speech: The Constitutionality of Agricultural Disparagement Statutes*, 10 Depaul Bus. L.J. 191 (1998).

93. *See* Defense of Marriage Act, 28 U.S.C. § 1738(c) (Supp. 1997).

94. *See* Thomas Ross, *Innocence and Affirmative Action*, 43 Vand. L. Rev. 297, 299–301 (1990).

95. *See generally* Bell, *Interest-Convergence, supra* (putting forward argument that elite whites' interests dictate course of antidiscrimination law).

96. *Id. See also* Charles A. Beard, An Economic Interpretation of the Constitution of the United States (1935).

97. Derrick Bell, *Racial Realism*, 24 Conn. L. Rev. 363, 364–72 (1992) (arguing that the racial situation of blacks is unlikely to improve but that the civil rights community must persevere nevertheless).

98. *See* David Stout, *A Black Businessman's Ordeal as a Suspect*, N.Y. Times, May 9, 1995, at B1. For accounts of other indignities suffered by black reporters, police officers, and lawyers, see generally Ellis Cose, The Rage of a Privileged Class (1993).

99. *See* Delgado & Stefancic, *supra*, at 721.

100. *See* Robert A. Williams, Jr., *The Algebra of Federal Indian Law: The Hard Trail of Decolonizing and Americanizing the White Man's Indian Jurisprudence*, 1986 Wis. L. Rev. 219, 298 n.248.

101. *See* Delgado & Stefancic, *supra*, at 719–20, 742.

102. *See, e.g.*, Chae Chan Ping v. United States, 130 U.S. 581 (1889) (Chinese Exclusion Case) (upholding immigration statute excluding certain Chinese from entering United States).

103. *See* Eva Hanks et al., Environmental Law and Policy 1–92 (1974) (detailing utilitarian and nonutilitarian reasons for environmental protection); Joseph L. Sax, *The Public Trust Doctrine in Natural Resources Law: Effective Judicial Intervention*, 68 Mich. L. Rev. 471 (1970) (natural resources are limited commodities that, if too rapidly consumed, will be unavailable for future generations). For the contrary, nonanthropomorphic view, see, for example, Aldo Leopold, A Sand County Almanac and Sketches Here and There (1949); Stone, *supra*.

104. *See* John Muir, My First Summer in the Sierra 110 (1991) ("[W]here we try to pick out anything by itself, we find it hitched to everything else in the universe."); *see also* Edward O. Wilson, The Diversity of Life 133 (1992) (pointing out intricate interdependence of life forms on each other for food, support, and, at times, control of numbers).

105. *See* Regina Austin & Michael Schill, *Black, Brown, Poor, and Poisoned: Minority Grassroots Environmentalism and the Quest for Eco-Justice*, 1 Kan. J.L. & Pub. Pol'y 69 (1991).

106. *See generally* Bruce Mazlish, The Fourth Discontinuity (1993) (noting that at several points in history, society has developed theories explaining why humans are separate from the rest of the natural world).

107. *See, e.g.*, Austin & Schill, *supra*, at 70: "[I]n the South, a sparse concentration of inhabitants is correlated with poverty which is in turn correlated with race. [']It follows that criteria for siting hazardous waste facilities which include density of population will have the effect of targeting rural black communities that have high rates of poverty.[']" Id. (quoting Conner Bailey & Charles E. Faupel, *Environmentalism and Civil Rights in Sumter County, Alabama*, in Proceedings

of the Michigan Conference on Race and the Incidence of Environmental Hazards, 159, 171 (1990)).

108. *See, e.g.*, William H. Frey, *America's True Colors on a National Level*, Orlando Sentinel, Aug. 9, 1998, at G1.

109. *See* Colleen Smith, *Crafty Canines Shake Off Efforts at Reduction*, Denv. Post Online-Lifestyles (visited Mar. 28, 1999) <http:// www.denverpost.com /life/nature0321.htm> (pointing out that coyotes do the same thing); *see also* Peter Singer, Animal Liberation 234 (2d ed. 1990) (discussing possibility that deer and other hunted animals exhibit similar behavior).

110. *See* Robert W. Kates, *Population, Technology, and the Human Environment: A Thread through Time*, 125 Daedalus 43 (1996).

111. *See* Charles E. Longino, Jr., & John R. Earle, *Who Are the Grandparents at Century's End?* 20 Generations 13 (1996); John Herberg, *Census Data Reveal 70s Legacy: Poorer Cities and Richer Suburbs*, N.Y. Times, Feb. 27, 1983, at G1.

NOTES CHAPTER 2

1. Jean Stefancic & Richard Delgado, No Mercy: How Conservative Think Tanks and Foundations Changed America's Social Agenda (1996).

2. Kowalsky had cited, *e.g.*, Robert A. Burt, *Judges, Behavioral Scientists, and the Demands of Humanity*, 143 U. Pa. L. Rev. 179, 183–85, 187–91 (1994).

3. *E.g.*, Shelden Novick, *Justice Holmes' Philosophy*, 70 Wash. U. L. Q. 703, 729 (1929).

4. *See e.g.*, Harlan Dalton, Racial Healing (1997); Richard Delgado, *Two Ways to Think about Race: Reflections on the Id, the Ego, and Other Reformist Themes of Equal Protection*, 89 Geo. L.J. 2279 (2001).

5. *See* Michael Olivas, *Breaking the Law on Principle*, 52 U. Pitt. L. Rev. 815 (1991) (describing career and disappearance of radical lawyer Oscar "Zeta" Acosta).

NOTES TO CHAPTER 3

1. On preventive detention, see John Kaplan et al., Criminal Law 59–70 (3d ed., 1996).

2. On emergency mental commitment, see Frank W. Miller et al., The Mental Health Process 301–17 (2d ed. 1976).

3. *See* chapter 4, this volume, on this and other wartime measures.

4. *See* chapter 4, this volume.

5. *Id.*

6. *See* Richard Delgado, *Rodrigo's Chronicle*, 101 Yale L.J. 1357, 1407–11 (1992) (Rodrigo posits selective disruption as possible strategy for social reform).

NOTES TO CHAPTER 4

1. *See* text and notes 6–25, 37–40, 50–52 *infra*.

2. *See* text and notes 36–37 *infra*; USA Patriot Act §§ 203, 213–15, 411–12, amending various sections of 8 U.S.C. 1182, 3123; 18 U.S.C. § 3123; 50 U.S.C. §§ 1804, 1823.

3. *See* chapter 3.

4. *See* Jim Ruttenberg, *Torture Seeps into Discussion by News Media*, N.Y. Times, Nov. 5, 2001; Walter Pincus, *Silent Suspects: U.S. May Get Tough*, Int'l Herald Trib., Oct. 22, 2001.

5. *Id.*

6. *E.g.*, Jack M. Balkin, *Using Our Fears to Justify a Power Grab*, L.A. Times, Nov. 29, 2001; Jack M. Balkin, *The New Regulation*, N.Y. Times, Nov. 28, 2001, at B7; Philip Shenon & Don Van Natta, Jr., *U.S. Says 3 Detainees May Be Tied to Highjacking*, N.Y. Times, Nov. 1, 2001, at A1.

7. Frank Rich, *Wait until Dark*, N.Y. Times, Nov. 24, 2001, at A25; Philip Shenon, *Justice Dept. Wants to Query More Foreigners*, N.Y. Times, Mar. 21, 2002, at A28.

8. Ruttenberg, *supra*.

9. Pincus, *supra*; Patricia Williams, *The Dangerous Patriot's Game*, Observer, Dec. 2, 2001 (naming Alan Dershowitz).

10. Amy Goldstein, *Detention Effort Aimed at Preventing More Terror*, Wash. Post, Nov. 6, 2001; Testimony of Attorney General John Ashcroft, Sen. Comm. on the Judiciary, Sept. 25, 2001. The bill that actually passed granted the Attorney General practically all that he had asked for. See USA Patriot Act, Pub. L. No. 107–56, 115 Stat. 272 (2001).

11. Katharine Q. Seelye, *Pentagon Says Acquittals May Not Free Detainees*, N.Y. Times, Mar. 22, 2002, at A13.

12. Somini Sengupta, *Ill-Fated Path to America, Jail and Death*, N.Y. Times, Nov. 5, 2001, at A1.

13. Testimony of John Ashcroft, *supra*; John Gibeau, *Winds of Change*, A.B.A.J., Nov. 2001, at 32.

14. Testimony of John Ashcroft, *supra*; Deborah L. Rhode, *Terrorists and Their Lawyers*, N.Y. Times, Apr. 16, 2002, at A9; *Feds Want to Monitor Attorney-Client Calls*, Boulder Daily Camera, Nov. 10, 2001.

15. Al Knight, *Immigration's New Looks*, Denver Post, Oct. 21, 2001, at E5; William Safire, *Threat of National ID*, N.Y. Times, Dec. 24, 2001 at A17 (mentioning

microchip implant technology, now used for straying pets, could be used for tracking humans).

16. Sarah Lyall, *Britain May Require ID Cards for All*, N.Y. Times, Sept. 23, 2001, at A8.

17. Knight, *supra*.

18. *Id.*

19. Lyall, *supra*.

20. *See* Mathew Purdy, *Bush's New Rules to Fight Terror Transforming Legal Landscape*, N.Y. Times, Nov. 25, 2001, at A1; Arlen Specter, *Questioning the President's Authority*, N.Y. Times, Nov. 28, 2001, at A27.

21. Specter, *supra*; Purdy, *supra*.

22. Pam Belluck, *Hue and Murmur over Curbed Rights*, N.Y. Times, Nov. 17, 2001, at B8; Robert Scher, *Abandoning Principles Won't Provide Freedom*, Boulder Daily Camera, Nov. 21, 2001, at 5A.

23. Purdy, *supra*.

24. William Safire, *Military Tribunals Modified*, N.Y. Times, Mar. 21, 2002, at A33. The new rules still permit the use of hearsay evidence, provide no civilian court review, no jury, and allow for indefinite detention before a suspect is tried.

25. Goldstein, *supra*.

26. Shenon & Van Natta, Jr., *supra* note 6.

27. Fox Butterfield, *Police Are Split on Questioning of Mideast Men*, N.Y. Times, Nov. 22, 2001, at A1.

28. Bob Herbert, *Rudy's No-Exit Strategy*, N.Y. Times, Oct. 1, 2001, at A23; *The Mayor's Dangerous Idea (Editorial)*, N.Y. Times, Sept. 28, 2001, at A30.

29. Balkin, *Grab, supra*; Paul Krugman, *Another Useful Crisis*, N.Y. Times, Nov. 11, 2001, at A13; David E. Rosenbaum, *Since Sept. 11, Lobbyists Use New Pitches for Old Pleas*, N.Y. Times, Dec. 3, 2001, at B1; Sharon Thelmer, *Groups Repackage Wish Lists as Vital*, Boulder Daily Camera, Nov. 26, 2001, at 7A.

30. Richard Reeves, *Patriotism Calls Out the Censor*, N.Y. Times, Oct. 1, 2001, at A23.

31. *E.g.*, Richard Cohen, *Thanks for the Gift of America*, Boulder Daily Camera, Nov. 25, 2001, at 3D; Frank Rich, *The End of the Beginning*, N.Y. Times, Sept. 29, 2001, at A23.

32. Richard Delgado, When Equality Ends: Stories of Race and Resistance 127–42 (1999).

33. *Id. See also* chapter 2, at text and note 3.

34. Reeves, *supra*.

35. *Id.*; Timothy Egan, *In Sacramento, A Publisher's Questions Draw Wrath of Crowd*, N.Y. Times, Dec. 21, 2001 at B1, col. 1 (audience booed newspaper publisher who questioned U.S. policy); *see also* Diana Jean Schemo, *New Battles in Old War over Freedom of Speech*, N.Y. Times, Nov. 25, 2001, at B6 (attacks on professors, students, and others critical of administration's war policy).

36. *See also* Robert H. Giles, *Why Are We Hiding bin Laden?* N.Y. Times, Nov. 11, 2001, §4 at 13.

37. *E.g.*, Richard Delgado et al., Words That Wound (1993); Richard Delgado, The Coming Race War? And Other Apocalyptic Tales of America after Affirmative Action and Welfare 66–67 (1996).

38. William F. Wechsler, *Terror's Money Trail*, N.Y. Times, Sept. 26, 2001, at A23; *5 Months after Sanctions against Somali Company, Scant Proof on Qaeda Tie*, N.Y. Times, Apr. 13, 2002, at A10; Donald G. McNeil, *How Blocking Assets Erased a Wisp of Prosperity*, N.Y. Times, Apr. 13, 2002, at A19.

39. Linda Greenhouse, *In New York Visit, O'Connor Foresees Limits on Freedom*, N.Y. Times, Sept. 29, 2001, at B5.

40. *Id.*

41. *Id.*

42. *Id.*

43. David Cole, *Liberties in a Time of Fear*, N.Y. Times, Sept. 25, 2001, at A29.

44. *Civil Liberties vs. Threats to Society through U.S. History*, N.Y. Times, Nov. 10, 2001 (unsigned).

45. *Id.*

46. *Id.*

47. *Id.*

48. *Id.*; Diana Z. Anhalt, A Gathering of Fugitives (2002).

49. Richard Delgado, *Derrick Bell's Toolkit: Fit to Dismantle That Famous House?* 75 N.Y.U. L. Rev. 283 (2000).

50. *Threats to Society, supra.*

51. *Id.*

52. Greenhouse, *supra.*

53. *Id.*

54. *See Questions about Military Tribunals* (box), N.Y. Times, Dec. 26, 2001, at B6, implying that recent measures, including new wartime tribunals, might violate the Third Geneva Convention on the treatment of prisoners of war. *See also* Hugo Young, *Guantanamo Could Be Where America and Europe Part Company*, (London) Guardian, Jan. 17, 2002.

55. William Safire, *Colin Powell Dissents*, N.Y. Times, Jan. 28, 2002, at A21, col. 5.

56. Katharine Q. Seelye, *A P.O.W. Tangle: What the Law Says*, N.Y. Times, Jan. 29, 2002, at A14, col. 1. But the government seems to have returned to its earlier position. See Dirty Bombz and Civil Rights (Editorial), N.Y. Times, June 17, 2002, at A20 (describing the case of Jose Padilla, deemed an enemy combatant subject to indefinite detention).

57. William Pfaff, *Bush Warning to Allies Grates on European Nerves*, Int'l Herald Tribune, Nov. 12, 2001, at 8. *See also* Natasha Hearst, *Rethinking Pacifism: The Quaker's Dilemma in a Time of War*, Amer. Prospect, Dec. 3, 2001, at 14

(reporting that a prominent columnist called pacifism, in today's setting, "evil" and "on the side of murderers").

58. Neil A. Lewis, *Ashcroft Defends Antiterror Plan, Says May Aid U.S. Foes*, N.Y. Times, Dec. 7, 2001, at A1; Frank Rich, *Confessions of a Traitor*, N.Y. Times, Dec. 8, 2001, at A25, col. 1.

59. Gaylord Shaw, *First Lady, Justice Launching Civics Project*, Boulder Daily Camera, Jan. 28, 2002, at 8A, col. 3.

60. Richard Delgado, The Rodrigo Chronicles, chapter 6, Black Crime, White Fears: On the Social Construction of Threat (1995).

61. Text and notes 1–22, 30–31, 33–45 *supra*.

62. Text and notes 30–31, 40–45 *supra*.

NOTES TO CHAPTER 5

1. On this and other exceptions to the rule of informed consent (and on the doctrine itself), *see, e.g.*, William Prosser, Handbook of the Law of Torts § 18 (4th ed. 1971).

2. *Id.*

3. *Id.*

4. *E.g.*, Amy Goldstein, *Detention Effort Aimed at Preventing More Terror*, Wash. Post, Nov. 6, 2001; Anthony Lewis, *It Can Happen Here*, N.Y. Times, Nov. 11, 2001.

5. The doctrine holds that Congress has unlimited ("plenary") power to enact rules, unreviewable by courts, in this area of law.

6. U.S. Const. Amend IV.

7. On these and other exceptions to the warrant and good cause requirement, *see, e.g.*, Ronald N. Boyce & Rollin M. Perkins, Criminal Law and Procedure 136–94 (8th ed. 1999).

8. *Id.*

9. *Id.*

10. Prosser, *supra*, at §§ 93, 95, 97.

11. *Id.* at § 97.

12. *Id.*, John W. Wade et al., Cases and Materials on Torts 807–8 (9th ed. 1994).

13. Robert M. Cover, *Violence and the Word*, 95 Yale L.J. 1601, 1609 (1986).

14. *Id.*

15. Alfredo Mirandé, The Mexican Exception (in progress 2001).

16. *Id.*

17. *See* Richard Delgado, *Rodrigo's Chronicle*, 101 Yale L.J. 1357, 1377–78 (1992).

18. *Id.* at 1377.

19. *Id.* at 1368.

20. *Id.* at 1377–78.

21. Martin Luther King, *Letter from a Birmingham Jail,* in Why We Can't Wait 76–95 (1964).

22. Delgado, *Chronicle, supra,* at 1377–78. *See also* Richard Delgado, The Rodrigo Chronicles 53 (1995).

23. *See generally* chapter 4.

24. Delgado, *Chronicle, supra,* at 1379.

25. Chapter 2, this volume.

26. Delgado, *Chronicle, supra,* at 1369–75.

27. *Id.* at 1364–65.

28. *Id.* at 1377–78.

29. We never had that conversation, at least during the period I'm recounting. What formative experiences, which certain Western countries supposedly lacked, was Rodrigo referring to? Presumably, he meant to include the United States. Would he take the position that, like children denied the opportunity to play in the sandbox with other children, we had grown to national maturity without learning lessons we needed to know? I made a mental note to ask him about it sometime in the future.

30. Delgado, *Chronicle, supra,* at 1378; *see also* Martin Crutsinger, *Are Terrorism, Globalization Two Sides of the Same Coin?* Boulder Daily Camera, Apr. 3, 2002, at 1A.

31. *See* Alexander Stille, *What Is America's Place in the World?* N.Y. Times, Jan. 11, 2002, at A17 (setting out six alternative strategies in effort against terrorism).

32. *Cf.* Saad Mehio, *How Islam and Politics Mixed,* N.Y. Times, Dec. 2, 2001, at 15 (op-ed).

33. *See* Arundhati Roy, *The Algebra of Infinite Justice,* Guardian, Sept. 29, 2001.

34. *Id.*

35. *Id.*

36. Courtland Milloy, *Good vs. Evil vs. Greed,* Boulder Daily Camera, Nov. 25, 2001, at E1. *See also* Paul Krugman, *The Scrooge Syndrome,* N.Y. Times, Dec. 25, 2001, at A19, col. 6; George McGovern, *The Healing in Helping the World's Poor,* N.Y. Times, Nov. 2, 2001, at A23, col. 3.

37. Delgado, The Rodrigo Chronicles, *supra,* at 46–56.

NOTES TO CHAPTER 6

1. On the black-white binary of race, which holds that the experiences of only two groups—the black and the white—define the terms of racial discussion,

so that Asians, Latinos, Indians, and other groups enter into the analysis only to the extent that they succeed in analogizing themselves to blacks, see Richard Delgado, When Equality Ends: Stories about Race and Resistance 109–25 (1999); Juan Perea, *The Black/White Binary Paradigm of Race: The "Normal Science" of American Racial Thought*, 85 Calif. L. Rev. 1347 (1997).

2. Cultural nationalism is the view that the prime business of any minority group of color is to advance its own interests and tend to its own community first.

3. *See, e.g.,* the Spike Lee film *Jungle Fever*, which draws attention to this tension in black thought.

4. On Malcolm X's attitude toward his white forebear, see Cornel West, Race Matters 103 (1993).

5. *See They're (Nearly) All Centrists Now*, Economist, July 7, 2001 (reporting National Alliance's victory in Member of Parliament race for seat representing Naples of candidate Alessandra Mussolini).

6. *See, e.g.,* Delgado, When Equality Ends, *supra*, at 1–22.

7. 388 U.S. 1 (1967).

8. Aimee Welch, *When Voters Are the Legislators*, Insight on the News, Dec. 11, 2000, at 22.

9. For a discussion of this and other, competing theories of racism, *see* Richard Delgado et al., *Fairness and Formality: Minimizing the Risk of Prejudice in Alternative Dispute Resolution*, 1985 Wis. L. Rev. 1359.

10. For a discussion of this and similar interpretations by social scientists, *see* Derrick Bell, Race, Racism, and American Law 334 (3d ed. 2001). *See also* Rachel Moran, Interracial Intimacy (2002).

11. Bell, *supra* at 333.

12. *Id.* at 335 (summarizing view of Joel Kovel).

13. *Id.* at 334 (describing views of social scientists Grier and Cobbs).

14. *Cf. id.* at 335.

15. *See* William F. Schmidt, *Birth to 59-Year Old Briton Raises Ethical Storm*, N.Y. Times, Dec. 29, 1993, at A1 (describing laboratory of Italian physician who successfully implanted a fertilized egg donated by a younger woman in a post-menopausal patient, who went on to give birth to a healthy infant).

16. Patrick Buchanan, The Death of the West (2002).

17. W. E. B. Du Bois, The Souls of Black Folk 2–15 (1903)

NOTES TO CHAPTER 7

1. Richard Herrnstein & Charles Murray, The Bell Curve: Intelligence and Class Structure in American Life (1994).

2. *See* Richard Delgado, When Equality Ends: Stories about Race and Resistance 1–25 (1999).

3. *Id.* at 3–5, 17.

4. *Id.* at 6–15.

5. *Id.*

6. Ian Haney Lopez, White by Law: The Legal Construction of Race (1997).

7. *Id.* at xiii, 1, 49–109.

8. *Id.* at 49–109, 223–25 (appendices A, B).

9. *Id.* at 146–50, 155–95.

10. Robert L. Hayman, The Smart Culture: Society, Intelligence, and Law (1998).

11. *See, e.g.*, Nicholas Lemann, The Big Test (1999); Richard Delgado, *Official Elitism or Institutional Self Interest? 10 Reasons Why U.C.-Davis Should Abandon the LSAT (and Why Other Good Law Schools Should Follow Suit) (2000 Edward L. Barrett, J. Lecture)*, 34 U.C.-Davis L. Rev. 593 (2001).

12. *See* Roe v. Wade, 410 U.S. 113 (1973).

13. *See* Maher v. Roe, 432 U.S. 464 (1977).

14. *See* Dandridge v. Williams, 397 U.S. 471 (1970).

15. *See* N.Y. Ed. Law §§ 340, 342(2) (2001).

16. *See* Skinner v. Oklahoma, 316 U.S. 535 (1942).

17. *See* Loving v. Virginia, 388 U.S. 1 (1967), which was decided thirteen years after Brown v. Board of Education, 347 U.S. 483 (1954).

18. *See* Jean Stefancic & Richard Delgado, No Mercy: How Conservative Think Tanks and Foundations Changed America's Social Agenda 45–81 (1990).

19. *Id.* at 33–44.

20. *See* William E. Schmidt, *Trial May Focus on Race Genetics*, N.Y. Times, Sept. 6, 1994, at A16.

21. *See* Jack West, Licensing Parents (1995); Howard B. Eisenberg, *A "Model" Proposal: State Licensing of Parents*, 26 Conn. L. Rev. 1415 (1994).

22. *See* Richard Delgado, *Two Ways to Think about Race: Reflections on the Id, the Ego, and Other Reformist Theories of Equal Protection*, 89 Geo. L. J. 2279 (2001).

23. Derrick Bell, Brown v. Board of Education *and the Interest-Convergence Dilemma*, 93 Harv. L. Rev. 518 (1980).

24. 347 U.S. 483 (1954).

25. Bell, *supra.*

26. Alan Freeman, *Legitimizing Racial Discrimination through Antidiscrimination Law: A Critical Review of Supreme Court Doctrine*, 62 Minn. L. Rev. 1049 (1978); Girardeau Spann, *Pure Politics*, 88 Mich. L. Rev. 1971 (1990).

27. Spann, *supra.*

28. *See, e.g.*, Peter Brimelow, Alien Nation: Common Sense about America's Immigration Disaster (1995).

29. *Id.*

30. Delgado, Two Ways, *supra.*

31. On formalism and its critique, see Robert Hayman, Nancy Levit, & Richard Delgado, Jurisprudence—Classical to Contemporary: From Natural Law to Postmodernism (2002). On the critique of the First Amendment version, *see* Richard Delgado, *First Amendment Formalism Is Giving Way to First Amendment Legal Realism*, 29 Harv. C.R.-C.L.L Rev. 169 (1994).

32. Stanley Fish, The Trouble with Principle (1999).

33. *See* chapter 9, this volume.

34. *See* chapter 10, this volume.

35. *See* chapter 11, this volume.

36. *See* Charles Lawrence, *If He Hollers, Let Him Go: Regulating Racist Speech on Campus*, 1996 Duke L.J. 431; Nadine Strossen, *Regulating Hate Speech on Campus: A Modest Proposal?* 1990 Duke L.J. 404.

37. *Id.*

38. *See Taking Part: FSM and the Legacy of Social Protest* (April 13, 2001) (conference program, on file with author). The speakers included Bettina Aptheker, Richard Delgado, Elaine Kim, Robert Moses, Carlos MuÒoz, Charles Muscatine, Orville Schell, Nadine Strossen, Jack Weinberg, Sheldon Wolin, & Reginald Zelnik.

39. *See, e.g.*, American Booksellers v. Hudnut, 771 F.2d 323 (7th Cir. 1985), *aff'd*, 475 U.S. 1001 (1986) (striking down Indianapolis antipornography ordinance).

40. *See, e.g.*, People v. Collins, 578 F.2d 1197 (7th Cir.), *cert. denied*, 439 U.S. 916 (1978).

41. Steven Shiffrin, Dissent, Injustice, and the Meanings of America 49–87 (1999). *See* Richard Delgado, *Toward a Legal Realist View of the First Amendment*, 113 Harv. L. Rev. 778 (2000) (discussing the dissent view).

42. *See id.* at 5–7, 9, 60–61, 63–87.

43. *See* Tamar Lewin, *Job Offer to Feminist Scholar May Mark Turn*, N.Y. Times, Feb. 24, 1989, at B10.

44. *See, e.g.*, Robert Stevens, Law School: Legal Education in America from the 1850s to the 1980s, at 6–10, 22–28 (1982); Hayman et al., *supra* at 2–6.

45. Hayman, *supra* at 2–5; Stevens, *supra* at 3–6.

46. Stevens, *supra* at 35–41; Christopher Columbus Langdell, *Teaching Law as a Science*, 21 Am. L. Rev. 123, 123–25 (1887).

47. *See* Langdell, *supra;* Stevens, *supra.*

48. *See* Jerome Frank, Law and the Modern Mind (1930); Felix Cohen, *Transcendental Nonsense and the Functional Approach*, 35 Colum. L. Rev. 809 (1935); Karl Llewellyn, *Some Realism about Realism: Responding to Dean Pound*, 44 Harv. L. Rev. 1222 (1931); Roscoe Pound, *Mechanical Jurisprudence*, 8 Colum. L. Rev. 605 (1908).

49. *E.g.*, Cohen, *supra*; Pound, *supra.*

50. *See* Richard Delgado & Jean Stefancic, Critical Race Theory: An Introduction 2–6 (2001); Delgado, *First Amendment Formalism, supra.*

51. *See* Delgado, *First Amendment Formalism, supra.*

52. *Id.* at 170.

53. Interview with University of Colorado administrator, Oct. 2000, in Boulder, Colo.

54. *See* Delgado, *Legal Realist View, supra* (positing a similar legal-realist analysis).

55. *Id.* at 794–95

56. Richard Delgado, *Words That Wound: A Tort Action for Racial Insults, Epithets, and Name-Calling,* 17 Harv. C.R.-C.L. L. Rev. 133 (1982).

57. *See* Catharine MacKinnon, Only Words 54–55, 109–10 (1998); Richard Delgado & Laura Lederer, eds., The Price We Pay: The Case against Hate Propaganda and Pornography 163–68 (1995).

58. *See* MacKinnon, *supra* at 109, 141 n. 28; Jack M. Balkin, *Some Realism about Pluralism: Legal Realist Approaches to the First Amendment,* 1990 Duke L. J. 375.

59. Delgado, *Legal Realist View, supra* at 794–95.

60. Richard Delgado & Jean Stefancic, Must We Defend Nazis? Hate Speech, Pornography, and the New First Amendment 88–89 (1997).

61. *Id.*

62. Thurgood Marshall, *Essay, The Constitution's Bicentennial: Commemorating the Wrong Document?* 40 Vand. L. Rev. 1337 (1987) (reprinting address to the Hawaii patent bar).

63. *Id.* at 1342.

64. *Id.* at 1338–39.

65. *Id.* at 1338.

66. The Thirteenth Amendment, which abolished slavery, entered into force in 1865.

67. *See, e.g.,* Juan Perea, Richard Delgado, Angela Harris, & Stephanie Wildman, Race and Races: Cases and Materials for a Diverse America 758–76 (1999); Richard Delgado & David Yun, *Bloodied Chickens: An Analysis of Paternalistic Objections to Hate-Speech Regulation,* 82 Calif. L. Rev. 871, 881–82 (1994).

68. Walker v. City of Birmingham, 388 U.S. 307 (1967).

69. *Id.*

70. *See* Balkin, *supra.*

71. Delgado & Lederer, The Price We Pay, *supra* at 163–68. On the role of the ACLU on expanding protection for commercial speech, *see, e.g.,* Samuel Walker, In Defense of American Liberties (1990); Robert Dreyfuss, *Philip Morris Money,* Am. Prospect, Mar. 27, 2000, at 20; Morton Mintz, *The ACLU's Tobacco*

Addiction; American Civil Liberties Union Receiving Donations from Tobacco Industry, The Progressive, Dec. 1995, at 17.

72. *See* Dinesh D'Souza, Illiberal Education: The Politics of Race and Sex on Campus (1991) (complaining of oppressive liberalism and political correctness at U.S. universities).

73. On the erosion of the Fourteenth Amendment, *see, e.g.,* Richard Delgado, When Equality Ends: Stories of Race and Resistance 1–77 (1999).

74. I am grateful to Joe Thome, Professor of Law, University of Wisconsin, for this suggestion.

75. Thanks to Mark Tushnet for this suggestion.

76. *See, e.g.,* Diana Jean Schemo, *Ad Intended to Stir Up Campuses More than Succeeds in Its Mission*, N.Y. Times, Mar. 21, 2001, at A1.

77. *See* Julie Bosman, *The (No) Free Speech Movement*, Wall St. J., Mar. 14, 2001, at A22, praising Horowitz for raising tough issues.

78. *See* Archive, The Free Speech Movement, in Bancroft Library, University of California, Berkeley.

79. On this aspect of the First Amendment, see Delgado & Stefancic, Defend Nazis, *supra* at 89.

80. *Id.* (showing how accepted ideas acquire aura of truth by means of this mechanism).

81. *Id.*

82. Morris Berman, The Twilight of American Culture 36 (2000).

83. David Skover & Ronald Collins, The Death of Discourse 5 (1998).

84. Berman, *supra* at 47–48; Andre Schiffrin, *For Serious Publishing, How Good Were the Good Old Days?* Chron. Higher Ed., Feb. 25, 2000, at B9.

85. *Id.*

86. Leslie Walker, *Buried Under a Mountain of Spam*, Wash. Post, May 3, 2001, at E01.

87. Berman, *supra* at 33.

88. *Id.* at 35.

89. *Id.* at 35–37.

90. *Id.*

91. *Id.* at 48.

92. *See, e.g.,* Delgado & Stefancic, Defend Nazis, *supra* at 66–68.

93. Alexander Tsesis, Destructive Messages (NYU Press, 2002).

94. *See* Frank Michelman, *Civil Liberties, Silencing, and Subordination*, in Delgado & Lederer, The Price We Pay, *supra* at 272.

95. 376 U.S. 254 (1964).

96. *Viz.,* ordinary communications that inadvertently turn out to be false and defamatory, or to violate norms of privacy and commercial secrets.

97. *See* Leslie Berger, *Program Hopes Girls' Lives Imitate Art: Pieces Show Beauty Is More than Thin Deep*, N.Y. Times, July 23, 2000, at A1–38 (on native girls

in remote villages who, soon after the arrival of cable TV, began dieting to lose weight).

98. *Cf.* Marshall Windmiller, *Berkeley Revolt, in* The Berkeley Student Revolt 414–15 (Seymor Martin Lipset & Sheldon S. Wolin, eds. 1965) (observing that the San Francisco Examiner portrayed the free speech protestors at UC Berkeley as little more than vandals).

99. *See* Cal. Const. art. I, § 31 (prohibiting any consideration of race in university admissions and governmental contracts).

NOTES TO CHAPTER 8

1. Stanley Fish, The Trouble with Principle (1999).

2. *Id.* at 3–4, 9–10, 43–45.

3. *Id.* at 3–4.

4. Stanley Fish, Doing What Comes Naturally: Change, Rhetoric, and the Practice of Theory in Literary and Legal Studies (1989).

5. Stanley Fish, Is There a Text in This Class? The Authority of Interpretive Communities (1980).

6. Stanley Fish, There's No Such Thing as Free Speech, and It's a Good Thing, Too (1994).

7. Fish, Trouble with Principle, *supra* at 95–150; 4, 20–21, 26–35, 310; 34–35; 153–284.

8. *E.g., id.* at 1–8, 89–94.

9. *E.g., id.* at 1–8, 89–94, 242–43.

10. *E.g., id.* at 3, 8–10, 44–46, 115–17, 142–46.

11. *Id.* at 7.

12. For example, courts often expect lawyers to recite cases (a type of principle) in support of their position, and in close cases tolerate arguments based on public policy.

13. Fish, *supra* at 5–19, 11–13, 43 (questioning whether any policy can treat fairly and equally groups with radically different histories and current situations).

14. *Id.* at 21–26.

15. *Id.* at 26.

16. *Id.* at 3, 4–7, 9, 12–14, 146, 242, 287, 293. When an argument is framed in a way that "labels itself a higher morality [it ends up being] so high that, from its lofty perspective, we are unable to see either the forest or the trees."

17. *Id.* at 29–34.

18. *Id.* at 93–94.

19. *Id.* at 89.

20. *Id.*

21. *Id.*

22. Oliver Sacks, The Man Who Mistook His Wife for a Hat, and Other Clinical Tales (1985).

23. *See id.* at 42–52 (ch. 3, *The Disembodied Lady*).

24. *Id.* at 42–44.

25. *Id.* at 44, 50–52.

26. *Id.* at 44, 50, 52.

27. *See* Fish, Trouble with Principle, *supra* at 20–21, 67–71, 88, 142–46, 242–43.

28. *Id.* at 75, 89, ch. 6. Like the patient whose proprioception is compromised, legal thinkers can go through their professional lives slightly (or in some cases, greatly) "out of touch," but unable to quite put their finger on why. Like the patient, their sense of self is skewed, their positional senses dictated by principles that, rather than being full of meaning and, therefore, providing some semblance of guidance, are literally empty—waiting to be spewed to fit any agenda, waiting to be filled in the blank to justify whichever outcome is sought. The contradictory results that Fish cites—restrictions on affirmative action, protecting speech that ends up suppressing other voices, the hypocrisy of academic freedom, our schizophrenic view of religion—are each a result of this artificial guidance system. *See* Jack M. Balkin, *Court Defers to a Racist Era*, S.F. Chron., May 21, 2000, at 7 (noting that the Supreme Court and Congress view much of civil rights legislation as based on interstate commerce clause, when a more natural home would be the Fourteenth Amendment). Just as Sacks's Christina "consciously or automatically adopted and sustained a sort of forced or willful or histrionic posture to make up for the continuing lack of any genuine posture" (Sacks, *supra* at 44), by relying on a flawed guidance system, the legal actor backs into awkward, inauthentic results.

Who, then, will be the neurologist for our society? We will have to dismantle our rhetoric, suggests Fish, and realize that to hide behind principle is like kicking someone underneath a glass table—you are fooling no one. When we step away from the constraints of principle, we will walk straight again. For example, when we step back from the notion of a color-blind Constitution we will recognize that it does make a difference if the active party is the KKK or the NAACP. Similarly, when we are free from the clutches of a lofty but empty notion of individual rights, we will see that a Shakespearean sonnet and hard-core pornography are distinct. By recognizing that one cannot have a procedural mechanism that is not "hostage to judgments of substance" (Fish, Trouble with Principle, *supra* at 2, 74, 117) one will no longer be forced to defend speech acts one despises, nor brush one's values aside for the sake of procedural purity.

29. *Id.* at 301, 306.

30. *Id.* at 306.

31. *See* Chapter 4, Justice at War.

32. Except for one person—Karl Marx, On the Jewish Question (Helen Lederer trans., 1958)—and in an obscure passage, at that.

33. That is, the gap between the ostensibly egalitarian focus of the public law, and the selfish individualistic thrust of private law, has been justified by the supposed ability of anyone, regardless of his or her initial economic position, by dint of hard work to rise and gain access to the public sphere. *See, e.g.,* Nicholas Lehmann, The Big Test 24–30, 67–78 (1998); David Broder, *Democracy Derailed*, Sunday Daily Camera (Boulder, Colo.), Apr. 20, 2000, at E1.

34. *See, e.g.,* Holly Sklar et al., *The Growing Wealth Gap*, Z Mag., May 1999, at 47. Decrying gross inequity as dangerous to democracy, see Jack M. Balkin, *The Declaration and the Promise of a Democratic Culture*, 4 Widener L. Symp. J. 167 (1999).

35. *See* Roger C. Altman, *The Fourth World; On a Global Scale, Technology Has Created a Huge Gap between the "Haves" and the "Have-Nots,"* L.A. Times, Dec. 12, 1999, at M1; Sklar, *supra; Brother, Can You Spare a Billion?* Z Mag., Dec. 1999, at 23.

36. Lemann, *supra* at 24–30, 67–78 (1998).

37. *See* Symposium, *Campaign Finance as a Civil Rights Issue*, 43 Howard L.J. 5 (1999); Molly Ivins, *Soon the Word "Politics" Will Mean "Money,"* Boulder Daily Camera, Mar. 8, 2000, at 9A.

38. Laurence Tribe, American Constitutional Law 1454–1553, 1590–93, 1620–13 (2d ed. 1998).

39. *E.g.,* John Noonan, Jr., Bribes (1984).

40. *E.g.,* Lawrence A. Sullivan, Handbook of the Law of Antitrust 1–6, 11–12, 19–40, 114–40 (1977) (discussing antitrust doctrines aimed at normalizing economic efficiency, deterring monopolies, and price fixing).

41. *E.g.,* Harry G. Henn & John R. Alexander, Laws of Corporations 644–56, 823–36 (3d ed. 1983) (describing policies against insider trading).

42. That is, that structure is not only poorly adapted to counter official oppression, but it is unlikely to sustain any sort of coherent social program, at least on its own.

43. *See* note 30–31, *supra.*

NOTES TO CHAPTER 9

1. *See* Stanley Fish, *Condemnation without Absolutes*, N.Y. Times, Oct. 15, 2001, at A19.

2. J. E. Zimmerman, Dictionary of Classical Mythology 146 (1964). The theme of zealous, overbroad retribution runs through many classical myths and tales. *See e.g., id.* at 146 (tale of the Marathonian Bull), 175 (Latona's revenge), 179 (Oeax's dangerous lighthouse), 212 (Atreus's gruesome dinner). *See also* The

History of Herodotus 2 (George Rawlinson trans., Manuel Komroff ed., 1939) (recounting that, at one point a group of Greeks kidnapped some Asian women. While not responding directly, some time later the Asians did the same to a single Greek girl. Thereafter, "for the sake of a single Lacedaemonian girl [the Greeks] collected a vast armament, invaded Asia, and destroyed the kingdom of Priam.").

For a similar parable of sweeping retribution, see New Amer. Bible, *Judges* 9:1–45 (Saint Joseph ed.), in which Abimelech governed Chechem, having risen to power after slaughtering his brothers. After learning that Gaal had publicly criticized him, Abimelech sent his army out to fight the people of the city. The villagers retreated within the confines of the city. The next day, when they went out to work the fields, Abimelech's men attacked, killing everyone, destroying the city, and finally, salting the earth.

3. Mari Matsuda, *On Causation*, 100 Colum. L. Rev. 2195 (2001).

4. *Id.* at 2195 (introductory précis); 2211–15. Matsuda also urges two additional measures—that we mourn others' pain, and act to relieve it. See *id.* at 2219–20. *See also* text and notes *infra* (discussing a third, personalistic account).

5. *Id.* at 2211.

6. *Id.*

7. *Id.* at 2215–18.

8. *Id.* at 2218.

9. *Id.*

10. *Id.*

11. *Id.* at 2218.

12. *Id.* at 2201 ("No person is ever an individual acting without consequences to others. Individual bad deeds . . . cause our collective illness"); 2209 ("advocat[ing] a broadly collectivist notion of cause and responsibility"); 2217 ("We must see the web of connection and hold our collective selves responsible for any harm to another human being.").

13.

> no man is an island, entire of itself;
> every man is a piece of the continent a part of the main;
> . . .
> any man's death diminishes me, because I am involved in mankind;
> and therefore never send to know *for whom the bell tolls;*
> it tolls for thee.
> —John Donne, John Donne: Selections from Divine Poems, Sermons,
>   Devotions and Prayers 272 (John Booty ed., 1990).

14. *See* F.R.C.P. 23.

15. *See* F.R.C.P. 18–24.

16. *E.g.*, Kallenberg v. Beth Israel Hosp., 45 A.D.2d 177, 357 N.Y.S.2d 508 (1974), *aff'd* N.Y.2d 719, 337 N.E.2d 128, 374 N.Y.S.2d 615 (1975); Joseph H. King,

Jr., *Causation, Valuation, and Chance in Personal Injury Torts Involving Preexisting Conditions and Future Consequences*, 90 Yale L.J. 1353 (1981).

17. Summers v. Tice, 33 Cal.2d 80, 199 P.2d 1 (1948) (extending causation-in-fact rules to shift burden of proof onto each of two defendants who acted separately and in negligent fashion toward plaintiff).

18. *See* Sindell v. Abbott Laboratories, Inc., 26 Cal.3d 588, 607 P.2d 94, 163 Cal. Rptr. 132, *cert. denied*, 449 U.S. 912 (1980) (applying *Summers v. Tice* rule in a products liability suit against nine defendants).

19. *Id.*

20. *See* Rubanick v. Witco Chem. Corp., 593 A.2d 733 (N.J.) 1991); Richard Delgado, *Beyond Sindell: Relaxation of Cause-in- Fact Rules for Indeterminate Plaintiffs*, 70 Calif. L. Rev. 881 (1982).

21. Delgado, *Beyond Sindell, supra.*

22. United States v. Allen, 588 F. Supp. 247 (D. Utah 1984), *rev'd*, 816 F.2d 1417 (10th Cir. 1987).

23. *Id.* at 327–29.

24. *Id.* at 416–25.

25. In re Agent Orange Product Liability Litigation, 597 F. Supp. 740 (E.D. N.Y. 1984) (memo justifying class settlement).

26. *Id.*

27. A few states have begun holding parents liable for such acts. *See* La. Stat. Ann. § 2318 (2000); Fla. Stat. § 741.24 (2000); Haw. Rev. Stat. § 577 (2000); William Prosser & H. Page Keeton, Handbooks of the Law of Torts 199, 318, 384, 912, 914 (1994).

28. *See* David E. Sanger, *A Top Japanese Politician Calls U.S. Work Force Lazy*, N.Y. Times, Jan. 21, 1992 at D1 (Yoshio Sakurauchi, then speaker of Japan's lower house of Parliament, claimed the economic recession in the United States could be blamed on lazy workers and illiteracy).

29. *See, e.g.*, George Lipsitz, The Possessive Investment in Whiteness 142–43 (1998); William Raspberry, *Fact-Based Education*, Wash. Post, Nov. 29, 1996, at 71; Glenn Wolceshyn, *Socializing Students for Anarchy: In Eschewing Rational, Individual Thought, "Progressive" Education Foments Violence*, L.A. Times, Feb. 18, 1997, at 7.

30. *See, e.g.*, Kevin Vaughan, *Rocker Manson Blames Society for Columbine*, Rocky MT. News, June 2, 1999, at 7A.

31. *See, e.g.*, Chuck Green, *Jocks Still Hold Sway at School*, Denver Post, May 23, 1999, at B01.

32. *See, e.g.*, Kieran Nicholson et al., *Columbine Report Rips Police, Schools, Red Flags Ignored, Governor's Commission Says*, Denver Post, May 18, 2001, at A1.

33. *See, e.g.*, Mark Obmascik et al., *Tracing a Deadly Trail*, Denver Post, Apr. 27, 1999, at AA1.

34. *See, e.g.*, Patricia Callahan & Karen Auge, *Schools Seek Way to Defuse Bullying*, Denver Post, Apr. 23, 1999, at A1.

35. *See, e.g.*, Jessica Crosby, *Video Game Violence: Pushing the Wrong Buttons, Industry Zapped by Growing Controversy*, Wash. Post, Oct. 25, 1993, at C1.

36. *See, e.g.*, Lance Hannan & James Defronzo, *Welfare & Property Crime*, 15 Justice Q. 273 (1998).

37. Dinesh D'Souza, The End of Racism: Principles for a Multicultural Society 3, 16–17, 23, 260–62, 482–86 (1995); Stephan Thernstrom & Abigail Thernstrom, America in Black and White: One Nation, Indivisible 267 (1997).

38. *See, e.g.*, Thernstrom & Thernstrom, *supra*.

39. *See* Richard Delgado, When Equality Ends: Stories about Race and Resistance 37–54 (1999).

40. *See supra* this chapter.

41. See Mari Matsuda, *Looking to the Bottom: Critical Legal Studies and Reparations*, 22 Harv. C.R.-C.L. L. Rev 323 (1987) (advocating reparations as remedy for racial and other wrongs).

42. *See* Felicia R. Lee, *Foes of War Say Kerrey Was a Victim, Too*, N.Y. Times, May 6, 2001, at S4–1.

NOTES TO CHAPTER 10

1. Richard Delgado, When Equality Ends: Stories about Race and Resistance 55–78, 223–35 (1999); Jean Stefancic & Richard Delgado, No Mercy: How Conservative Think Tanks and Foundations Changed America's Social Agenda (1996).

2. Mary Dudziak, Cold War Civil Rights: Race and the Image of American Democracy 3–6 (2000).

3. Dudziak, Cold War, *supra*.

4. Mary L. Dudziak, *Desegregation as a Cold War Imperative*, 41 Stan. L. Rev. 61 (1988).

5. Derrick Bell, Brown v. Board of Education *and the Interest-Convergence Dilemma*, 93 Harv. L. Rev. 518 (1980).

6. Dudziak, Cold War, *supra* note 2, at 5–6, 11–17, 252.

7. *See, e.g.*, Derrick Bell, Race, Racism, and American Law (3d. ed. 2001)(landmark statement of this position).

8. *Id.* at 21–80 (ch. 2, American Racism and the Uses of History).

9. 163 U.S. 537 (1896).

10. 347 U.S. 483 (1954).

11. *See, e.g.*, Derrick Bell, Faces at the Bottom of the Well: The Permanence of Racism (1992); Richard Delgado & Jean Stefancic, *The Social Construction of*

Brown v. Board of Education: *Law Reform and the Reconstruction Paradox*, 36 Wm. & Mary L. Rev. 547 (1995).

12. *See* Richard Delgado, *Two Ways to Think about Race: Reflections on the Id, The Ego, and Other Reformist Theories of Equal Protection*, 89 Geo. L.J. 2279 (2001).

13. *Id*. *See also* Richard Delgado & Jean Stefancic, *Images of the Outsider in American Law and Culture: Can Free Expression Remedy Systemic Social Ills?* 77 Cornell L. Rev. 1258 (1992).

14. On this "social contact" hypothesis for reducing racism, *see, e.g.*, Richard Delgado, *Fairness and Formality: Minimizing the Risk of Prejudice in Alternative Dispute Resolution*, 1985 Wis. L. Rev. 1359.

15. *E.g.*, Mari J. Matsuda, Richard Delgado et al., Words That Wound: Critical Race Theory, Assaultive Speech, and the First Amendment (1993); Mari J. Matsuda, *Public Response to Racist Speech: Considering the Victim's Story*, 87 Mich. L. Rev. 2320 (1989).

16. Consider, for example, the proliferation of diversity seminars at workplaces and campuses. On storytelling and counter- storytelling as means of changing thought patterns, *see, e.g.*, Patricia Williams, Alchemy of Race and Rights (1991); Derrick Bell, *Foreword: The Civil Rights Chronicles*, 99 Harv. L. Rev. 4 (1985); Mari J. Matsuda, *Affirmative Action and Legal Knowledge: Planting Seed in Plowed-Up Ground*, 11 Harv. Women's L.J. 1 (1988).

17. Delgado, *Two Ways, supra*; Bell, *Interest-Convergence Dilemma, supra*.

18. *E.g.*, Bell, *Interest-Convergence Dilemma, supra*; Derrick Bell, *Racial Realism*, 24 Conn. L. Rev. 363 (1992).

19. *See, e.g.*, Alan D. Freeman, *Legitimizing Racial Discrimination through Antidiscrimination Law: A Review of Supreme Court Doctrine*, 62 Minn. L. Rev. 1049 (1978); Alan D. Freeman, *Race and Class: The Dilemma of Liberal Reform*, 90 Yale L.J. 1880 (1981).

20. *See* Delgado, *Two Ways, supra*.

21. Dudziak, Cold War, *supra*.

22. Bell, *Interest-Convergence Dilemma, supra* at 515, 524–26.

23. *Id*. at 524; Bell, Race, Racism, *supra* at 159–65.

24. 347 U.S. at 495.

25. Bell, *Interest-Convergence Dilemma, supra* at 524–25. *See also* Dudziak, Cold War, *supra* at 23.

26. Bell, *Interest-Convergence Dilemma, supra* at 523–26.

27. *Id*. at 524–25; Bell, Race, Racism, *supra* at 65–79.

28. Dudziak, Cold War, *supra at* 38, 80, 142–45, 147, 160, 169–70, 175, 183, 188–89, 203, 208–11, 213, 215–19, 234–35, 237–45 (memos); 18–23, 26–27, 29–46, 107–11, 119–26, 134–38, 159, 164, 182, 194–97, 205, 209–10, 215, 223–35, 237–45 (press releases and statements).

29. *Id*. at 77–80.

30. *Id.* at 104–6 (Supreme Court justices who decided *Brown* were concerned over international appearances).

31. *Id.* at 80.

32. *Id.* at 77.

33. That is, the elites who treated black breakthroughs as chess moves in the Cold War expected blacks to be grateful and assist in that effort.

34. And they did. *See* text and notes *infra*.

35. *Id.* at 15, 62–63, 71, 77, 220. *See also id.* at 250 (stating that blacks who spoke out of turn, especially to international audiences, were silenced). That is, when elite groups acted in blacks' interests in the 1950s and 1960s, they did so to improve America's position vis-‡-vis international communism. As a corollary, blacks were expected to demonstrate Americanism and distance themselves from black radicals and fellow travelers such as Baker and Robeson.

36. Dudziak, Cold War, *supra* at 67–77.

37. *See* W. E. B. Du Bois, The Autobiography of W. E. B. Du Bois 132–54 (1968); Peter Jon Perla, *From Left to Center: The Appropriation of Anti-Communist Rhetoric by the Black Press and Leading Black Opinionmakers, 1946 through 1948,* at 99–104 (unpublished honors diss., on file with author) (analyzing black press coverage of Robeson's fall from grace during this period). On the role of DuBois's "talented truth," see Eric Foner, *The Remarkable Life of W. E. B. Du Bois* (book review), J. Blacks in Higher Education, Winter 2000/2001, at 132.

38. *See, e.g.*, Eldridge Cleaver, Soul on Ice (1969).

39. David Ray Papke, Heretics in the Temple: Americans Who Reject the Nation's Legal Faith 118–28 (1998).

40. *See* Malcolm X & Alex Haley, The Autobiography of Malcolm X 184–85, 187–88, 203–5, 244–45, 306, 423–24 (1973).

41. *See* Tradition and Conflict: Images of a Turbulent Decade 1963–1973 86 (Mary Schmidt Campbell ed., 1985); Ward Churchill, *The FBI's Secret War against the Black Panther Party: A Case Study in State Repression,* in Race in 21st Century America 271–79 (Curtis Stokes et al., eds., 2001); George Lipsitz, The Possessive Investment in Whiteness 186, 189, 205 (1998) (noting that other groups followed suit); Papke, *supra* at 128–32.

42. *E.g.*, Robert L. Allen, Black Awakening in Capitalist America: An Analytic History 3–15 (1969); Mark Dowie, American Foundations 203–207 (2001); (speculating that the purpose of this wave of spending may have been co-optation) (2001); Herbert H. Haines, Black Radicals and the Civil Rights Mainstream, 1954–1970, at 179 (1988); J. Craig Jenkins, *Channeling Social Protest, in* Private Interests and the Public Good (William Powell & Elizabeth Clemens, eds. 1997). Some pointed out that truly radical groups were at first shunned by America's grant-makers. Dowie, *supra* at 208.

43. *See* Rodolfo Acuna, Occupied America: A History of Chicanos 409 (4th ed. 2000) (describing how Coors Brewing bought itself out of a boycott by Chi-

cano activists by investing $250 million into the Chica
supra at 61–63, 121–27, 188–89; Leslie G. Carr, "Col(
(1997); Dowie, *supra* at 31–32, 203–13.

44. *German Minister Condemns Violence at G8 Su*
Monitoring Europe, July 23, 2001; Roberto F. de Ocamp
Challenge of the New Trilateralism, Bus. World, July 5, 2001, at 4.

NOTES TO CHAPTER 11

1. Richard Delgado, When Equality Ends: Stories about Race and Resistance 109–26 (1999).

2. Cynthia Kwan Lee, *Beyond Black and White*, 6 Hastings Women's L.J. (1995).

3. Elizabeth Martinez, *Beyond Black/White*, 20 Soc. Just. 22 (1993).

4. Vine Deloria, Jr., Custer Died for Your Sins 168–96 (1969).

5. Juan Perea, *The Black/White Binary Paradigm of Race: The "Normal Science" of American Racial Thought*, 85 Calif. L. Rev. 1213 (1997).

6. *See*, in addition to the above sources, Richard Delgado, *Derrick Bell's Toolkit: Fit to Dismantle That Famous House?* 75 N.Y.U. L. Rev. 283 (2000); Richard Delgado, *Rodrigo's Fifteenth Chronicle: Racial Mixture, Latino-Critical Scholarship, and the Black-White Binary of Race*, 75 Tex. L. Rev. 1181 (1997).

7. *E.g.*, Perea, *supra* at 1213–14, 1219.

8. *Id.* at 1221–22, 1257–58.

9. *Id.*

10. Andrew Hacker, Two Nations: Black and White, Separate, Hostile, Unequal (1992).

11. Cornel West, Race Matters (1993).

12. Joe Feagin & Melvin P. Sikes, Living with Racism: The Black Middle-Class Experience (1994).

13. Joel Kovel, White Racism; A Psychohistory (1984).

14. Perea, *supra* at 1220–21.

15. On the differential racialization approach, *see* generally Juan F. Perea, Richard Delgado, Angela P. Harris, & Stephanie M. Wildman, Race and Races: Cases and Resources for a Diverse America (2000).

16. *See generally* Mari Matsuda, *Voices of America: Accent, Antidiscrimination Law, and a Jurisprudence for the Last Reconstruction*, 100 Yale L.J. 1329 (1991).

17. *Id.*

18. *See* Delgado, *Toolkit, supra* at 291–93.

19. *Id.* at 299–300.

20. *Id.* at 294–95, 302–3.

21. Athena Mutua, *Mapping Intellectual/Political Foundations and Future Self critical Directions*, 53 U. Miami L. Rev. 1177, 1187–91 (1999).

22. Joe R. Feagin, Racist America: Roots, Current Realities, and Future Reparations 203–5 (2000); Mutua, *supra* at 1189–91.

23. Angela Harris & Leslie Espinoza, *Afterword: Embracing the Tar Baby*, 85 Calif. L. Rev. 1585 (1998).

24. *See id.* at 1596.

25. 347 U.S. 483 (1954).

26. 42 U.S.C. § 2000a et seq. (1964).

27. *See* Delgado, *Toolkit, supra*; Perea, *supra*.

28. 347 U.S. 483 (1954).

29. Delgado, *Toolkit, supra* at 289.

30. *I.e.*, the Civil War.

31. *See* Rudolph AcuÒa, Occupied America 43–49, 60–68 (4th ed. 1999).

32. Delgado, *Toolkit, supra* at 291.

33. *Id.* at 291–92.

34. *Id.* at 292.

35. *Id.*

36. Timothy Egan, *Win Major Round in Fight over Trust Accounts*, N.Y. Times, Feb. 23, 1999, at 15; *Redeeming a Historic Trust*, N.Y. Times, Apr. 30, 2001, at 18.

37. Virginia Groark, *First One Casino, Then Two. Now What?* N.Y. Times, Sept. 2, 2001, §14, at 1.

38. Stephen Kinzer, *Museums and Tribes: A Tricky Truce*, N.Y. Times, Dec. 24, 2000, §2, at 1.

39. *See* Juan Perea, *Demography and Distrust: An Essay on American Languages, Cultural Pluralism, and Official English*, 77 Minn. L. Rev. 269 (1992).

40. *See* 1994 Cal. Legis. Serv. Prop. 187 (West) (Proposition 187 as codified in scattered sections of Cal. Educ., Gov't, Health & Safety, Penal, Welf. & Inst. Codes); declared unconstitutional, in part, by consent agreement, League of United Latin American Citizens v. Wilson, 1998 WL 141325 (C.D. Cal. 1998).

41. Delgado, *Toolkit, supra* at 294.

42. *Id.* at 295.

43. *Id.*

44. *Id.* at 294.

45. *See* Perea *et al., supra* at 412–16.

46. 347 U.S. 483 (1954).

47. *See* chapter 10, this volume. *See also* Derrick Bell, Brown v. Board of Education *and the Interest-Convergence Dilemma*, 93 Harv. L. Rev. 518 (1980); *see also* Mary Dudziak, Cold War Civil Rights (2001).

48. *See* chapter 10.

49. *Id.*

50. *Id.*

51. *E.g.*, Perea, *supra* at 1228–30; Delgado, *Toolkit, supra* at 300–303.

52. For examples of the former, *see* Delgado, *Toolkit, supra* at 303; of the latter, Bill Piatt, Black and Brown in America: The Case for Cooperation (1997). Native Americans have sometimes declined to participate in civil-rights coalitions on the ground that they were not minorities, but sovereign nations.

53. 64 F. Supp. 544 (S.D. Cal. 1946).

54. *Id.* at 545, 551; Delgado, *Toolkit, supra* at 303.

55. Plessy v. Ferguson, 163 U.S. 537 (1896).

56. Delgado, *Toolkit, supra* at 303–4.

57. *Id.* at 304.

58. *Id.*

59. *Id.* at 304.

60. *Id.* at 305, citing *Brown*, 347 U.S. at 494, 495 n.11.

61. Delgado, *Toolkit, supra* at 305.

62. *Id.*

63. *Id.* at 306.

64. *Id.*

65. *See, e.g.*, Civil Rights Action Team, U.S. Dep't of Agric., *Civil Rights at the United States Department of Agriculture* (1997).

66. *See* Charlene Gilbert & Quinn Eli, Homecoming: The Story of African American Farmers (2000).

67. Thomas W. Mitchell, *From Reconstruction to Deconstruction: Undermining Black Landownership, Political Independence, and Community through Partition Sales of Tenancies in Common*, 95 Nw. U. L. Rev. 505 (2001).

68. *Id.* at 507 n.11.

69. *Id.* at 505–27.

70. *Id.*

71. *Id.* at 507, 511.

72. *Id.* at 510, 518–21.

73. For example, one sixty-fourth or one-hundred-twenty- eighth.

74. Mitchell, *supra* at 508 (inability to require owners out of possession to contribute to cost of repairs); 512 (unclear management assignments); *id.* (freerider problems); 517 (restrictions on alienability); 518, 522–23, 571 (inability to obtain financing); 516 (inability to secure collateral).

75. Mitchell, *supra* at 563–79.

76. Consider the English common, for example, *see* Garrett Hardin, *The Tragedy of the Commons*, 162 Science 1243 (1968), or Southwest water rights, Wells A. Hutchins, *The Community Acequia: Its Origin and Development*, 31 SW Hist. Q. 266 (1928).

77. *See, e.g.*, Pigford v. Glickman, 185 F.R.D. 82 (D.D.C. 1999). *See also* the consent decree in *id.*, No. 97–1978 (D.D.C., Apr. 14, 1999), described in Mitchell, *supra* at 506 nn.6–8.

78. *See* text and notes immediately *infra.*

79. *E.g.,* Perea et al., *supra* at 390–405 (1999).

80. *Id.* at 406–12.

81. *Id.* at 260–75.

82. *Id.* at 272–80. In some of these actions, the U.S. Attorney brought suit at the behest of Anglos to oust Mexican owners who had resided on the land for generations. Of course, the Supreme Court was the ultimate arbiter of these claims. *Id.* at 284.

83. Perea et al., *supra* at 178–79, 254–58, 326–31. *See* Derrick Bell, Race, Racism, and American Law 102–14 (4th ed., 2000). Indigenous people in Australia and New Zealand suffered the same fate; only the legal doctrines were slightly different. On the *Mabo* decision, which restored aboriginal lands in Australia, see *id.* at 108–9.

84. California Agrarian Action Project, Inc. v. Regents of the Univ. of Cal., 210 Cal. App. 3d 1245 (1989).

85. *Id.* at 1245–46; Richard Delgado & Jean Stefancic, *California's Racial History and Constitutional Rationales for Race-Conscious Decisionmaking in Higher Education,* 47 UCLA L. Rev. 1521, 1605 (2000).

86. Delgado & Stefancic, *California's Racial History, supra* at 1605.

87. *Id.*

88. *Id.*

89. Ann Draper & Hall Draper, The Dirt on California: Agribusiness and the University (1968).

90. Samuel P. Berger, Dollar Harvest: The Story of the Farm Bureau (1971).

91. *E.g.,* Jim Hightower, Hard Tomatoes, Hard Times (1973).

92. 210 Cal. App. 3d, at 1248–49.

93. *See* Delgado & Stefancic, *California's Racial History, supra* at 1606.

94. *Id.* at 1600–1605.

95. Boris Bittker, The Case for Black Reparations (1973).

96. Rhonda V. Magee, *The Master's Tools, From the Bottom Up: Responses to African-American Reparations Theory in Mainstream and Outsider Remedies Discourse,* 79 Va. L. Rev. 863, 888 (1993).

97. Michael A. Fletcher, *Putting a Price on Slavery's Legacy; Call for Reparations Builds as Blacks Tally History's Toll,* Wash. Post, Dec. 26, 2000, at A1. This approach is similar to the tack taken by Japanese Americans, a group of whose attempt at a class action suit for reparations was ultimately dismissed. Hohri v. United States, 586 F. Supp. 769 (D.D.C. May 17, 1984); *see* Magee, *supra* at 904–6.

98. *See* text and notes *infra.*

99. Bittker, *supra* at 4–5.

100. Tim Nickens, *Rosewood Bill Signed into Law by Governor,* Miami Herald, May 5, 1994, at 5B.

101. William Safire, *On Language; Stop Me Before I Apologize Again*, N.Y. Times, May 5, 1994, § 6, at 32.

102. 50 U.S.C. § 1989, et seq. (1988). *See also* Vincene Verdun, *If the Shoe Fits, Wear It: An Analysis of Reparations to African Americans*, 67 Tul. L. Rev. 597, 600 (1993) (listing the five waves of reparation movements).

103. Robert Westley, *Many Billions Gone: Is It Time to Reconsider the Case for Black Reparations?* 40 B.C. L. Rev. 429, 453–58 (1998).

104. *See* Magee, *supra* at 886; Calvin J. Allen, *The Continuing Quest of African Americans to Obtain Reparation for Slavery*, 9 NBA Nat'l B.A. Mag. 33 (Jun. 1995).

105. Allen, *supra*.

106. Conyers numbers the bill "forty" each year in reference to "forty acres and a mule." *See* Magee, *supra* at 877. Conyers also seeks to create a commission to study the unjust and often cruel treatment of African Americans subjected to slavery and discrimination since the close of the Civil War. Commission to Study Reparation Proposals for African-Americans Act, H.R. 40, 107th Congress (2001). *See also* Fletcher, *supra*. Given corporate America's role in slavery and the obvious economic power such companies wield, some argue that not just the government but corporate America as well should pay reparations. *See* Milner S. Ball, *Reparations and Repentance: A Response to Professor Cook*, 68 Geo. Wash. L. Rev. 1015, 1017 (2000).

107. This report is accessible online at http://www.yaleslavery.org. *See also* Kate Zernike, *Slave Traders in Yale's Past Fuel Debate on Restitution*, N.Y. Times, Aug. 13, 2001, at P1.

108. Verdun, *supra* at 631–32. *See* Westley, *supra* at 441.

109. W. Burlette Carter, *True Reparations*, 68 Geo. Wash. L. Rev. 1021, 1022 (2000).

110. Irma Jacqueline Ozer, *Reparations for African Americans*, 41 How. L.J. 479, 482–92 (1998).

111. Westley, *supra* at 473.

112. Anthony E. Cook, *King and the Beloved Community: A Communitarian Defense of Black Reparations*, 68 Geo. Wash. L. Rev. 959, 972, 977 (2000).

113. Charles Krauthammer, *A Grand Compromise*, N.Y. Times, Apr. 6, 2001, at A37.

114. Text and notes *supra*, this chapter.

115. John D. Skrentny, *Affirmative Action and the New Demographic Realities*, Chron. Higher. Educ., Feb. 16, 2001, at 7.

116. *See, e.g.*, Krauthammer, *supra*.

117. *Id.*

118. *Id.*

119. Orlando Patterson, *Race by the Numbers*, N.Y. Times, May 8, 2001, at A27.

120. National Language Act of 2001, H.R. 280, 107th Congress (2001).

About the Author

RICHARD DELGADO serves as the Jean Lindsley Professor of Law at the University of Colorado, where he teaches and writes in the areas of social justice and civil rights. He and his wife, legal writer Jean Stefancic, live in a cabin in the mountains outside Boulder.